Language Processing in
Children and Adults

£8-95+

Introduction to Modern Psychology

General editor: Max Coltheart
Birkbeck College, University of London

Language Processing in Children and Adults:

An introduction

Margaret Harris and Max Coltheart

Routledge & Kegan Paul
London and New York

For Frank, Myra, Veronika and Alice

First published in 1986 by
Routledge & Kegan Paul Ltd
11 New Fetter Lane, London EC4P 4EE
Reprinted 1987

Published in the USA by
Routledge & Kegan Paul Inc.
in association with Methuen Inc.
29 West 35th Street, New York, NY 10001

Set in Baskerville 10 on 12 point
by Columns of Reading
and printed in Great Britain by
St Edmundsbury Press Ltd
Bury St Edmunds, Suffolk

Library of Congress Cataloging in Publication Data

Harris, Margaret, 1951–
Language processing in children and adults.
(Introductions to modern psychology)
Bibliography: p.
Includes index.
1. Psycholinguistics.   2. Children—Language.
I. Coltheart, Max.   II. Title.   III. Series.
BF455.H2715   1986   401'.9   85-25767
British Library CIP data also available
ISBN 0-7100-9633-X
ISBN 0-7102-0801-4 (pbk.)

Contents

Figures

Part I

1 Introduction

Psychologists have long recognised that human minds feed on linguistic symbols. Linguists have always admitted that some kind of psycho-social motor must move the machinery of grammar and lexicon. Sooner or later they were certain to examine their intersection self-consciously. Perhaps it was also inevitable that the result would be called 'psycholinguistics'. (Miller, 1968)

1.1 Alternative approaches to the study of language

The development of theories about language is the concern not only of psychologists but also of those in many other disciplines. In particular, linguists and philosophers have had a great deal to say both about the nature of language and its use by speakers of a particular language. Psychologists are also interested in both of these issues, but what makes a *psychological* approach to the study of language unique is that psychologists are concerned with the nature of *language processing* – hence the title of this book. What we mean by this is that psychologists attempt to discover how people actually understand and produce language – in other words they are interested in the cognitive processes which are involved in the use of language.

Initially, psychological research into language processing was very heavily influenced by linguistic theory. The relation between the two disciplines existing in the mid-1960s and early 1970s is well illustrated by the quotation from Miller (1968) which appears at the beginning of this chapter. As this quotation explains, one immediate result of psychology's reliance on linguistic theory was that the term 'psycholinguistics' was created to describe this new approach to the psychological study of language. We write 'new' approach because it would be incorrect to assume that psychological research into language did not begin until the 1960s. However, what changed at that point was that psychologists became aware of the linguistic theory being developed by Noam Chomsky in *Syntactic Structures* (1957) and realised that it offered the basis of a model of language processing which could be experimentally tested.

We have not, however, used the term *psycholinguistics* in the title of our book. The reason for this is that although a great deal of psychological research into language was given a new impetus by Chomsky's writings, there were other areas of psychological research into language processing which were much less influenced by linguistic theory. In particular, research into reading and into memory and perception of language was largely unaffected by the radical developments in linguistic theory. One consequence of the close relation between linguistic theory and psychological theory and experimentation in psycholinguistics was that these other areas of psychological research concerned with language were frequently considered to be entirely separate areas within psychology. Thus many psychologists saw themselves as studying perception or memory or reading or psycholinguistics, and there was relatively little contact between researchers in these areas.

However, it would seem that there is much to be gained by an attempt to understand language processing as a whole, and this can only be accomplished through an awareness of the many different approaches to the study of language within psychology. We have attempted to reflect these different approaches in our book and to draw out the links between them. We have, therefore, included chapters on adult language use and chapters on the acquisition of language by children. We discuss language processing in the normal population and the processing of language by adults and children with language disorders. We discuss the processing of written language as well as the processing of spoken language, and consider the production of language as well as language comprehension.

Before we can begin to discuss these issues, however, we need to say something about the nature of language, and so in the remainder of this introductory chapter, we discuss some of the main features of language, and illustrate these features by considering different kinds of systems for the written expression of language.

1.2 Some important properties of language

Producing a satisfactory definition of 'language' is surprisingly difficult, as a consultation of dictionary definitions reveals. One reason for this difficulty is that the term 'language' is used to refer both to *particular* languages such as French, German and English, and to human language in general. Psychologists are concerned with both aspects of language processing since they attempt to answer general questions about how language is processed as well as more specific questions about how processing of one language might differ from that of another.

Another ambiguity in the term 'language' is that it is often used to describe a wide variety of human and animal communication systems – such usage appears in terms like 'animal language' and 'body language'. We do not want to spend time here considering the extent to which various kinds of communication systems are actually 'languages'. However, we do want to describe some of the most important properties of language and to define what essential properties a communication system has to have in order to be considered a language. It is theoretically important to be aware of such properties for two reasons. First, as we have already implied, these properties can be used to distinguish communication systems in general from communication systems which are also languages – a distinction which has important theoretical significance. Second, in order to develop satisfactory models of language processing it is essential to have a clear idea of what kind of tasks are involved in both the learning and use of a language; as we shall see, this is only possible in the light of a clear understanding of what the main properties of language are. Such an awareness will also allow distinctions to be made between aspects of processing which are common to all languages and aspects which are relevant only to a *particular* language and a particular mode of communication such as speech, writing or signing.

In developing models of language processing one of the most

important properties of language which has to be taken into account is **creativity** or **productivity**. What we mean by this is that someone who knows a language does not just know how to produce or understand a limited number of spoken, written or signed messages. Rather, a language user knows how to produce and understand an *infinitely large* number of messages, even messages which the language user has never previously encountered. This creativity in language is possible because the individual units of a language (which are fixed in number) can be combined in an infinite number of different ways. In the case of spoken English, for example, a limited number of different individual sounds (or **phonemes**) can be combined in an infinite number of ways to produce words, and words can, in turn, be combined in an infinite number of ways to produce clauses and sentences. It follows from this creative property of language that anyone who 'knows' a language must know how phonemes and words can be put together in a particular language (since only *some* combinations will be legal for a particular language) and also what particular ways of combining phonemes and words actually *mean*. So someone who understands English will have to know not only that the combination of words in an unusual sentence like 'The Martian was given a standing ovation by the House of Lords' is legal but also what message is being conveyed by this sentence which they are unlikely to have encountered before. Part of understanding the message will involve, for example, being able to understand the difference in meaning between that sentence and a similar one such as 'The Martians gave a member of the House of Lords a standing ovation'.

In linguistics, knowledge of a language is referred to as linguistic **competence**, and this is a term which has been adopted by psychologists who investigate language processing. It is important to distinguish what a language user knows about a language – competence – from the actual *use* of language in the production and comprehension of particular linguistic messages. This use of language is known as linguistic **performance**.

The actual use of language – performance – obviously depends on competence since, as we have just explained, the creativity of language often requires a language user to draw on general knowledge of how a language is organised rather than previous experience with particular clauses and sentences. However, performance will never be a perfect reflection of competence since language users make various kinds of errors when they use their linguistic knowledge to produce and understand particular messages. These errors arise because of the memory and attentional limitations of human beings. Thus, we may actually forget what we are trying to say or write or be unable to recall a particular word; or our attention may be diverted to some other task while we are in the middle of trying to produce or understand a particular message.

An understanding of language processing involves the understanding of both competence and performance, and of the relation between them. However, it is worth noting that, while there are various different ways of describing competence, only some of these ways (and ultimately one way) will be useful for understanding language *processing*. In order for an account of competence to be psychologically valid (that is, to explain something about the nature of language processing) such a description has to have what Chomsky (1965) refers to as **descriptive adequacy**. What we mean by this is that the description of competence has to provide a model of a language user's linguistic knowledge and to describe what a language user actually knows about a language. Such a model will thus provide insights into how such knowledge is actually organised and will suggest hypotheses about how this knowledge is used in the production and comprehension of language. (For a detailed discussion of the different levels of adequacy in linguistic theory see Smith and Wilson, 1979.)

We have just drawn a distinction between a description of the kind of linguistic knowledge which might be included in competence and hypotheses about how such knowledge might actually be used in language processing. It is important to recognise this distinction because there may be considerable evidence to suggest that a person who knows a particular language possesses a particular piece of linguistic knowledge about that language. However it does not necessarily follow that this piece of information is actually used in language production or comprehension. Consider the rule in English that the plural form of regular nouns (like *spoon*) is formed by adding an *s* to the singular form (to make *spoons*). There can be little doubt that speakers of English are aware of this rule because if you ask what has to be added to a word like *spoon* to make it plural the answer would almost invariably be correct. However, it is by no means clear that people actually form the plural form of a regular noun in this way when they want to use it in a written or spoken sentence. They might actually have two *separate* forms for each noun (singular and plural) which are used in language production. However, the '+ s' rule might be used in language comprehension. (We discuss some evidence relating to this issue in production in Chapter 8 and some evidence relating to comprehension in Chapter 3.) This distinction between rules which describe what a language user knows about the structure of a language and rules which are actually used in language processing explains why the linguistic notion of **descriptive adequacy** has to be sub-divided for the purpose of producing a model which explains how language processing actually operates.

The creativity of language raises various theoretical and empirical questions, as we have just seen. Another property of language which has important implications for the study of language processing is that language is an **arbitrary** form of communication. What this means is that there is no readily apparent systematic relationship between the form of a message and its meaning. In other words, if a message is conveyed in a purely arbitrary way it is impossible to guess at its meaning purely on the basis of what the message looks or sounds like – the relation between the form of a message and its meaning has to be *learned*.

There are some exceptions to this arbitrary relation between what a message actually means and how it looks or sounds. For example, with onomatopoeic words it is possible to guess meaning from sound since the sound of the word like 'woof' is actually supposed to represent the sound of a dog barking. However, even with words like this there is some degree of arbitrariness, since the way in which an onomatopoeic animal noise is represented varies from language to language. For example, in the Mandarin dialect of Chinese, dogs do not say 'woof', they say 'wang'.

The opposite of arbitrary representation of meaning is **iconic** representation in which it *is* possible to guess what a message means from the way it is expressed. Obviously a language would be very much easier to learn if messages were represented iconically, since the meaning of individual items in the language would not have to be learned. Many of the messages we need to convey cannot be represented iconically, however. One good way of appreciating the limitations of an iconic system of communication is to see how well you can mime a message without using any previously agreed signs for particular parts of the message. You will probably find that with a certain amount of ingenuity it is possible to convey messages about concrete ideas (the names of objects, for example) but it is almost impossible to convey more abstract concepts such as the verbs 'to be' or 'to believe'.

Arbitrary representation of meaning is thus essential for full creativity in a language. If a language were to restrict its users to the expression of messages that could be conveyed iconically then only a very restricted range of messages could be represented. The price that has to be paid for having a creative and arbitrary communication system is that languages have to be **culturally transmitted**. In other words, languages have to be *learned*, rather than being genetically transmitted from generation to generation. As we shall see in Chapter 2, there has been considerable debate about the extent to which language does have *some* genetically transmitted component. However, even those theorists who argue for a genetic component in the child's learning of language only argue for a genetic component in the transmission of those aspects of language that are common to *all* languages. Aspects of a language which are specific to a particular language *cannot* be genetically transmitted, since there is no guarantee that children will need to learn the same language as their parents.

Some of the difficulties that a child may encounter in learning a particular language arise because of the way in which linguistic messages are actually represented in that language. We will now turn our attention to differences between languages. However, rather than discussing *spoken* language, we will discuss different ways in which language can be represented in *written form*. We do so for two reasons: as we explain in the next section of this chapter, differences in the form of messages are particularly striking in the case of written language; as we explain in Chapter 6, psychological models of language processing have to be able to explain how spoken *and* written language is processed.

1.3 Writing systems

Language use involves more than the application of linguistic knowledge to the construction of messages in linguistic form. If we are to communicate such messages to each other, the messages must be expressed in physical form – as sequences of sounds, or as marks on paper, or as gestures in a sign language, for example.

The different languages of the world do not differ from each other in the methods by which they are given spoken expression. One can always identify for any language a basic set of elementary sounds – **phonemes** – out of which the spoken forms of words are built. Certain phonemes will be used in some languages and not in others, but the basic method for expressing the language in audible form (building the spoken word up from phonemic elements) is the same for all languages.

The written expression of language is a different matter: here there *are* absolutely fundamental differences between languages in the methods used for expressing the language in visible form. These differences have major implications for ideas about how children learn to read and write the different languages, and major implications for attempts to construct theories about skilled reading and writing. Unless one is content to restrict one's interests solely to the reading and writing of English – and we are not – it is necessary to consider the various forms which writing systems take, and the implications of these for our understanding of the acquisition and skilled use of written language.

Four basic kinds of writing system – four different principles by which language can be expressed in visible form – may be distinguished. These are referred to as **pictographic**, **logographic** (sometimes called **ideographic**), **syllabic** and **alphabetic**. These fall naturally into two categories, as we will see. Pictographic and logographic systems are 'word-writing' systems, in which individual characters generally stand for whole words. In contrast, syllabic and alphabetic systems are 'sound-writing' systems, in which individual characters generally stand for individual sounds within a word.

1.3.1   *Pictographic writing systems*

The earliest kinds of writing all used pictographic principles to convey meaning. Here the relationship of the visual symbol to the idea whose meaning it conveys is iconic, rather than arbitrary: an idea is represented by drawing a picture of it. Figure 1 (reproduced

from Gelb, 1952, Figure 8) illustrates this: as Gelb observes, 'the
design warns horsemen that a mountain goat could climb up the
rocky trail but a horse would tumble down'. This 'No Thorough-
fare' sign was drawn on a rock by American Indians in New
Mexico.

FIGURE 1   (From Gelb, I, 1952: *A Study of Writing*. U. Chicago
Press)

A major problem with any pictographic writing system is that in
any language many words will be abstract, and so difficult or
impossible to represent in pictorial form. Another difficulty is
grammatical distinction – how could a pictographic system
distinguish, say, *big* from *biggest*, or *depart* from *departing* and *will
depart*? Some ways in which writing systems can evolve to cope with
these and other difficulties inherent in pictographic systems are
illustrated in Figure 2 (reproduced from Jensen, 1970, Figures
126-130).

1.3.2   *Logographic writing systems*

As this figure shows, the writing system for Chinese was originally
pictographic. Over several millennia, it has evolved so as to
become much more stylised, and at the same time much more
inscrutable. The character for 'dog' for example, originally looked
like a dog, but in its modern form it no longer does. It is now
arbitrary rather than iconic. A writing system in which individual
characters stand for individual words, but do not represent them
pictorially, is known as a **logographic** system (the term **ideographic** is also sometimes used here).

It will be seen in these examples of Figure 2 that the problems

The East-Asian Group of Scripts

old form	mod. form	meaning	explanation
𠙘 𠀉	子	child	
米	木	tree	branches above roots below
門	門	gate, door	two leaves of a door
𦫼 𣥏	矢	arrow	
𢖽	心	heart	the heart muscle
𠱛	言	word, to speak	mouth with breath coming out
𩂏 雨	雨	rain	the vault of heaven with rain-drops falling from it
𤜌	犬	dog	head, body, legs and tail
巳	巴	large snake	
𠂇	手	hand	forearm with five fingers
貝	貝	treasure, wealth	cowrie-shell
田	田	field	field divided up into parcels

old sign	mod. form	meaning	explanation
𠃉	方	region	indicating the four quarters of the sky
勿	勿	not (in prohibition)	flag of warning
𡴭 言	言	to speak, word	mouth with breath coming out
中 中	中	middle	target with arrow
畺	畺	boundary	line between two fields

	old sign	mod. sign	meaning	explanation
1	孖孖	孖	twins	2 · child
2	覞	見見	to see together	2 · to see
3	竝	立立	side by side. together	2 people standing next to each other
4	川	巛	stream	3 · ditch
5	東東	東東	everywhere	2 · the East
6	炎	炎	very hot	2 · fire
7	馬馬馬	馬馬馬	to gallop	3 · horse
8	姦	女女	a quarrel	2 · woman

old sign	mod. form	meaning	explanation
囚	囚	prisoner, prison	human being in an enclosure
采	采	to pluck	a hand above a tree
明	明	bright	sun and moon
鳴	鳴	to sing	mouth and bird
聞	聞	to hear	door and ear

FIGURE 2 Examples of early and modern forms of Chinese characters (from Jensen 1970)

posed by abstractness can be dealt with in various ways. 'Very hot' is depicted by duplicating the character for 'fire'; the rapidity of 'gallop' is represented by trebling the character for 'horse'; conjoining the character for 'mouth' and the character for 'bird' produces a compound character 'sing'; and the conjunction of the 'door' and 'ear' characters gives us a compound character meaning 'listen'. In case you do not agree that such devices destroy the iconic (non-arbitrary) properties of the original system, consider the compound character 雜

If we tell you it is composed of the character 隹

(meaning 'bird'), the character 木

(meaning 'wood') and the character 衣

(meaning 'clothes'), can you thereby deduce what word the whole compound character represents? Try to work this out before you look at the footnote to this page, which gives you the answer.[1]

A property of logographic writing systems that is of fundamental importance is that a logographic character does not contain any representation of the individual sounds making up the spoken form of the word written by the character. For example, there is absolutely nothing in the character for 'yen' in Figure 2 that corresponds to the 'y' or the 'e' or the 'n' in the spoken word 'yen'. This has advantages and disadvantages. The big advantage is that people who speak different languages (and a considerable number of different languages exist in China) can use a single writing system. This cannot happen if the writing system directly reflects the spoken language. If you have to convey the concept of twoness to a Frenchman who speaks no English, writing *two* will not help; but writing *2* will. That is because *2* is a logographic character and so does not represent sound directly; hence the fact that the spoken

1 Did you try to think of something that 'bird', 'clothes' and 'wood' have in common, and so end up with an answer like 'scarecrow'? Unlucky. 'Bird', 'clothes' and 'wood' have nothing in common. That is why the compound character means 'miscellaneous'.

word for two in English and in French is different does not matter, as it does if you write alphabetically.

The disadvantage is that, if you are shown a word in logographically written form and you have never seen it before, you will not be able to understand it even if you are familiar with the word's spoken form, because there is no way of going from written form to spoken form if you have never seen the spoken form before. This is sometimes disputed by those who point out that many Chinese words are written by compound characters made up of two elements, the 'semantic radical' (giving some information about the very general meaning of the word) and the 'phonetic' radical' (said to give information about the pronunciation of the word). For example, the word for 'to dry-roast' in Chinese is *kǎo*, and it is written 烤

The two characters making up this compound are 火

which means 'fire' (and so is the semantic radical in many words describing methods of cooking) and 考

which is pronounced '*kǎo*' and so is the phonetic radical – it *means* 'to examine' but this is irrelevant here because it is the *pronunciation* of the character which is significant. Thus, if you had never seen the written word 'to dry-roast' before, and if you could decide that it was the right-hand half of the character that was the phonetic radical, and if you already knew the two characters from which the compound character is composed, you could reason as follows: the left-hand character must show that the whole word means a method of cooking, and the right-hand character shows it is pronounced '*kǎo*', so the whole thing must mean 'to dry roast'.

However, it is only very rarely that this decoding strategy could be successfully applied. Take the written word 炒

Now that we have taught you a little Chinese, you can recognise the left half of this as the character for 'fire', so this whole word is likely to refer to a method of cooking. The pronunciation of the right half of the character is '*shǎo*' and it means 'few' (but, again, this is irrelevant). So what method of cooking is pronounced '*shǎo*'? There isn't one. The whole compound character means 'to stir-fry' and the pronunciation is '*chǎo*'. So the pronunciation of the so-called phonetic radical here is not identical to the pronunciation of the whole word. Indeed, it is often the case that the two pronunciations are completely different. The reason is that the system of semantic and phonetic radicals originated in ancient Chinese, and the pronunciations in ancient Chinese are not the same as the pronunciations in any dialect of modern Chinese. Further ambiguities are introduced by the fact that the phonetic radical may itself have several different pronunciations. Almost the only way of compelling waiters in Chinese restaurants to serve you a dish of tripe (they normally either say that there isn't any today or else insist non-negotiably that you would not like it) is to astonish them by being able to write the word in Chinese. It is

肚

(which actually means 'stomach' and is pronounced '*dǔ*', but will do for the purpose of obtaining tripe). Now 月

is the semantic radical here, meaning 'meat'. The right-hand character can mean 'gentleman, officer' and this is pronounced '*shi*'; or it can mean 'earth' which is pronounced '*tǔ*', but *neither* of these pronunciations is the pronunciation of the word 'tripe'.

Finally, there are some words written as compound characters with no phonetic radicals at all – for example, the word for 'good', pronounced '*hǎo*' is written 好

The two elements here are both semantic radicals (one means 'woman', the other means 'child') and neither has anything to do with the pronunciation of the word 'good'.

We have gone into some detail here so as to illustrate a property of logographic scripts which is not possessed by the two sound-writing scripts (the syllabic and the alphabetic), namely, that if you have never seen the logographically written form of a word before, you will not only fail to understand it, you will not be able to read it aloud. Hence even if the spoken form of the word is known to you, this will not help. In contrast, you can use spelling-to-sound rules when you see an unfamiliar word written in a syllabic or alphabetic script, and this will give you the pronunciation of the word: hence, if the word's pronunciation is known to you, this provides a means for comprehending its printed form, a means not available in logographic writing systems.

Another unique property of logographic scripts is the difficulty of producing dictionaries for them. If you come aross an ideographic character you do not recognise, and so need to look it up in a dictionary, how will you find it in the dictionary? One principle that is used is classification by semantic radical: all words with a common radical are grouped together. This helps, provided you can identify the semantic radical in the character that you do not recognise. A second principle is to arrange characters in order of the number of strokes making them up. Figure 3 illustrates this.

This list of ladies, obtained from the Metro Ballroom in Singapore, is arranged in alphabetical order, from top left to bottom right, depending upon the number of strokes in the first name of each person, from Ting Yiu Ling (two strokes) down to Tse Ping (nineteen strokes, we think).

1.3.3   Syllabic writing systems

In these systems, each written character represents a syllable, so, for example, any trisyllabic word will be written as a sequence of three characters. Such writing systems are only suitable for languages in which the number of possible syllables is small. The number of legal syllables in Englsih runs into several thousand, so if English were written using a syllabic system we would have to learn several thousand different characters. Other languages have many fewer syllables – Japanese has 69 for example (its writing system is discussed in Section 1.3.4). The two most extensively used syllabic systems are Devanagari, using for writing several languages in India (accounts of this system may be found in Byng, Coltheart, Prior and Riddoch, 1984, and in Karanth, 1985) and Kana, used in Japan and described in Section 1.3.4.

1.3.4   The Japanese writing system

Japanese is written in a mixture of two different writing systems. There is an ideographic system known as Kanji and directly derived from the Chinese writing system; and there is a syllabic system known as Kana, with one character for each of the 69 syllables used in spoken Japanese (for an account of the Japanese writing system, see Sasanuma, 1980, 1985).

瓊 樓 佳 麗

ALL BEAUTIFUL LADIES FOR YOUR CHOICE

姓名 Name	語言	姓名 Name	語言	姓名 Name	語言
丁燕玲 Ting Yin Ling	粵國	李晶瑩 Ada	粵英國	陳亮華 Chan Leung Wah	粵國
小韻 Fanny	滬粵國英	余情 Yu Ching	粵國	徐綺雲 Tsui Yee Wan	粵國
王小紅 Wong Shiu Hung	粵國	克萍 Hak Ping	粵國	許慧兒 Kathleen Choi	粵英
王丹妮 Wong Danny	粵國	林麗萍 Francine	粵英	飛鳳 Fai Fung	粵英國
王秋雲 Wong Chow Wan	粵國	金敏華 Ronnie	粵國英葡	莎玲 Sar Ling	粵滬國英
文靜 Mona Lee	粵英國	金淑華 Mary Ann Kam	粵英國	莊潔 Cheong Kit	粵英國
方茵 Fong Yan	粵國	周露文 Chow Lo Man	粵越國	黃秋紅 May Wong	粵英日
方敏 Fong Man	粵國英日	美儀 Mai Yee	粵國	張白玲 Cheung Pek Ling	粵國
白皓 Pek Ho	粵國	胡露玲 Wu Ngoi Ling	粵國	張玲珊 Cheung Ling Shan	潮粵廈國
江麗 Kong Lai	粵國	韋芳 Wai Fong	粵滬國英	張綺華 Cheung Yee Wah	粵國
江竹玲 Kong Chuk Ling	粵國	徐玲 Jeanett	粵國	綺媚 Yee May	粵國
田珍 Judy	粵英國	唐夢 Tong Mung	粵國	夢玲 Mung Ling	粵國
妃妃 Fei Fei	粵滬國英	唐玲 Tong Ling	粵英國	嘉玲 Ka Ling	粵國
李皓 Lee Ho	粵滬國英	陳淑華 Chan Suk Wah	粵英國	嘉敏 Carmen	粵英
李湘雲 Lee Sheung Wan	粵	陳錫芬 Chan Shek Fan	粵國	謝萍 Tze Ping	粵廈國潮

Please mark with √ on the name that you choose

FIGURE 3   List of ladies – Metro ballroom, Singapore

How did this dual system arise? It was because of a property of the Chinese writing system to which we have already alluded, namely, that Chinese logographs do not represent sounds. When Chinese and Korean traders came to Japan in the first millennium AD, the Japanese had no writing system. Soon they began to use the Chinese system to write Japanese; and this was only possible because the system was a logographic one. For example, the Chinese word for 'water' is 'shwĕi' whilst the Japanese word is 'mizu' but the character 水

can be used to write either word, since it says nothing about how it is to be pronounced (exactly as, for example, 2 can be used to write the words 'two', 'deux', 'zwei', 'due', etc.). Thus much Japanese writing can be understood by readers of Chinese because of close similarities between Japanese Kanji characters and Chinese characters.

However, obstacles arose for the use of the Chinese system to write Japanese because of major differences in the grammatical structure of the two languages. Japanese is like English in being a highly inflected language, that is, prefixes and suffixes are extensively used. Chinese is not like this – other means are generally found to express, say, number or tense. Japanese and English express the plural or the past tense by adding to the ends of nouns or verbs elements which in themselves are meaningless (-s, -ed); the Chinese language does not possess such elements. Therefore it does not possess characters corresponding to them. How, then, could the Japanese write anything to represent the suffixes on their spoken words?

Exactly this fundamental difficulty was encountered, at a very different time and in a very different place, by Tarzan of the Apes. He learned to speak the language of the Apes, but was, of course, not taught to read. However, at the age of ten years or so, he came across some books (a primer, children's readers, picture books, and a dictionary). By detecting that a picture of a boy almost always accompanied the printed word BOY, he learned the meaning of this printed representation, and by the same means eventually acquired the ability to read many words. But he did not learn to read aloud, of course, because he knew nothing of spoken English. He had learned to read English logographically (even though it is written alphabetically) because he could not use the fact that a printed English word contains elements that correspond to elements in its spoken form. How he came to be able to write TARZAN, a word whose spoken form he knew but which he could never have seen in any of his reading materials, we cannot understand.

Then he met, and incurred the gratitude of, the French explorer D'Arnot, whom he asked to teach him to speak the language of men. So, when Tarzan pointed to the printed word MAN, D'Arnot told him that it was pronounced 'homme' – and APE was pronounced 'singe'. Such correspondence he learned rapidly, not at all impeded by the lack of any relationship between the written elements of MAN and the spoken elements of 'homme', since he had not learned printed words as sets of elements, only as wholes – **logographs** (but how could he have learned to write TARZAN?). However, when he came to try to read sentences, the grammatical differences between English and French led to confusion for him. Word order is different in the two languages, for example; and the English article THE is sometimes 'le', sometimes 'la', and sometimes 'les'.

Burroughs (1912) does not tell us how these problems were resolved. We do, however, know how the Japanese resolved the problems they encountered in adopting the Chinese system for the writing of Japanese. Consider the Japanese suffix *-te* (meaningless in itself and having a purely grammatical function). It sounds a little bit like the Chinese word *t'ien* (meaning 'sky' in Chinese). So the Chinese character for 'sky', 天

came to be used to write the suffix *-te* when Japanese was being written. But notice the major consequence this had. When the Japanese reader saw the character 水

(meaning 'water') he would have to attend to its meaning and ignore its Chinese pronunciation, whereas he had to do the opposite (ignore meaning and attend to Chinese pronunciation) with a character like 天

when it was representing the suffix *-te* (since the meaning 'sky' is utterly irrelevant here). Eventually, a different Chinese character was adopted (on the basis of its pronunciation) to represent each of

the 69 syllables of Japanese. This set of 69 characters formed the
Kana syllabary.

Over centuries of use, these 69 characters became simpler and
simpler in form – for example, the Kana character for *-te* is now

テ

– and in current Japanese the Kanji and the Kana look completely
different. The Kanji are generally large, handsome, complex,
Chinese-looking characters. The Kana are simple characters
looking like squiggles.

Figure 4 shows a page from a contemporary Japanese book.
Even if you cannot read Japanese, it is easy to tell which characters
are Kanji and which are Kana. Written next to some Kanji are
their Kana representation. This is to help less skilled readers, who
will not have learned to recognise all the Kanji they might come
across. When they find a Kanji they do not recognise, they can
obtain its pronunciation, and hence understand it, by reading its
Kana representation. This device (accompanying the Kanji by
Kana) is known as **furigana**.

椒魚の失敗にして
の花吹雪格闘事件
しいと�せられ
題して先生が山椒
てなかなか忘れ難
るほどの人物であ

FIGURE 4　Extract from a contemporary Japanese book

1.3.5 Alphabetic writing systems

Syllabic writing systems have sprung up independently in various places and at various times; this is true of logographic systems and of pictographic systems too. But the alphabetic system was developed only once, by the ancient Greeks about three thousand years ago. Alphabetic writing is defined as writing in which the individual characters of written words represent the individual basic sounds (phonemes) of spoken words. The two major alphabets currently in use (both of which developed out of the Greek alphabet) are the Roman alphabet (used to write most European languages) and the Cyrillic alphabet (used to write Russian and also used in Serbo-Croatia).

There are subtle differences (but differences which are important if we are considering the cognitive processes involved in learning to read or skilled reading) between languages in the way they use alphabetic writing systems. These differences are discussed in some detail by Coltheart (1983) and will be reviewed here in relation to the way English employs the Roman alphabet.

(a) Mapping of letters to phonemes

It is not really true to say that in the writing system used for English each letter stands for a phoneme.[2] It is often the case that a phoneme is represented by a sequence of two or even more letters. The word *thick* has five letters but only three phonemes; the word *thatcher* has eight letters for its four phonemes. A useful concept here is **grapheme**. This means the written representation of a phoneme. So *thatcher* is composed of four graphemes, which are ‹th›, ‹a›, ‹tch› and ‹er›. In English, there is (by definition) a one-to-

2 It is not even strictly true to say that English is written entirely alphabetically. There are elements of English writing which are pictographic (such as the Roman numerals I, II and III, or the X in Xmas) and there are elements which are logographic (such as most Arabic numerals, and symbols such as &, + or £). Even syllabic writing can occasionally be found in English (as in BAR-B-Q), and indeed even in Chinese. Consider the four-character Chinese word 可口可樂

These characters mean, respectively, ‘be able’, ‘mouth’, ‘be able’, and ‘laugh’, but here none of their meanings are relevant. The characters are pronounced ‘ke kou ke le’ and the whole expression is the Chinese word for Coca-Cola.

one relationship between graphemes and phonemes, but not between letters and phonemes. This is equally so for French, Spanish and Italian, for example. In contrast, for some languages employing an alphabet, there *is* always a one-to-one relationship between letters and phonemes – for example, Serbo-Croatian. As Coltheart (1985) discusses, in some forms of reading disturbance produced by neurological damage, the reader of English has a specific difficulty in grouping letters into graphemes, so this grouping process is a psychologically significant one – but one which does not occur in the reading of such languages as Serbo-Croatian.

(b) Homophones
In English, the same phoneme can be written in various ways – *f* and *ph* are pronounced the same way, for example. Because of this, one can have words with different spellings and meanings but the same pronunciation – homophones such as *knows/nose* or *eye/I*. This also happens in French and Spanish. But it does not happen in Italian, where any phoneme has only a single written form, so that if two words have the same pronunciation, they *must* also have the same spelling.

(c) Regularity of spelling-to-sound correspondences
As we have seen, the alphabetic system in English is one in which each grapheme in the written form of a word maps onto a single phoneme in the word's spoken form. But the correspondences between graphemes and phonemes are not uniform across all words: for example, in the words *splint, hint, mint,* and many others, the grapheme *i* maps onto a short 'i' sound, but there is one word, *pint,* for which this is not true. If one draws up a table of all the graphemes of English, and specifies what phoneme normally corresponds to each grapheme, then there will be a set of words which disobey these normal correspondences. Such words are known as 'exception words' or 'irregular words'; examples are *sew, yacht, gauge and colonel.* The same thing happens in French, but it does not happen in Spanish or Italian. Every word in these languages conforms to a standard set of grapheme-phoneme correspondence rules: there are no exception words at all.

We will be arguing, in Chapter 4, that there is a phase during the acquisition of reading where the child makes extensive use of rules relating spellings to sounds when attempting to read unfamiliar material. Three difficulties for the child can arise here. Firstly, the child may not appreciate that the relationship of letters to phonemes is not one-to-one. Secondly, the child who reads *sail* by using such rules will not know whether it is about ships or shops. Thirdly, such rule use will fail when applied to exception words. All three of these difficulties can occur when the child is trying to learn to read in English or in French. The Spanish child can meet only the first and second of these difficulties. The Italian child can be confronted only by the first one; in contrast, this is a difficulty that the Serbo-Croatian child will never come across. Similar points can be made when we are thinking about the processes involved in the skilled reading of English, French, Spanish, Italian and Serbo-Croatian. Consequently, although all five of these languages are written using a single kind of alphabetic writing system, there may be considerable differences between them in how reading is learned and how skilled reading occurs, differences engendered by subtle variations in the way in which the languages employ the Roman alphabet.

1.4   Overview

In this chapter we have outlined some of the main properties of language. We have distinguished between properties of language in general and properties which distinguish particular languages from others. Both kinds of properties have to be taken into account when we are attempting to formulate theories about language processing.

The next four chapters of the book, which constitute Part II, deal with various aspects of the acquisition of language. We consider the processes involved in the early acquisition of the ability to speak and to understand speech, and we discuss the subsequent acquisition of the ability to process printed language – the ability to read, write and spell. There are various ways in which children may fail to acquire one or other aspect of language processing; these developmental disorders of language are considered in Chapter 4.

Part III concerns the skilled language processor – the adult in whom the processes of language acquisition have been completed. The tasks of skilled fluent language comprehension and production depend, we will argue, upon a complex information-processing system consisting of a set of processing modules, each responsible for one specific language-processing job. We discuss how such a model can be used in attempts to describe all the things the skilled language user can do with language. We also consider acquired disorders of language – impairments in language processing caused by damage to the brain of someone who had previously been able to use language normally – and show how such disorders can be interpreted as patterns of damage to particular modules of the language-processing system with other modules remaining intact.

Part II

Language processing in children

2 Learning to talk: the earliest stages

2.1 Introduction

As we saw in Chapter 1, learning to talk requires the child to master an enormously complex linguistic system. This task is particularly difficult because, since language is arbitrary, the meanings of words are often difficult to discover. Having discovered what certain words mean the child then has to determine the complex ways in which particular words may be combined to form sentences. However, the child does not only have to discover the meaning of sentences which other people use but also to learn to produce sentences which have not been heard before. A consideration of the enormous amount of knowledge which is required to enable the child to do this might lead to the conclusion that language acquisition is an almost impossible task. Yet almost all children do learn to talk, and by five years of age most children are able to use language with a great deal of skill to talk about the world, and to ask questions about it. This chapter begins by considering some of the theories which have been advanced to account for the speed and apparent inevitability with which children learn to talk. It goes on to describe some of the research which has been carried out to gain insight into the kinds of processes which might be involved in language acquisition.

2.2 Theoretical perspectives

Several theoretical perspectives have been adopted in order to explain how children acquire language. Put at its simplest, the

29

question which distinguishes these perspectives is the extent which language acquisition is viewed as being similar to other kinds of learning. The mere fact that the term 'acquisition' is often used to refer to the child's learning of his native language might suggest that at least some theorists have seen the processes involved in learning to talk as being different in some way from those involved in other kinds of learning.

One extreme view of language learning is that it is merely a complex form of conditioning, in which the child's utterances are 'shaped' until they finally become like those used by adults. According to this view, the child plays a very passive role in the acquisition process, which is seen as being no different in kind from other learning demonstrated by man and animals, and as being heavily dependent on the child receiving appropriate linguistic input and reinforcement. Diametrically opposed to this view is one which emphasises the enormous complexity of language, and proposes that a child can acquire language only if born already equipped with very specific linguistic skills. According to this nativist view, language-learning is different from other kinds of learning in that it requires specific linguistic skills which are assumed to be innate.

Research which has been more influenced by a consideration of the kind of environment in which the child learns language has been concerned with the kind of linguistic experience which the child gains. Research which has been influenced by a more nativist view of language acquisition has sought to determine what kinds of linguistic skills the child might be using. The view of language acquisition which the researcher adopts will, therefore, play a crucial part in determining what kind of experiments he or she will carry out. Before going on to discuss some experimental studies of children's language, we will consider some of the alternative theoretical positions in more detail.

2.2.1 Skinner's view

The first view mentioned, that language-learning should be seen as a conditioning process, was advanced in great detail by B.F. Skinner in his book *Verbal Behavior*, published in 1957. As Walker (1984) has pointed out the scope of Skinner's vast work has been traditionally under-rated. The greater part of *Verbal Behavior* is not concerned with how children learn their native language, but with adult language. Poetry and metaphor are considered, as are the behavioural origins of such works as *Finnegans Wake* by James Joyce and of more prosaic utterances such as 'Pass the salt'. However, it is for Skinner's views on language acquisition that *Verbal Behavior* is best known.

The main reason that psychologists have a limited view of Skinner's views on language is that Chomsky's searing critique of *Verbal Behavior* (Chomsky, 1959) is more often read than the book itself. In order to expose what he saw as the incorrectness of Skinner's views, Chomsky summarised them in an extreme form. However, Skinner did propose that language acquisition could be explained by extending the model of operant conditioning which he had used to account for learning in laboratory animals. He also claimed that children learned language as a result of the reinforcement provided by their parents, which served to 'shape' their initially incorrect utterances so that these eventually became adult-like. However, Skinner certainly did not claim that rats could be trained to talk, because animals use vocal communication in a fixed way for expressing emotional states such as fear or anger. This is quite different from the open-ended communication in which humans engage. Moreover, he did not claim that children learned language only by copying what they heard, or by having each individual utterance reinforced. Indeed, Skinner even points out that language is made up of 'units' which can then be 'composed' into new combinations. However, Skinner was labouring under the disadvantage of not possessing an appropriate linguistic framework for exploring the significance of this insight. He was more at home discussing the environmental influences on the child rather than what might be going on in the child's head.

It is also probably fair to say that because Skinner did not have a suitable model of the nature of linguistic knowledge he did not highlight the essentially productive or creative nature of language. Thus his attempt to explain language acquisition was unsuccessful because it does not satisfactorily account for the child's rapid acquisition of the skills necessary to produce and understand any sentence in a language. However, as we will see, Skinner's views and those of Chomsky are perhaps not as diametrically opposed as it would initially appear.

2.2.2   *Chomsky's view*

Chomsky's critique of *Verbal Behavior* was published in 1959 and attacked Skinner's use of a conditioning paradigm to explain language acquisition. Although Chomsky probably did not do Skinner justice in dismissing his account of language as a system of habits acquired through extensive training, Chomsky's own account of language acquisition had a radically different point of departure which offered a significantly different picture of the child's task.

Taking as his starting point the fact that language is creative (i.e. productive, see Chapter 1), Chomsky argued that Skinner in no way explained how it is that speakers of a language learn to produce and understand *novel* utterances, which is the most important aspect of language. While admitting that reinforcement does play a part in learning to talk, Chomsky emphasised that the most important processes require the active involvement of the child. He also argued that language is only in the most marginal sense 'taught', and that parents do not normally give their children systematic linguistic instruction. Indeed, most of the time small children hear speech containing incomplete or ungrammatical sentences. This is because much of adult speech is not a perfect reflection of what speakers know about a language. When we are talking we often make mistakes; we begin sentences which are not finished, we may forget a particular word which we want to use, we may hesitate or repeat outselves. Therefore, Chomsky argued, the young child has to master a complex linguistic system on the basis of incomplete and inaccurate information. Since almost all children do acquire language, Chomsky argued that some innate mechanism must ensure that language develops in spite of these difficulties. According to Chomsky, children are born with specific linguistic skills and specific linguistic knowledge, and this enables them to learn to talk.

Although there has been much debate about the nature and existence of innate linguistic knowledge, and about whether there are such things as specific linguistic skills, most people have accepted what Chomsky went on to say about what was involved in learning to talk. He wanted to explain how a child can learn to produce and understand *any* sentence in a language. As a linguist he set out to describe the kind of knowledge which someone who knew a language would need in order to be able to do this. This knowledge is referred to as **linguistic competence** (see Chapter 1).

Chomsky argued that language can best be described as a set of rules, and that the child's task is to discover what these rules are. Chomsky proposed that the child is able to do this by generating his own rules as a result of listening to and analysing the speech he hears around him. The child can then try out these rules by producing his own sentences using the rules he has worked out. Initially the child's rules will be very simple and general, and although these rules will often produce 'correct' utterances, they will also result in utterances which an adult would never use. With time, the child modifies and adds to the set of rules he is using, until they finally produce adult speech and only adult speech.

So far there may seem little to object to in Chomsky's view of language acquisition. The suggestion that children seek to discover the rules of the language they are learning might be taken to indicate that language acquisition is essentially a process of hypothesis testing, and so is like other kinds of complex problem solving. However, Chomsky saw the kinds of processes which operate during language acquisition as unique in that they cannot operate without innate knowledge about the nature of language. In later writing, Chomsky (1965) devotes considerable space to discussing how children are capable of distinguishing correct from incorrect hypotheses about language. He argues that if the child had to work through all possible hypotheses, language acquisition could not possibly take place as rapidly or indeed as inevitably as it does. Thus Chomsky makes powerful claims about the extent to which language is pre-programmed, and therefore is acquired as the result of maturation rather than learning.

As we have already hinted, Chomsky's emphasis on the innateness of language acquisition has not gone unchallenged. We will return to this aspect of his views later but, for the moment, it is important to realise what a significant change in ideas about the nature of children's language these views represent. Before Chomsky, there had been a tendency to view early child speech as merely an incorrect imitation of adult speech. Chomsky's picture of the child as a rule-user suggested that it was important to look for internal consistencies in the child's utterances. Furthermore, as a guide to the kind of rules which the child might be using, utterances which sounded strange to adult ears were more important than those which appeared to follow adult rules. Chomsky's theoretical perspective was therefore important for psycholinguistics because it suggested what kind of patterns should be sought as evidence that language acquisition is an active process of rule-learning.

2.2.3   Piaget's view

So far we have briefly considered Chomsky's and Skinner's contrasting views about language acquisition. Needless to say, modifications of both views have been put forward; but rather than discussing these we want to consider next a somewhat different perspective on language development, which has been highlighted by Piaget. (See Piaget and Inhelder, 1966 for a summary and Karmiloff-Smith, 1979a for a recent discussion of Piaget's views on language.)

Although Piaget never made a comprehensive study of the acquisition of language, he has discussed the place of language in cognitive development. He has argued that it is impossible to isolate language from cognitive development, which he sees as preparing the way for linguistic development.

During the first eighteen months or so of life, the child learns about the world by acting upon it. Anyone who has observed a young baby will immediately notice the way in which objects are touched, smelled, held and often put in the mouth. According to Piaget, it is through exploration of this kind that the infant finds out about the world and about the way in which objects and people behave. It is only once this first stage of life (the sensori-motor stage) nears its end that language appears.

Piaget points out that once language begins the child's ability to represent the world is greatly increased. Possession of the ability to represent events linguistically allows the child to go beyond present time and space; representation through action is much more restricted in its scope. Piaget also emphasises, however, that language is only part of a much wider ability to act symbolically, for at the same time as children begin to use language they also begin to draw, to imitate previously observed actions, and to use symbolic play (e.g. the game of pretending). For Piaget, language is only possible after the capacity for symbolic action and symbolic representation has developed (at the end of the sensori-motor period), and he argues that in later stages of development too it is cognition that affects language and not the other way round. The development of new cognitive processes is a prerequisite for the acquisition of new aspects of language.

While Piaget's views are compatible with much of what Chomsky said, Piaget's emphasis on the centrality of cognitive development led him to reject Chomsky's claim that the child's ability to acquire language stems from innate, specifically linguistic structures. Piaget (1970) argues that child language appears neither as the result of conditioning processes, nor as the result of maturation of an innate neurophysiological programme, but instead through the completion of the processes involved in sensori-motor development. The completion of this developmental stage also paves the way for the development of thought through the later stages outlined by Piaget.

It is interesting to note that more recently Chomsky (1976) has admitted that the relation between the language faculty and cognitive capacity remains to be discovered. While still taking the view that there is an autonomous cognitive system capable of generating linguistic rules, he does admit that language may result only from the interaction of several mental faculties, one being the faculty of language. Chomsky concludes, 'There may be no concrete specimens of which we can say, these are solely the product of the language faculty; and no specific acts that result solely from the exercise of linguistic functions.' (1976, p.43).

Chomsky has considered this argument particularly in the context of naming things. He argues that there is probably no sharp distinction between the properties of a named object or person which are strictly linguistic, and those which form part of common-sense understanding. For example, the word 'tiger' only has meaning if we draw on our general knowledge of tigers and call up non-linguistic information about their shape, size, colour and behaviour. Our linguistic knowledge may provide information about more abstract semantic properties like male/female or human/non-human, but in order to produce or understand sentences we need *both* kinds of information. In this way the knowledge held in our linguistic system is used hand-in-hand with our non-linguistic knowledge. It is for this reason that Chomsky claims that the 'language faculty' does not operate in isolation from other cognitive processes which organise and store information about the world.

Of course it is important to note that even if it can be shown that language does have its roots in the early sensori-motor experiences of the child, and that later language development and cognitive development go hand in hand, it does not necessarily follow that Chomsky's view of language as a rule-discovering process is incorrect, because two separate issues are involved here. One concerns possible differences between linguistic knowledge and other kinds of knowledge which the child has available, and whether such linguistic knowledge is innate or acquired. The second issue is concerned with the way in which the child goes about language-learning. These two issues are at the heart of experimental studies of child language. We will go on to look at some of the studies which have been carried out in recent years to see what light they shed on the theoretical viewpoints we have examined. Since somewhat different issues are of particular importance at particular stages of language development, we will begin by considering the early stages of development.

2.3 The social context of early linguistic development

During the last decade developmental psychologists have become increasingly aware that very young children not only possess complex perceptual and motor skills, but also exhibit a wide range of social behaviours. This awareness that the very young child is a highly social creature has had important implications for the study of language development, as we will see later.

2.3.1 Early mother–child interaction

One area of particular interest has been the development of turn-taking in social situations. This has been observed in feeding, where bursts of sucking are interspersed with pauses which seem to act as signals to the mother to interact with her child by stroking, jiggling or through some other appropriate behaviour. This pattern of sucking followed by activity is typical of a great deal of adult–infant interaction in that it consists of first one partner then the other being active. Schaffer (1975) has noted that turn-taking of this kind is a particular feature of mother–baby vocalisations. He found that mothers and babies rarely vocalised at the same time, and the alternations they produced sounded remarkably like adult conversation. Schaffer suggests that this alternation results from the infant's natural tendency to vocalise in bursts, just as he sucks in bursts. As with sucking, it is the mother who fills the pauses. So, in the early stages, the regular alternation of the two sets of responses is due to the mother letting herself be paced by the infant's periodic behaviour.

A similar pattern of synchrony between mother and baby emerges when their looking behaviour is studied. Schaffer and his co-workers have observed mother–baby pairs in an unfamiliar environment. The baby sat on the mother's knee in a room which was bare except for a number of brightly coloured toys. Analysis of videorecordings made at each session revealed that there was a significant tendency for mother and infant to be looking at the same object at the same time. Closer analysis revealed that it was usually the baby who led and the mother who followed. That is, the baby looked at various toys in turn and the mother closely followed the baby's direction of gaze. Interestingly, this pattern of the mother following her child's looking behaviour continued up until the end of the first year of life, after which the baby increasingly began to follow the mother's looking.

Although in both the cases described above (vocalisation and looking) it is the mother who adapts her responses to fit in with the baby's behaviour, other evidence shows that the baby has an important part to play in eliciting behaviour from the mother. Trevarthen (1975) has compared the responses which babies make to people with the responses they make to objects, during the first six months of life.

Even when babies were just a few weeks old, they behaved in two distinct ways. Their response to *objects* was to track them, to explore them visually, and to try to grab hold of them. In contrast, they responded to *people* by waving their hands, and by a peculiar piece of behaviour which Trevarthen called 'pre-speech'. This consisted of silent movements of the tongue and lips which looked as though the child was trying to talk. It is tempting to suggest that such tongue and lips movements have some significance for the later development of speech; but at the moment their significance is not clear. However, the important thing is that the child's responses, particularly smiles, will induce adults to communicate with the child.

Normally a child has very intense and prolonged interaction with one or two adults, of whom one is usually the mother. Trevarthen (1975) has shown that over a period of time mother and baby develop a particular and individualistic style of communication which is specific to each mother and baby. They develop games like 'Round and round the garden' and 'Peekaboo'. They develop routines in which the mother might build up a tower of bricks which the baby then knocks down, or in which the mother holds out a toy for the child to take. The older the baby gets, the more complex these communication routines become.

By seven months, the age at which most babies become anxious when separated from their mothers or familiar adults, mother and baby (and often father and baby) typically have a well worked-out routine for communicating with each other nonverbally. Bower (1977) suggests that this communication routine cannot be carried out by someone who is unfamiliar with it, and that this unfamiliarity may explain why children show separation anxiety at about seven months. At this age the child has come to expect a certain pattern of interaction, and is prepared to respond accordingly. When unable to communicate with a familiar adult, and so to engage in a predictable routine, the baby is isolated from communication and so in effect alone, even when other people are present.

2.3.2   Bruner's view

The idea that mother and baby develop a communication routine, in which the child knows both what to expect and how to respond, has been seen by Bruner (1975 a and b) as vital for the emergence of language. He has also illustrated the importance of shared regard which Schaffer noted. Bruner argues that the child learns about language in the highly familiar context of the social exchanges he has with his mother. Because of this, the child is able to use his knowledge of the social situation to help work out the meaning of the speech the mother uses to comment on and interpret the situation. As Bruner puts it, such knowledge allows the child to 'crack the code' of the linguistic utterances that are heard. It is perhaps surprising that such an idea was not considered earlier; but, as Bruner points out, the fact that researchers had tended to concentrate on the creative aspect of language led them to ignore the fact that early language emerges in highly familiar contexts that have already been well establbished. Utterances may be novel: the situations in which they are emitted are familiar. These familiar contexts provide an opportunity to learn about concepts which the child will later come to express linguistically. For example, the children come to learn about the concept of **agent** (the person who carries out an action) and **experiencer** (the person on the receiving end of an action) through the turn-taking games played with the mother. Through these games they learn that they can do things and can, in turn, have things done to them. They learn about objects and the relations of objects to agents, by learning to play give-and-take games in which they first take an object from their mother and later give it back to her. Eventually the mother's comments on these exchanges will lead the child to discover a verbal way to express these concepts using non-adult forms of early verbal expression.

The fact that babies and their mothers tend to look in the same direction is crucial for such learning, because it is only when mother and child are attending to the same thing that a mother's comments about the actions and objects involved in their interaction can be interpreted. If the mother is commenting on one thing while the child is attending to another, familiarity with the situation the mother is describing will be of little use to the child.

In many ways, Bruner's ideas about the social context of language acquisition are related to Piaget's argument that a child needs to grasp a concept before learning to express it linguistically. However, Bruner differs from Piaget in stressing the importance of the **social** environment for development. Bruner also differs from Chomsky in suggesting that what may be innate about language acquisition is not specific linguistic skills, but something about human action that permits the rules of language to be derived by observing the ways in which language is used. Bruner points out, however, that the existence of the kind of processes he is describing does not necessarily preclude the existence of innate linguistic skills. It may merely suggest that they cannot operate until the child has gained appropriate experience of the underlying relationships involved in social exchanges.

2.4   Adult speech to children

2.4.1   *The nonverbal context of adult speech*

Initial support for Bruner's claim that mothers provide their children with a linguistic commentary that serves to interpret events taking place was provided by studies carried out by Messer (1978; 1980). Messer showed just how closely what mothers are saying at any moment is related to the shared activity of mother and child. He videotaped mothers and their children playing with a number of toys. The children were aged between 11 and 24 months. Analyses of the manipulation of toys and of the mothers' utterances revealed that between 73 and 96 per cent of all references to toys were made at the same time as the toy was being manipulated.

When the mothers' speech was broken down into verbal episodes, (i.e. sequences of utterances concerned with the same object), it was the case for a high proportion of episodes that the beginning of an episode could be related to the manipulation of a new toy. Since the end of one episode and the beginning of another was also marked by a long pause, the manipulation of a new toy served as an additional cue to the start of a new episode. Mothers often provided additional information about the start of a new episode by naming more often at the beginning of an episode than at other points. Thus children were presented with speech which was clearly divided into clearly marked verbal episodes, each referring to particular objects and actions to which the child's attention was simultaneously drawn. An extract from one of the interactions Messer recorded makes this clear:

Mother's utterances	Action
EPISODE A	
(1) It's a bus	child picks bus up
(2) You make it go	

EPISODE B
(3) Oh that's a super car   mother brings car to child
(4) You like cars don't you?   both hold it
(5) What are you going to do   child retains it
     with it?
(6) Are you going to make
     it go?

Messer also found that there was considerable repetition in the
mothers' speech. This would also tend to make the information in
the verbal episodes easier for the child to interpret. In particular,
the repetition of a toy name would make it easier for a pre-verbal
child to become familiar with the appropriate name for such objects.

A similar picture of the close relation between maternal speech
and the nonverbal context in which it occurs has emerged from a
longitudinal study carried out by Harris, Jones and Grant (1983).
They videotaped pairs of mothers and infants aged between 7 and
10 months. Analysis of relations between the mothers' speech and
the nonverbal context revealed that mothers constantly commented
on and interpreted their children's actions while they were playing
with their children. Almost all maternal utterances concerned the
child's immediate environment; 70% referred to an object on
which the child was currently focusing attention and 40% related to
actions which were actually being carried out, or could be predicated
from past experience of similar sequences. The following extract is
typical of the kind of exchanges which Harris et al. observed.

Mother	Child (aged 7 months)
	reaches for large teddy bear
You want to hold him don't you? (pushing bear closer to child)	putting hands around bear's nose
He's too big to hold	
He's such a. . . . He's such a *big* bear (standing bear in front of child)	

A comparison of the patterns which emerged at 7 months with those at 10 months revealed that this close meshing between language and nonverbal context was achieved by the mother taking her lead from the child. The most common pattern was for a mother to respond to what her child was looking at, or to what the child was doing. At 7 months, mothers often took the child's direction of gaze as the cue to begin a new topic of conversation. By 10 months, however, all mothers paid less attention to gaze and more to the child's activity. This change reflects the consistency with which mothers attempted to engage in child-centred conversation. At both 7 and 10 months, about 67 per cent of changes in topic were responses to a change in the child's activity. This high proportion at 7 months was only possible because a mother was prepared to take a relatively small change in her child's activity as the signal to start a new topic of conversation.

Where a mother chose to initiate a new topic, initial references to it were almost always accompanied by an action which served to make the general meaning of her utterance clear. In order to ensure that the child was attending appropriately, a mother typically waited until the child turned to look at her before making any verbal comment. In this way, a mother was able to match her speech to the child's focus of attention either by responding to the prior focus, or by changing the child's attention through her own action. These strategies resulted in the very high proportion of maternal utterances that referred to an object receiving current attention.

A recent paper by Schaffer, Hepburn and Collis (1983) has also emphasised that mothers tend to monitor what their children are doing, and to time directives so that the child is focusing on the relevant object before being asked to carry out some action with that object. The data from Harris et al. suggest that this pattern extends beyond the situation where mothers are actually trying to get children to carry out some action. When talking to their children, mothers appear to spend a considerable time watching the child's activities so that they can make appropriate comments about what the child is doing.

Demonstrating that there is a clear relationship between a mother's speech and its nonverbal context does not, however, explain how (or indeed whether) such a relation might be important in language acquisition. One hypothesis which both Schaffer et al. and Shatz (1983) have examined is that maternal speech and maternal action might have some consistent correspondence. This is an attractive hypothesis in that the task of learning language should be easier if there are two parallel systems of input for the child (verbal and nonverbal). If this were the case, understanding of one system should provide direct aid to understanding the other. However, neither Schaffer et al. nor Shatz were able to identify any consistent relation between maternal speech, action and gesture.

Shatz argues that this is because any analogies which may exist between linguistic and nonlinguistic systems are not transparent or direct. They have to be teased out by the child. Therefore, the argument that the context in which the child encounters language may aid the task of learning to talk does not detract from the claim that this task involves very complex processing. Indeed, raising the whole question of how the child learns about relations between language and the world makes language acquisition appear more, rather than less, difficult. It will probably turn out to be necessary to emphasise *both* the environmental aspects *and* the internal cognitive aspects of language acquisition in order to provide a satisfactory model of how children learn to talk.

2.4.2   *Maternal speech to children: motherese*

Another aspect of the child's environment which has been studied in some detail is the linguistic input children receive from their mothers and other adults. Research in this area stemmed initially from a reaction to Chomsky's claim that children hear incomplete and ungrammatical speech from the adults around them. As we mentioned earlier in this chapter, adult speech is often filled with hesitations and errors. As we saw in Chapter 1, this is because spoken language (i.e. performance) is an imperfect reflection of the knowledge possessed by language users (i.e. competence). Spoken language is affected by such factors as memory limitations and divided attention, and so is subject to error. However, language specifically directed towards *children* may not be so imperfect and incomplete, since it is not necessarily the case that adults talk to children in the same way they talk to other adults; and indeed recent research has shown that speech to children (known as 'motherese') has its own particular characteristics. These include peculiarities of syntax and content as well as paralinguistic features such as intonation and pitch. We will begin by discussing this latter aspect.

Garnica (1977) argued that the speech which adults use to children is systematically different in pitch and intonation from the speech adults use to other adults. She also predicted that adults' speech to younger children would differ from their speech to older children. When she compared mothers' speech to an adult with mothers' speech to their own children in standardised situations, Garnica found that mothers spoke in a higher pitched voice to a 2-year-old child than to both a 5-year-old and an adult. Garnica suggests that this use of higher pitch serves to mark a message as being intended for a young child, and so allows the child to distinguish such speech from normal adult–adult communication. Some of the mothers' comments about the need to get the child's attention when they spoke supported this hypothesis.

Another interesting feature of mothers' speech to 2-year-olds was that sentences often ended in rising pitch, even when they were not actually questions. This use of rising terminal pitch may cue the child to expect to make a response, since it is usually questions which end in rising pitch, and questions normally require a response.

Garnica also found that, within sentences, mothers emphasised important words when talking to children. For example, when mothers were explaining how to take a coloured wooden puzzle to pieces, they prolonged verbs and colour words, giving instructions like: *Push in* the *blue* piece. For the 2-year-olds, mothers also emphasised important words by stressing them, so that whereas sentences to adults normally contain only *one* primary stress, sentences to the 2-year-old often contained *two* stressed words. Garnica suggests that the longer duration of key words, plus the additional use of stress, helped the child to identify the most important words in the sentence. Since the younger children would not normally have the ability to understand every word in a sentence, making the key words stand out was particularly helpful.

A comparison of speech to the younger and older children revealed some interesting differences. Most of the features present in the speech to the 2-year-olds had disappeared in the mothers' speech to 5-year-olds. By this age, a child's attention span and linguistic knowledge has greatly increased, and so the child does not require so many cues about what should be attended to and about when responses should be made. However, mothers still tended to emphasise colour names in the puzzle task and, occasionally, to use higher pitch. This suggests that even when the children were 5 years old, mothers still felt that they needed some help to understand instructions.

Other researchers have concentrated on the syntactic aspects of motherese. One of the best known studies was carried out by Snow (1972). She asked mothers to talk to a 2-year-old and a 10-year-old and found that, on several measures of grammatical complexity, mothers used more complex and longer sentences when speaking to the older children than when speaking to the younger children. In order to see how much mothers' speech was influenced by the child's responses, Snow also asked mothers to imagine they were talking to an absent child. On every measure of syntactic complexity, mothers used simpler speech when the child was actually present.

At first sight, this might suggest that the simplified form of motherese results from the feedback which the child provides about his ability to understand language. However, another of Snow's findings suggests that this explanation may be too simple. When women who were not mothers were asked to record some suitable instructions for a 2-year-old who was not present, Snow found that the speech of mothers and non-mothers was almost identical. Experienced mothers were only slightly better at predicting the kind of simplified speech which would be best suited to young children, suggesting that familiarity with children does not affect motherese. Of course, it is not possible to make the critical comparison between mothers and non-mothers speaking to a child who is present; so the extent to which the characteristics of motherese are determined by immediate feedback, rather than general familiarity with young children, is not clear. Since mothers spoke more simply when the child was present, and also used slightly shorter and less complex sentences than non-mothers, Snow's experiment suggests that linguistic feedback from the child is important for determining the fine-tuning of motherese, but perhaps not for determining its general characteristics. This is an issue we will return to later.

As a result of her study of motherese, Snow concluded that, contrary to what Chomsky had claimed, children are *not* presented with a confusing input of complex and ungrammatial sentences. Rather, young children hear organised, simplified and redundant sentences which provide an ideal basis for language learning. Snow's findings about the nature of mothers' speech to children have been confirmed by several subsequent studies, including one carried out by Phillips (1973). She found that motherese was syntactically less complex than normal speech, with sentences being shorter and containing fewer verbs, modifiers and function words such as adverbs. Phillips also found that true motherese did not reliably appear until children were old enough to respond to it, that is, towards the end of the first year of life.

This again raises the question of what determines the character of motherese. Cross (1977, 1978) has argued in favour of a linguistic feedback hypothesis. This emphasises the importance of the linguistic feedback which young children provide about their attentional and language comprehension skills, and is based on the finding that motherese is adjusted to the receptive maturity of the child. In other words, motherese is simplified most for children with the least mature comprehension skills. A later paper by Snow (1977) proposed what has become known as the 'conversational hypothesis', which emerged from her longitudinal study of two infants. Snow noted that, for both infants, their mothers produced simplified speech long before the children were capable of providing detailed feedback. What seemed to be important was each mother's expectation that the child was capable of interacting with her. Thus, the most marked change in the way the two mothers talked to their children came not when the children had developed some comprehension skills, but at about 7 months. When the children reached this age the mothers ceased to talk about the child itself, and began to talk about items and events in the child's immediate environment. (This is supported by the pattern which emerged from the Harris et al. (1983) study discussed earlier.) The mothers also became more demanding about the kind of vocalisations they would respond to.

With 3-month-old children, the mothers produced a large quantity of speech with very little response from the child. By 7 months, however, the interaction had assumed much more of a turn-taking pattern, even though the children's repertoire of responses had not greatly increased. This was because the mothers waited for the children to make some sound which could be interpreted as a contribution to the conversation.

Although Snow saw the conversational hypothesis about the determinants of motherese as an alternative to the linguistic feedback hypothesis discussed earlier, more recent research has suggested that a multi-factor account is necessary. A recent paper by Cross, Johnson-Morris and Nienhuys (1980) reported findings from a study of mothers' speech to hearing and hearing-impaired children. A study of the latter provides the opportunity to see how much motherese is affected by feedback from the child, and how much by mothers' expectations of the child's potential to become a fully participating conversational partner. The 2-year-old hearing-impaired children were similar to much younger normal children in that they could not understand any words, but their linguistic *potential* was not the same as that of younger normal children.

Three main patterns emerge from the Cross et al. study. First, mothers speaking to hearing children addressed them differently from hearing-impaired children, matched either for age, or for level of spontaneous language use. This confirms the hypothesis that variation in the linguistic **receptivity** of the child is a crucial determinant of motherese, since the comprehension skills of the hearing and hearing-impaired children differed even though their level of spontaneous language use was the same. However, linguistic receptivity cannot be the sole determinant because, on some of the measures of mothers' speech used by Cross et al., there were no differences between speech to the hearing children and speech to the hearing-impaired children with the same level of spontaneous speech. This suggests that some aspects of motherese are determined by the current level of the child's conversational skills, rather than a general ability to understand language.

The third important finding was that mothers spoke more simply to pre-linguistically deaf children than to hearing infants of the same age, who had begun to use language. Cross et al. interpret this as evidence that a mother's awareness of hearing-loss does, in itself, lead to simplification of maternal speech. The differences between mothers' behaviour to the older hearing-impaired children and behaviour to the hearing children, which Cross et al. attribute to differences in linguistic receptivity, might also have been due in part to a similar maternal reaction to having a child who does not hear normally. Cross et al. conclude their paper by arguing for a multifactor account of the determinants of motherese, in which the linguistic receptivity of the child is seen as the major determinant; but such factors as a child's ability to take part in a conversation, and his mother's expectations about his potential skills, are also seen as important.

2.4.3   *Relations between adult speech and children's language development*

Analysing the factors which determine the form which motherese takes does not, however, shed light on another very important question which we raised earlier in the context of comments by Shatz (1983) on the relation between maternal speech and the nonlinguistic environment. This question concerns the possible influence of the kind of speech which children hear on the speed with which they master language. Even though it would appear that Chomsky's claims about the nature of the child's linguistic input are incorrect, this does not necessarily mean that children actually *require* simplified language in order to acquire language themselves. Wells and his co-workers have carried out a longitudinal study of the development of children's spoken language, in which they have assessed the influence of the speech which children hear on the rate at which they develop language.

Data reported by Ellis and Wells (1980) reveal that children's rate of linguistic development is *not* related to the length and complexity of the adult utterances addressed to them. However, rate of development is related to differences in the frequency of particular styles and topics of conversation in parental speech. In particular, children showing the earliest and most rapid linguistic development received more acknowledgments of their own utterances, more directives, and more questions. Presumably, acknowledgments provide the child with feedback and reinforcement. The reason why directives appear to be helpful is less obvious, but Ellis and Wells point out that the kind of directives which are used to small children usually refer to objects or actions with which the child is involved at the time of speaking. Adults typically ask young children to do something which is related to their present situation. They also tend to ask questions which are closely related to the child's current activity or environment. Thus, both directives and questions may aid linguistic development because they present a symbolic encoding of information which the child is already likely to have represented non-linguistically. Since the acquisition of language involves the teasing out of relations between the linguistic system and the world, providing linguistic information about something the child is familiar with should make this task easier.

Ellis and Wells also report that children showing accelerated language development received more adult speech which referred to activity in which the child alone was engaged. Furthermore, there was a trend for conversations with the earliest and most rapid language learners to concern current household business. Since routine household activities become familiar through repetition, as do the child's own activities, it would seem that children benefit most from adult speech which can be related to familiar activities about which the child already has considerable non-linguistic knowledge.

This picture of the relation between adult speech and children's linguistic development fits in well with Bruner's view that language is acquired in a highly familiar social context which serves to aid cracking of the linguistic code. It also fits in with the picture of maternal speech which emerges from the Harris et al. study. Taken together, Bruner's hypothesis about language development and the experimental studies we have discussed suggest that language acquisition is not aided by the *syntactic* simplicity of motherese, so much as by the simplified relation which adult speech to children bears to the child's world. Indeed, we might suggest that the typical syntactic simplification of motherese comes about as a consequence of the restricted nature of the conversation which most people have with young children.

Before leaving our consideration of the relation between adult speech and children's language development, we will discuss one final experiment which suggests that the different strategies adopted by mothers when they talk to their children may have some influence on language development. Howe (1980) reports a study of the linguistic development of a group of children initially aged between 20 and 22 months. At this stage the children all showed similar levels of language development. However, when the children were filmed with their mothers three distinct patterns of conversation between mother and child emerged.

In all mother–child pairs, the children rarely initiated conversation by requesting information from their mothers, or responded to their mothers by giving anything other than minimal replies; but there were interesting differences in the mothers' speech. In one group, mothers rarely initiated conversation by a request for information, but frequently responded to children's comments by expanding on them and giving the child additional information. Howe refers to this kind of reply as 'extended'. An example of the kind of conversation which typically went on between a mother and child in this first group is shown below:

(Mother and Oliver play with animals)
M.   Look, a little monkey.   (provision of information)
O.   Monkey   (acknowledgment of old
                                      information)
M.   Yes, he's trying to drive a   (extended reply)
     lorry, isn't he?
O.   Drive. Drive.
M.   Drive, uhm.
O.   Drive.

In a second group, mothers often began a conversational exchange by asking the child for information, but they rarely gave extended replies to their children's comments. The following conversation between Ian and his mother typifies this pattern:

(Mother shows Ian another car)
M.   What colour's that one?   (request for information)
I.   Yellow   (provision of information)
M.   It's a yellow one.   (minimal reply)

     What colour's this one?
I.   Yellow.
M.   No it's red.
I.   It's yellow.

In a third group of mothers and children, both features of the other two patterns were present. Mothers frquently requested information, as well as responding to the children's comments with extended replies, as the following example illustrates:

(Mother and Kevin look at pictures)
M.   And what are those?   (request for information)
K.   Shells.   (provision of information)
M.   Shells, yes.
     You've got some shells   (extended reply)
     haven't you?

     What's that?
K.   Milk.

Howe was interested in finding out whether these different conversational patterns would have an effect on the children's language development. When she assessed their linguistic skills three months later, she found that differences had emerged between children in the three groups. As one would expect, the language of all children had advanced, but children in the third group showed the greatest advance. Children in the second group were ahead of those in the first group on one semantic measure.

Howe attributes the greater linguistic development of children in the third group to the kind of linguistic experience which they gained through conversation with their mothers. Since children in this group showed greater syntactic and semantic development than children in *both* other groups, this suggests that both characteristics of the group three pattern were important. That is, children benefited most from requests for information, together with extended replies to their own comments.

The importance of extended replies, that is elaborating upon something which the child has just said, has been highlighted in earlier research, notably that by Cross (1978). The reason why linguistic experience of this kind appears to be useful is that it provides the child with an ideal opportunity to extend his or her linguistic knowledge. However, Howe's findings suggest that this is not the only important factor. Since children in group three showed greater linguistic development than those in group one, who also received extended replies, the additional factor of requesting information from the child seems to be important too. If children have the opportunity only to acknowledge information provided by the mother, they are forced into a relatively passive conversational role. Asking children for information which they can provide gives them an opportunity to play an active role in conversation and to display their developing linguistic skills. This experience may motivate linguistic development to a greater extent than merely allowing a passive role. A similar explanation can be given for the superiority on one semantic measure of children in group two over those in group one. Children in group two were given frequent opportunities to provide information while those in group one were not.

2.5   Overview

The theoretical and experimental evidence which we have discussed in this chapter suggests that the context in which children learn to talk is of great importance. Children do not learn about language in isolation. They learn to talk at the same time as they are developing knowledge about people, objects and events in their world. Theories of language acquisition must take account of this, and must attempt to explain the complex relation between the child's internal processes and the linguistic and non-linguistic experience the child is gaining from the environment. This chapter has concentrated mainly upon experimental studies of how the young child's linguistic and nonlinguistic environment influences the course of language acquisition. We will now go on to consider the internal processes underlying language acquisition – that is, to consider experimental evidence about the way in which the child attempts to work out the rules which govern spoken language.

3 Learning to talk: later developments

3.1 Introduction

As we saw in the previous chapter, Chomsky's claim that children have to learn language by listening to adult speech which is full of errors has not been supported by studies of the way adults talk to children. However, although the linguistic data which children have available to them is simplified, repetitive and relatively error-free, the process by which they discover the rules on which language is based remains a complex one. This chapter is concerned with some of the experiments which have been carried out to investigate the kinds of cognitive processes which are involved in acquiring and storing information about the structure of language.

Although we chose to discuss studies of the child's linguistic environment in the chapter before this one, it should be remembered that such studies began relatively recently, whilst the research which we will be discussing in this chapter began a decade earlier, in the 1960s and was therefore strongly influenced by Chomsky's claim that language acquisition was an innately based process of rule-learning. What particularly captured the imagination of researchers in child language was Chomsky's view that what had to be explained was the child's ability to acquire the necessary knowledge to produce and understand *any* sentence in his native language. It was widely accepted that any model which was based on imitation was implausible because it could not cope with the creativity of language. Miller (1968) calculated that in order for a child to learn all the 20-word sentences of English by hearing each one only once, he would have to have a childhood lasting

100,000 million centuries, during which he did nothing but listen to sentences. You may recognise that this is a somewhat unfair attack on Skinner's view of language development; but this calculation does emphasise that the probability of having heard any particular 20-word sentence before is extremely low.

3.2   Rules in early child language

Chomsky's proposal that children have to learn rules which tell them how to produce and understand speech was spelled out in detail in 1965. It stimulated a series of studies which attempted to find out whether early child language showed evidence of rule use. The basic procedure was to record samples of children's spontaneous speech, and to look for regular patterns in the way they constructed utterances. Once these regularities had been determined, researchers attempted to write a series of rules which would account for these regularities. These rules formed the **grammar** which described the speech of the particular child being studied. The exact theoretical status of rules and grammars derived in this way was not always clear. As we saw in Chapter 1, a satisfactory linguistic description may not be a satisfactory psychological one. That is, a set of rules may describe the language a child is using without telling us anything about the way in which that child actually combines words into utterances or performs any other linguistic activity.

Another important question about rules is whether they are specific for each child, or specific to particular languages, or universal. Chomsky's claim that language is acquired as the result of specific linguistic knowledge and skills, which are innate, implies that the rules children develop during the course of language acquisition are universal. For this reason, much of the research carried out into the grammar of early child language was directed towards the discovery of universal rules, which would account for patterns found not only in English, but also for patterns found in the acquisition of other languages. It should be noted, however, that although innateness requires universality, universality is in itself not necessarily evidence that a particular process is innate. (See Cromer (1974; 1979) for a discussion of this point.)

3.2.1 Grammars of early child language

The studies of children's language which were carried out in the mid 1960s in the United States have been described in detail elsewhere. (See Brown (1973) and de Villiers and de Villiers (1978).) We will therefore mention only two studies, those of Braine (1963) and Brown and his co-workers (Brown and Bellugi, 1964; and Brown and Fraser, 1964).

Braine studied three children for a period of four months beginning from the time they began to use two-word utterances – in this case, when they were aged between 1.7 and 1.11, i.e. 19 and 23 months. His analysis of all interpretable utterances, except those which appeared to be imitations of immediately preceding adult utterances, revealed a common pattern. The children appeared to be grouping words into two classes. One class consisted of a small number of words which occurred frequently, and were always placed in initial position. Braine called these **pivot** (P) words. The other class of words was much larger. These words occurred less frequently than pivot words, and they did not have a fixed position in the children's two-word utterances, although they most frequently occurred in second position. Braine called these **open** (O) words.

The most common pattern to appear in the two-word utterances of the children Braine studied was of a pivot word followed by a word from the open class i.e. P + O. However, there were also some utterances which consisted of an open word followed by a pivot. Since these pivot words were not the same as those which occupied initial position, but they came from a small class, were used frequently, and had a fixed position, Braine called these P_2 words to distinguish them from initial-position pivots (P_1). Some of the children's other utterances were formed from two open-class words, and there were also some which consisted of a single open-class word. Pivot-class words did not occur on their own. Examples of some of the two-word utterances produced by Gregory, one of the children studied by Braine, are shown overleaf.

The study carried out by Brown and his co-workers adopted a similar method of analysing children's speech. This time two children, who were given the pseudonyms Adam and Eve, were studied; and later another child, Sarah, was also studied. Samples of their speech were taken at various stages in the early development of their language, from the point when they were just beginning to produce multi-word utterances.

$P_1 + 0$	$0 + P_2$	$0 + 0$
see boy	push it	mommy sleep
see sock	move it	milk cup
pretty boat		oh-my see
pretty fan		
more taxi		
more melon		
bye-bye melon		
bye-bye hot		

One of the points which Brown noted was that many of the two-word utterances produced by the children were not like adult speech. If you look back at the extract from Gregory's speech you will observe that this was also true of the utterances in Braine's study. Brown was particularly interested in non-adult utterances because he felt that these provided clear evidence that children acquire language actively by constructing their own rules, rather than passively. Application of these rules sometimes leads to rather bizarre utterances, as the following samples of Adam's and Eve's early speech reveals. Non-adult utterances are marked with an asterisk.

A coat	My stool	Poor man
*A celery	That knee	Little top
*A Becky	More coffee	Dirty knee
*A hands	*More nut	That Adam
The top	*Two sock	Big boot
My mummy	*Two tinker-toy	

Looking carefully at this group of utterances, which are all noun phrases (NP), it is possible to see that they have a common pattern. The second word is always a noun, and the first word gives more information about it. Brown concluded that Adam, Eve and Sarah were constructing noun phrases by adding any modifier (M) word in their vocabulary to any noun (N). This can be expressed as:

$$NP \rightarrow M + N$$

Close inspection of the modifier category reveals that it does not correspond to any grammatical category used by English-speaking adults. It contains articles, a possessive noun, a quantifier, a cardinal number, some descriptive adjectives, and a demonstrative adjective. For Adam, Eve and Sarah all these different words seem to function as a single class having a common privilege of occurring before nouns; it is this which leads to the production of sentences that an adult would consider ungrammatical. However, as the children's language developed, they began to differentiate between the different kinds of word in their modifier class. Initially, articles (Art) and demonstrative pronouns (Dem) were distinguished from other modifiers, and this led to the use of more complex rules, for example:

$$NP \rightarrow Art + M + N \qquad \text{e.g. The driver's wheel}$$
$$NP \rightarrow Dem + M + N \qquad \text{e.g. That mommy sandwich}$$
$$NP \rightarrow Dem + Art + N \qquad \text{e.g. That a page}$$

Brown saw this progression from very simple, general rules to more complex and specific ones as support for Chomsky's claims that the first rules which children use are very simple and general; and that although children often produce adult-like utterances, they also produce sentences which an adult would never use. However, the conclusions which were drawn from the studies of early child grammar we have just been considering have been the subject of criticism from several sources.

One of the most influential critiques was made by Bowerman (1973). She reviewed data from a number of studies of English-speaking children as well as data from children acquiring Finnish, Luo (a Kenyan language), and Samoan. Bowerman's aim was to see whether the patterns of rule use which emerged from the Braine and Brown studies were universal. She concluded that Braine's pivot grammar did not even accurately represent the speech of young American children, let alone the early utterances of children acquiring languages other than English. There were certain similarities between the speech of Braine's children and those considered by Bowerman. In particular, all the children tended to use a small number of words in relatively fixed positions, a finding which subsequent studies have confirmed. However, Bowerman found that the children's words rarely incorporated all the properties which Braine had ascribed to pivots, i.e. fixed position, not occurring alone, not occurring in conjunction with another pivot word. On the other hand, none of the children appeared to be using a large undifferentiated class of non-pivot words. They appeared to divide words into several different classes. However, it may have been that the children Bowerman considered were more advanced than those studied by Braine, since we have seen that differentiation of word classes increases with age.

3.2.2   *Semantic development in early child language*

An even more serious criticism of Braine's findings was concerned with another matter, which also affects other studies of child grammar carried out during the same period, including Brown's study. Bloom (1970) argued that such studies failed because they did not accurately represent the extent of the child's early grammatical knowledge. This was because they had described the *syntactic* structure of children's early language and had ignored the vital point that language is used to convey *meaning*. Therefore they had said nothing about the early meanings which children might be trying to express by their utterances.

Studies of children's language carried out in the 1970s attempted to remedy this omission, and the decade saw the beginning of what became known as 'rich' interpretations of child speech. These involved going beyond the form of children's speech to include an interpretation of what the child intended to say.

One of the first of these studies was carried out by Bloom in 1970. She realised that it was important to record not only what children said, but also to make a note of what was happening at the time of each utterance. This additional information about the context allowed Bloom to ascribe a wide variety of meanings to children's two-word utterances. For example, Kathryn, one of the children observed by Bloom, said 'party hat' as she picked up a hat worn for parties. Bloom classed this as an **attributive** utterance because it referred to a hat which had to do with parties. Some other examples of Kathryn's utterances, together with Bloom's interpretation of them, are shown below:

Utterance	Context	Classification
sweater chair	K. puts her sweater on the chair	locative
mommy sock	K. picking up mother's sock	possessive
mommy sock	K. having sock put on by mother	subject-object

You will notice that the last two examples are formally identical but, since they were used by the child in two distinct situations, Bloom interprets their meaning differently. One is concerned with the ownership of a sock, the other with what mommy did to the sock. Thus Bloom is suggesting that different semantic relations can be expressed by apparently identical utterances; and that within the syntactic restrictions of two-word utterances, the child intends to express a wide and varied set of semantic relations between the two words being used.

A similar point was made by Slobin (1971), who compared the semantic functions of two-word utterances in a number of different languages including German, Russian and Finnish. He found that there was a remarkable consistency in the types of relation which were expressed. Some examples are given below:

Semantic relation	Examples
locative, name	there book, that car, see doggie
demand, desire	more milk, give candy, want gum
negation	no wet, no wash, not hungry, allgone milk
possessive	my shoe, mama dress

Brown (1973) presents a detailed review of the other attempts which were made to interpret the semantic development of early language. Various problems have been raised about particular interpretations, but rather than discussing these, we will consider some of the more general problems inherent in attempting a rich interpretation of early utterances. One of the most serious of these is that, even when there appears to be a clearly observable context for a particular utterance, the researcher's interpretation of the child's intended meaning remains subjective. For example, it may be that the child does not construe the contextual situation in the same way that an adult would; and even if child and researcher do view the situation from the same perspective, there remains the problem of deciding what particular aspect of the situation the child is referring to. For these reasons, some independent justification for assigning a rich interpretation to child speech is needed.

As we will see later in this chapter, one way to provide additional evidence is to carry out controlled experiments. However, these are extremely difficult with children in the first stages of language acquisition (usually under 2 years of age). An alternative approach is to carry out longitudinal studies of children, and to discover what kinds of meaning they appear to be expressing in the early stages before they have developed differential ways of expressing such meanings by the choice of different grammatical and semantic forms. The next stage in the investigation is to see if it is these previously identified meanings which appear later, once the child has discovered ways of distinguishing them grammatically. For example, in English, different verb tenses have different endings, and children eventually have to learn to use all of these. The question is whether the particular tenses which children seem to be aware of early on (when they only use one verb form) are the ones which they use when they first use different verb endings, or **inflections** as they are called.

Brown (1973) looked at the way in which verb inflections were acquired by Adam, Eve and Sarah. In the earliest stages they used verbs in their uninflected form, e.g. come, fall, break, drink. Nevertheless, the way in which the children used these verbs suggested to their parents, as well as to Brown, that they were aware of several different types of meaning. One of these was the description of an action of temporary duration which was occurring while the child was speaking. In adults, this would be described by use of the present continuous tense. A second meaning was reference to an action in the immediate past, and a third concerned the child's immediate wishes or intentions. A fourth use of verbs was as imperatives.

Brown noted that the children soon learned ways of modifying the simple verb form they had previously used on all occasions. They began by marking the past tense by use of the regular *-ed* ending, for example 'It dropped', as well as some irregular past tense forms such as 'It fell'. They also modified the verb by using it in conjunction with semi-auxiliaries such as 'gonna', 'wanna', 'hafta', when they wanted to convey intentionality or to refer to something just about to happen, e.g. 'I wanna go', 'It's gonna fall'.

A third way in which Adam , Eve and Sarah modified the verb was by using a primitive progressive form consisting of the *-ing* ending without an auxiliary. For example, they might say 'Fish swimming', rather than the adult '(The) fish *is* swimming'. Note that these three modifications correspond exactly to three of the four meanings which had appeared to be present at the uninflected stage, namely, reference to the immediate past, the immediate future, and to a currently occurring event. The fourth meaning, the imperative, is not marked by an inflection in English, but instead by tone of voice. However Adam, Eve and Sarah found a way round this problem. At the same time as the other three tenses were distinguished by inflections, the children began to add 'please' to signal the imperative. No doubt this was a direct result of parental training.

Several other studies have provided similar evidence that children appear to be aware of meanings early on in their language development which only later become capable of differential expression through use of inflections. Bloom (1970) noted that the children she studied appeared to use the word 'no' in three rather different ways in two-word utterances. The first was to express **rejection** as in 'No dirty soap', spoken as a piece of dirty soap was pushed away. The second was to describe **non-existence** which was used when the child was talking about something not present, as in 'No pocket', spoken as the child handled a piece of cloth which had no pocket. The third meaning of 'no' was **denial**, as in 'No truck', spoken in response to a car.

Bloom noted that ways of expressing each of these three kinds of negation appeared in a fairly consistent developmental order of rejection, non-existence and finally denial. Rejection was expressed mainly by use of 'don't', replacing 'No pants' by 'I don't need pants off', and 'No eat' by 'Don't eat it'. Non-existence was usually marked by 'more', as in 'No people' becoming 'No more people', and 'No lights' becoming 'No more lights'. Denial was usually indicated by the use of 'not', as in 'That not lollipop' and 'It's not cold' replacing 'No lollipop' and 'No cold'.

A more recent study by McShane (1980) of six children during their second year of life has confirmed these early uses of negation, and has added two further uses which appear to emerge at the same time. These are the uses of 'no' to comment on the child's failure to carry out some action which he or she was attempting, and a conversational use of 'no' to deny or contradict something someone else has said. These uses of 'no' are different from the four identified by Bloom because they are not modified later, and they can appear on their own.

The studies by Brown, Bloom, and McShane support the idea that the child begins to expand his use of particular words before he has acquired the ability to reflect this expansion by the use of a different form for each different function. There is thus some support for the claim that contextual information about early language use can provide an insight into aspects of development which might otherwise escape attention. However, while it useful to chart subtle changes in the development of word usage in this way, it may be unwise to make strong claims about the semantics of two-word utterances, as a 'rich' interpretation has traditionally done. It must always be remembered that children's meaning systems, and their construction of the world, are not necessarily the same as those of adults. Any interpretation of what the child means must be seen as an approximation. As we will discover, in some cases children's routes to the discovery of adult meanings may lead them up some blind alleys.

3.3   Strategies in sentence comprehension

So far we have considered the evidence for looking upon language as a rule-learning process. We have seen that there is considerable evidence that children attempt to use the words they know in a wide variety of different constructions which are often unlike those which an adult would use. Such attempts lend support to Chomsky's view that language acquisition is an active process in which children are developing hypotheses (or rules) about their native language. However, so far it has not been possible to draw firm conclusions about whether the linguistic hypotheses which children develop and test out are the same for all children. We will consider this question by reviewing some of the experiments which have been carried out to investigate the acquisition of various kinds of complex syntactic form.

One advantage of considering the later stages of language acquisition is that it is possible to carry out controlled experiments. The studies we have mentioned so far in this chapter, as well as those in the previous chapter, were essentially observational. That is, they observed the way in which children use language spontaneously. This kind of approach is extremely useful, particularly for studying the earliest stages of lexical and semantic development. However, observation of language *use* does not necessarily provide an accurate reflection of lingusitic *competence* since, on the one hand, children may well understand much more than they are capable of producing and, on the other, they may be producing linguistic forms they do not fully understand. The use of different experimental paradigms allows a researcher to build up a more detailed picture of how much a child knows about language at particular points in development. In order to illustrate this approach we will begin by considering how information is built up about one particular syntactic form, namely the passive.

3.3.1   Strategies for interpreting the passive

One reason why the passive has been the subject of a large number of experiments is that it is a syntactically complex form which takes a considerable time to acquire. By assessing what children know about the passive at different points in their development, it is possible to gain some insight into the processes involved in acquisition.

One of the first experimental investigations of the acquisition of the passive was carried out by Bever (1970). Bever hypothesised that the passive is not correctly understood by many children because they adopt an incorrect strategy which correctly interprets the majority of active sentences, but which leads to an incorrect interpretation of passives. This strategy, known as the NVN strategy, involves the assignment of the interpretation actor-action-object to any noun-verb-noun sequence. For example, in a sentence like *The girl kisses the baby* the NVN strategy would interpret the first noun, *girl*, as being the actor and the second noun, *baby*, as being the object. Since this is an active sentence, this interpretation is correct. However, if the same strategy is followed with a passive sentence like *The baby is kissed by the girl* an incorrect interpretation arises, with *baby* being treated as though it were an actor rather than an object, and *girl* being incorrectly treated as an object rather than an actor. This leads to an interpretation which is the reverse of the correct meaning.

What is particularly interesting about Bever's claim is his suggestion that from about the age of 3 years the way children interpret passive sentences is affected by *the kind of event* described in the sentence. Bever suggests that children do not use the NVN strategy if this leads to an interpretation which is inconsistent with the child's experience of what is likely in the world. For eample, a child might attempt to interpret a passive sentence like *The flowers are being watered by the girl* using the NVN strategy. This would lead to the interpretation that flowers are watering a girl. If the child has had sufficient experience of events in the world to realise that such an interpretation is very unlikely to be correct, the NVN strategy will be rejected for that particular sentence, and a more plausible interpretation accepted.

Bever's investigation of children's comprehension of active and passive sentences confirmed that young children frequently interpreted passive sentences incorrectly. However, children of three years and over were able to understand passives in which one noun was clearly the actor, and the other the object. For example a sentence like *The dog is patted by the mother* was correctly understood by 3-year-olds, but a sentence like *The horse is kissed by the cow* was not. This latter kind of sentence, where each of the nouns is equally likely to be the actor, is known as a **reversible** passive. Sentences like the first one, in which one noun is more likely to be the actor, are known as **nonreversible**.

Several subsequent studies have confirmed that nonreversible passives are understood correctly before passives in which there is no indication of which noun is the actor. (See Sinclair, Sinclair and de Marcellus, 1971; Strohner and Nelson, 1974; Harris, 1976.) These experiments support the idea that children use their knowledge of the world, that is, their nonlinguistic knowledge, in order to augment their linguistic skills. As we saw in the previous chapter, this process of relating linguistic and nonlinguistic knowledge is one which begins in the earliest stages of development.

Another way in which children are able to augment their current linguistic skills is by using information about the linguistic context of a particular utterance. This process has been illustrated in an experiment carried out by Dewart (1975). She presented children aged between 3 years 5 months and 4 years 10 months with sentences which were prefaced either by an appropriate context which set the scene for the sentence, or by an inappropriate context which did not. In the following examples, example (a) has an appropriate context, and examples (b) and (c) show the same sentence with an inappropriate context.

(a) Poor duck.   The duck is bitten by the monkey.
(b) Bad duck   The duck is bitten by the monkey.
(c) Poor monkey. The duck is bitten by the monkey.

Dewart asked the children who took part in her experiment to act out the sentences using hand puppets. She found that her subjects were much better at assigning a correct interpretation to the sentences prefaced by an appropriate context, like (a).

Later in this chapter we will describe some further evidence that children are able to make use of information provided by the linguistic context when trying to interpret particular syntactic structures. However, before doing so, we will continue our discussion of factors involved in the acquisition of the passive by considering another of the experiments carried out by Dewart (1975) which examined the effect of animacy on children's comprehension of active and passive sentences.

Dewart presented 4-year-old children with sentences containing one nonsense word in place of a noun. The children's task was to decide which of several toys the nonsense word referred to. Half the toys were animate (dolls or animals) and the other half were inanimate objects. The children showed a clear pattern of preference. If the nonsense word was the *first* noun in the sentence, children usually selected an *animate* toy as the one being referred to, whereas if it was the *second* noun an *inanimate* was usually selected. This pattern was the same for actives and passives, and suggests that 3- and 4-year-old children assume that the first noun in a sentence is animate and the second inanimate.

This might appear a rather unlikely strategy for children to adopt; but there is evidence from an experiment by Harris (1978) that this strategy plays a part in sentence production as well as comprehension. Harris presented children aged between 5 and 10 years with line drawings in which the animacy of both actor and acted-upon (i.e. object) was systematically varied. The children's task was to describe what was happening in each of the pictures; and the animacy of actor and acted-upon proved to have a strong influence on the kinds of description which the children gave. When the actor was more animate than the acted-upon, a picture was invariably described using an active. For example, one such picture was invariably described as depicting *A policeman riding a bicycle*. In contrast, when the acted-upon was more animate than the actor, passives were often used in descriptions. A typical 'passive' picture was described as *A boy being knocked down by a car*. Furthermore, a passive was most likely to be used when the acted-upon was human and the 'actor' inanimate, as in this example. Fewer passives were used when an animal and an inanimate object were depicted, and even fewer when a human and an animal were shown.

These two experiments suggest that animacy is an important cue which children use in interpreting and producing passive sentences. They provide an interesting illustration of the way in which an aspect of the child's *non-linguistic* environment (i.e. relations between animate and inanimate things) becomes an important part of his linguistic knowledge. However, some of the knowledge which the child uses in the process of acquiring new syntactic forms is based on his existing *linguistic* knowledge.

Harris (1976) has illustrated the way in which children pick up syntactic cues, as well as semantic ones, while they are in the process of discovering how to interpret passive sentences. She pointed out that the majority of English passives are not like those we gave in the previous examples in that they do not contain a by+agent phrase at the end. Typical passives are like the following: *The boy was run over. The girl was kicked.*

Passives of this kind are usually known as **truncated**, although in terms of their greater frequency this term is something of a misnomer. One important difference which this commonly occurring passive has from many active sentences is that is contains only *one* noun. Therefore, passives without agents cannot be interpreted using the NVN strategy, which we mentioned earlier. Harris therefore predicted that truncated passives would be interpreted correctly at an earlier age than passives with agents. This prediction was tested by presenting children with pairs of pictures in which the object and actor in one picture were the actor and object in the other. For example, one picture in a pair showed a dog licking a lamb, and the other a lamb licking a dog. Children were read a sentence and asked to point to the picture it described.

The results of the experiment revealed that the youngest children (who were under 5 years) found passives with and without agents equally difficult; they also found reversible and non-reversible passives equally difficult. Children of 6 years were capable of understanding all the different types of passive. The most interesting results came from the children between these ages, who were in the process of acquiring the passive. These children found passives without agents easier to understand than those with agents; and non-reversible passives easier than those in which either noun could be a plausible actor. Non-reversible passives without agents were the easiest of all and reversible passives with agents, like *The lamb is licked by the dog*, the most difficult of all. This pattern of difficulty suggests that children rely both on linguistic knowledge, and on non-linguistic knowledge, as they discover how to interpret unfamiliar syntactic forms.

3.3.2 *Individual differences in comprehension strategies*

So far we have considered experimental evidence for strategies which all children seem to use while they are acquiring language. However, there is an increasing body of evidence which suggests that different children may use different strategies. One of the studies carried out by Dewart (1975) demonstrated that children's interpretation of a particular kind of sentence followed several distinct patterns. The sentences which Dewart used contained two nouns which were direct object, and indirect object respectively. For example in a sentence like *Send the cat to the dog*, the first noun is the **direct object** and the second noun is the **indirect object**. However, in a slightly different sentence like *Send the dog the cat*, the first noun is the **indirect object** and the second noun is the **direct object**.

Dewart asked children to act out sentences like these, and other similar ones using toy animals in carts. In this way, it was possible to see which of the two animals mentioned in each sentence was interpreted as being the direct object. Not all the children treated the sentences in a consistent way, but of those who showed consistent strategies, some always treated the first noun as direct object; others always chose as direct object the noun not marked by *to* sentences where this preposition occurred. One child used the strategy that the noun nearest the verb was the direct object, while another always chose the second noun as direct object. In other words, at least one child used each of the possible strategies consistently.

The experiment by Harris (1976) on children's comprehension of different kinds of passive sentences, which we described earlier, also provided evidence of different strategies being used by different children. While the overall results showed that both non-reversibility and the absence of an agent improved children's understanding of passives, some children were only aided by non-reversibility and not by truncation, while others were aided by truncation but not by non-reversibility. A third group of children were only capable of understanding passives which were both truncated *and* non-reversible.

Recent experiments by Nicolaci-da-Costa (1983) and Nicolaci-da-Costa and Harris (1983) have provided further evidence of individual differences in children's use of comprehension strategies. These experiments were concerned with acquisition of a somewhat different aspect of English, namely number markers (ways of distinguishing singular and plural forms). One experiment used a picture-pointing task to investigate children's comprehension of the contrast between sentences like *That sheep is jumping* and *Those sheep are jumping*. These particular sentences contain *two* number markers indicating that the first sentence refers to one sheep and the second to two sheep. Compare them with two sentences like *That girl is jumping* and *Those girls are jumping*, which contain *three* number markers, namely a demonstrative, a regular noun, and an auxiliary verb. Nicolaci-da-Costa's experiment was concerned with the effect which increasing the number of markers would have on children's ability to interpret sentential number. She hypothesised that children would be more successful in deciding whether a sentence was singular or plural if number was marked in several different ways. This proved to be the case. However, an analysis of the way in which the presence of *particular* number markers affected individual children revealed that redundant number marking produced three different patterns of response.

The first response pattern was one of consistent use of one particular marker. For example, some children correctly understood the number of all sentences containing regular nouns (like girl/girl*s*). Other children did not reliably understand number in sentences containing only one number marker, but they were able to understand sentences in which two or more number markers occurred together. A third group of children combined both of these strategies, and understood all sentences containing one particular marker, as well as some sentences which contained two other markers, which were not reliably interpreted when they occurred alone.

These three different studies which we have just described all lend support to the idea that different children use different strategies while they are in the process of discovering the meaning of particular aspects of syntax. Before we end our discussion of individual differences in the use of strategies, we should point out that there is also evidence that such differences between children appear in the very early stages of language development.

A seminal study by Nelson (1973) investigated the acquisition of the first fifty words by eighteen children. One of the most interesting things to emerge from her study was that the children differed greatly in their use of early words. Nelson found that she was able to divide the children into two groups. One group, which she called the **referential** group, was object oriented and had a large number of object names in their first fifty words. The other, the **expressive** group, was more oriented towards people, including themselves. They used language mainly to express their feelings and needs.

Nelson followed the development of these children to see whether there would be other differences associated with these two different patterns of use. She found that both groups of children acquired their first ten words at the same rate. However, the subsequent vocabulary development of the referential group was faster. They acquired more words per month than the expressive group, and had attained a higher vocabulary by two years. However, the expressive group showed a faster rate of *syntactic* development. They acquired their first ten phrases faster than the referential group. By two years of age, the expressive group were producing more complete grammatical utterances (like *Don't do it*) than the referential group, who produced simpler utterances, like *More car*. These differences have been confirmed by several later studies, including that by Barrett (1979).

The mounting evidence that there are important differences in the patterns which children show during language acquisition implies that a strict nativist account of acquisition cannot be correct. Language is not acquired in an identical way for all children. Therefore those aspects of acquisition which are innate must be general, rather than specific. The kind of model which best accounts for individual differences is one which regards language acquisition as a process in which the child develops hypotheses, and tests them out. While there will be underlying similarities in these hypotheses, the precise details will differ from child to child, although the nature of language itself, and its relation to the world, means that the range of hypotheses which the child will develop and test out will be circumscribed.

3.4   Developing linguistic hypotheses about language

As we have seen from our discussion of the kinds of strategies whch children use in acquiring language, much of language acquisition involves the use of non-linguistic knowledge. However, some of the problems which the child has to solve about language are purely linguistic ones, which have no non-linguistic counterpart. One clear example is the gender system, which has no clear semantic basis. For example the word 'soap' is masculine in French, feminine in German and neuter in Russian. The acquisition of the gender system in French has been investigated by Karmiloff-Smith (1979a). Of course, languages like English do not have a comparable system, but Karmiloff-Smith's experiments are of general interest because they illustrate the acquisition of a purely linguistic system, and so shed light on the kind of processes which may be involved generally in language acquisition.

Although the French gender system has no clear semantic basis, it is closely related to the form of particular word endings. The pattern of these endings is apparent both in written and spoken French. For example, the 'on', 'eau' and 'ois' endings typically indicate a masculine noun, whereas the 'elle', 'ienne' and 'ette' endings are typically feminine. For the child, it will initially be the phonological rather than orthographic characteristics of word endings like this which are noticed, although later their orthographic regularity may become important. Karmiloff-Smith was interested in discovering whether young French children would be able to use this phonological regularity to predict the gender of unfamiliar words, or, alternatively, whether the children would initially relate gender to semantic distinctions when possible.

Theories which have emphasised the importance of relating linguistic distinctions to non-linguistic ones would predict that semantic distinctions are important for acquiring the gender system.

Karmiloff-Smith investigated children's knowledge of the French gender system by presenting them with pictures to which were given, as names, nonsense words which had either masculine or feminine endings; for example, *bicron* and *coumeau* should be masculine, whilst *podelle* and *forsienne* should be feminine, according to their endings. The children were asked various questions involving the nonsense words, and their replies were analysed to see which gender they had ascribed to a particular word. Perhaps surprisingly, even the youngest children (who were 3 years old) were sensitive to the phonological regularities of gender. In the condition in which the nonsense words were preceded by articles (le/la; un/une) all the children performed much better when the information given by the article was consistent with the noun suffix. Even more surprisingly, when the children were presented with a picture of an obviously masculine or feminine figure, the children followed the phonological cue for gender until ten years of age. While older children did take account of the apparent gender of a depicted figure, where there was a discrepancy between apparent gender and phonological gender, the phonological information was treated as paramount.

What Karmiloff-Smith's findings illustrate is that children are capable of detecting internal consistencies within their linguistic environment, even when these consistent patterns do not have an exact parallel in the child's non-linguistic environment. This ability is crucial for language acquisition because, even when the pattern of non-linguistic events is a good guide to important linguistic distinctions, the child still has to discover the precise nature of the linguistic pattern which reflects the non-linguistic one. For example, although children need to discover that number markers are used to reflect the singularity and plurality of real objects, they also have to discover that different nouns are made plural in different ways; and that verbs and demonstratives, as well as nouns, have to be marked for number. Learning to talk requires children to detect patterns both in the language they hear and in the events which language describes, for it is only then that the child can detect the crucial, but often tenuous, links between the two.

3.5   Acquiring communicative competence

There remains one important area of language acquisition, which we have not so far mentioned because it is one not considered in any of the theoretical perspectives we considered in Chapter 2. Up to this point, we have been concerned with how children acquire a knowledge of what is syntactically and semantically appropriate. However, as Hymes has pointed out in an influential book entitled *On Communicative Competence* (1971):

> We have to account for the fact that a normal child acquires knowledge of sentences, not only as grammatical, but also as appropriate. He or she acquires competence as to when to speak, when not, and as to what to talk about with whom, when, where, in what manner.

Hymes describes this latter kind of knowledge as **communicative competence**. It has been the subject of much research, particularly in sociolinguistics, where issues such as sociocultural influences on language have received much attention. In developmental psycho-linguistics, one aspect of communicative competence which has been seen as particularly important is the acquisition of the conversational skills which allow children to take account of their listeners, and to modify their own speech accordingly.

3.5.1   Egocentrism in child speech

Long before Hymes' book, Piaget (1926) suggested in *The Language and Thought of the Child* that children were generally bad at modifying what they were saying for the benefit of a listener. Piaget claimed that one illustration of this inability came from an experiment in which he had asked children to explain the operation of a water tap, where the handle had to be turned in order to let water run out. Having established that the children understood the process themselves, Piaget asked them to explain the operation of the tap to another child, who did not know how the tap worked. Even children of 8 years found this task very difficult. They did not provide enough information, and took it for granted that the other child would understand certain crucial terms and expressions. The following explanation of the operation of the tap was provided by a boy of 7 years 6 months:

'It's a fountain. It either runs or it doesn't. When it's like that it runs. And then there's the pipe the water goes through. And then, when it's lying down when you turn the tap, it doesn't run. When it's standing upright, and then you want to turn it off, it's lying down . . . And then when it's standing upright it is open and when it is lying down it is shut.' (p.108)

With hindsight, it seems reasonable to suggest that many adults would have difficulty in giving a verbal explanation of the operation of a tap. However, most would probably be more successful than this boy, and the other children tested by Piaget. The main reason that the above decription is so confusing is that pronouns are used without their referents first being defined. How can a description which includes so many references to an undefined 'it' possibly be clear?

Piaget argued that children of 8 years and below are bad at explaining things to other people because their speech is **egocentric**. By this Piaget meant that children are encased in their own point of view when they are trying to explain their own thoughts, or to understand those of others. Because of this, children are often unaware of the differences between their own knowledge of the world and that of others; and whereas adults make an effort to understand and to be understood, children think that both states can be achieved without effort.

Recent research has, however, suggested that children are far more aware of the needs of their listener than Piaget suggested. Such awareness seems to begin very early in development, although it takes some considerable time for the child to acquire all the linguistic skills needed to communicate efficiently. Keenan and Klein (1975) observed the social interaction of twin boys during a twelve-month period beginning when the twins were 2 years 9 months old. The twins' conversation during the early hours of the morning was recorded since it was carried on without the presence of an adult. Sometimes the twins' attempts to communicate with each other were minimal, and the utterance of one bore no relation to the preceding utterance of the other, as the following extract illustrates:

Twin 1   goosey goosey gander . . .
Twin 2   [i:] moth, [i:] moth
Twin 1   goosey goosey gander, where shall I wander
Twin 2   [i:] moth, [i:] moth, [i:] moth, [i:] moth
Twin 1   upstairs downstairs in the lady's chamber . . .
Twin 2   [i:] moth, [i:] moth, [i:] moth

Finally, the singer of the nursery rhyme takes notice and stops singing:

Twin 1   [i:] moth?
Twin 2   gone moth, all gone

Keenan and Klein found that the twins frequently took note of what had just been said, and responded to one another's utterances. Sometimes one twin would simply repeat what the other had said, but often their exchanges contained agreement or denials, like the following:

Twin 1   cradle will rock, cradle will fall, cradle will rock
Twin 2   no cradle will fall

Twin 1   you silly
Twin 2   no you silly.

On other occasions one twin would add further information to the other's previous utterance:

Twin 1   flower broken. flower . . .
Twin 2   many flowers broken

Of course, it could be argued that twins are particularly good at communicating with one another. However evidence from an experiment by Maratsos (1973) suggests that children who are not related at all are sensitive to the kind of response which is best suited to a particular situation. In this experiment, children aged between 3 and 5 years had to explain to an experimenter which of several toys should be placed in a toy car. In one condition, the experimenter put her fingers over her eyes so that it appeared she could not see the toys, whereas in the other condition, the experimenter looked at the toys.

Maratsos was interested to find out whether the children would be sensitive to the fact that they would need to give more explicit information when the experimenter could not see the toys than when she could see them. Even the 3-year-olds showed evidence of realising this, with all age groups giving more explicit information when the experimenter had her eyes covered. For example, when the experimenter was looking at the toys, the children often just pointed to the toy which should be put in the car, whilst, when she could not see, the children almost never just pointed.

Since pre-school children in Maratsos' study were able to give more explicit information when necessary, this raises the question of why Piaget's subjects failed to be sufficiently explicit in their descriptions of the tap. One explanation may lie in the fact that Piaget's subjects had to describe something which was extremely complicated. Perhaps it was not that they were unaware of the needs of their listeners, but that they were unable to take these into account in their explanations because so much of their attention was devoted to remembering what they had to say. After all, it is normally easier to produce a simple and clear explanation of something you understand very well, than it is to describe something you can only just understand yourself.

An experiment by Peterson, Danner and Flavell (1972) suggests that it is important to distinguish between the child's awareness of what kind of information is needed in a particular situation, and his ability to provide that appropriate information. Peterson et al. asked 4- and 7-year-old children to describe a nonsense figure to an experimenter in such a way that he could pick it out from several other similar figures. The experimenter responded in one of three predetermined ways to the child's description. He either gave the child a puzzled and bewildered look, but did not say anything; or he made some comment to the effect that he did not understand which figure the child was referring to; or he explicitly told the child how the child should help him. In this last condition he said things like, 'Look at it again. What else does it look like?' and 'Can you tell me anything else about it.?'

Neither 4- nor 7-year-olds were very good at realising that they should reformulate their descriptions when only the experimenter's expression indicated that he did not understand. However, when the experimenter *said* that he did not understand, there was a difference between the age groups; the 7-year-olds frequently reformulated their descriptions but the 4-year-olds did not. In the explicit condition (where the experimenter suggested how the child might help him) both 4- and 7-year-olds frequently provided more information. Thus, the difference between the age groups lay not in their ability to provide additional information about the figure, but in their awareness that this was what was required. This is illustrated by the fact that several of the younger children attempted to provide 'helpful' information when the experimenter indicated that he did not understand which figure they were referring to. However, the information which they provided was inappropriate and essentially useless because it was not additional information about the figure. For example, they said things like 'Look harder' or 'Maybe look over on the other side'. Only the 7-year-olds realised that when the experimenter requested more information, they should provide additional information about the defining features of the target figure.

Providing the right kind of information is, of course, only one aspect of communicative competence. Another aspect is selection of an appropriate speech style. What is appropriate varies from situation to situation. For example, presenting a political speech involves one particular style, which is quite different from the style normally used in private conversation. Learning *how* to talk to different kinds of people is an essential part of learning to become a competent language user.

3.5.2 Taking account of the listener

Martlew, Connolly and McCleod (1978) recorded the spontaneous speech of a 5-year-old boy, Jamie, in three different situations; playing alone, playing with a friend of the same age, and playing with his mother. Several differences between Jamie's speech in the three conditions emerged when the transcripts were analysed. One of the most obvious was that Jamie's speech to his mother contained many more elaborate utterances than were typical of the other two conditions, and far more questions, but fewer commands. This was because many of the conversations Jamie had with his mother consisted of his replying to her questions. In contrast, the two play situations were frequently concerned with fantasy.

However, there were important differences between these two situations. When playing alone, Jamie's talk consisted almost entirely of dramatic dialogue in which the invented characters had appropriate voices. In this situation, Jamie did not need to describe the scene he imagined; but when playing with his friend he often gave precise details of the scene. This sometimes led to trouble when there was disagreement about the details:

Jamie   Look the coach comes along here you know.
Friend   No but – I know – but this car knows, so the
         robbers . . .
Jamie   No it's not.
Friend   No it says yes 'cos don't forget there's no coaches or
         buses travelling.
Jamie   There is.
Friend   There's not.
Jamie   I don't care the game doesn't have to be the same as
         anything.
Friend   Well it can be. Do it yourself.
Jamie   I'm not going to play with you then.
Friend   You're not to.
Jamie   All right then, shoo. Have all your stuff.

It is interesting to compare this exchange between two equals with the conversations Jamie had with his mother, in which he had a subordinate position:

Jamie   Where can these two go?
Mother   They could go in the zoo couldn't they?
Jamie   Where there's some fields.
Mother   Well maybe they use tractors in zoos sometimes for
         pulling something along, something heavy.
Jamie   Oh yes.
Mother   If there's a heavy cage to lift or something like that.

Such a comparison suggests that Jamie had already acquired one aspect of communicative competence. In Hymes' words, Jamie had learned 'what to talk about with whom . . . [and] in what manner'.

Martlew et al.'s findings that Jamie's speech was more complex to his mother than to either himself or his friend is in line with several earlier studies carried out by Shatz and Gelman (1973). They recorded 4-year-old children talking about a toy to adults, to 2-year-old children, and to peers, and found that the 4-year-olds spoke in a different way to the three kinds of listener. When talking to the 2-year-olds, as opposed to peers or adults, they produced shorter utterances. They also used less complex sentences, avoiding co-ordinate and subordinate constructions. They were also more inclined to use words which would attract and hold the younger child's attention.

Sachs and Devin (1976) also found that pre-school children did not talk to younger listeners in the same way that they spoke to their mothers or peers. These differences did not depend solely on the child responding to feedback from the younger children, because the children simplified their speech both in response to a younger child and when they were asked to talk to a doll.

A recent experiment by Evans (1980) has confirmed these earlier findings. She recorded the speech of pre-school children explaining a simple game involving the movement of a toy bus along a road. The bus stopped to set down and pick up passengers. The following extracts are from the instructions which 4-year-old Adriana gave to her mother, and to her 2-year-old brother Dominic:

(to her mother)
Adriana   Mum. Can you do this game? All the people have to
         get in and stop. And put some in the field. Then go on
         and go to the house and get out.
(Experimenter   You show her what to do.)
Adriana   There's the lady that goes in the middle. That's a girl.
         There's a dog. A boy, another boy, and it goes off. It
         drops two off in the field. It drops two off in there.
         That one can be the bus driver. That can. Then it
         goes back to the people in the field. Then it stops at
         the station.
(Experimenter   Where's the station?)
Adriana   Then it stops at the station and all the people get out
         and then they get back on the bus again.
(to Dominic)
Adriana   Dominic, I'm putting some people in the bus. Now
         drive off. Now drive off. Down to the end. Drop some

people off. Drive off to the next village.

Mother	He can't hear you.
Adriana	Drive off down to the village, darling. They stay there. Now are you going to do that?
	You have to go down here. Stop here you do. Drop some people on, off there.
	Then go back to the village and drop some people off there. Now you push this bus and you go off down the lane. Drop two people down here. And down here . . .
	There is one bus stop.
	And another bus stop here . . .

As these extracts reveal, Adriana tended to use shorter sentences when she was talking to her brother, and to give simpler instructions. When the mean length of her ten longest utterances to her mother was compared with that of her ten longest utterances to Dominic there was a striking difference; 12.4 morphemes to her mother compared with 9.5 morphemes to Dominic. This illustrates just how sensitive even young children are to the way in which language has to be adapted to suit particular situations.

3.6 Overview

In this chapter we have discussed some of the complex aspects of spoken language which children have to learn about before they can become fully competent speakers and listeners. We have seen that children not only have to discover the relationship between syntactic and semantic aspects of language, but also about the pragmatic aspects of language which are essential if the child is to use language appropriately in its social context. We have described studies of child language which have explored a variety of these aspects, and we have included both recent studies and studies which were carried out some time ago.

We will end this chapter, and our discussion of the acquisition of spoken language, by noting some of the changes which have occurred in the overall picture of development emerging over the past twenty years. During this time there have been countless experimental and observational investigations of children's language (and we have only had space to describe a few of these in Chapters

2 and 3). Needless to say, the picture of language development which has emerged from these studies is a complex one. However, if we compare the views which were held in the early 1960s with those appearing today, there seems to be fairly general agreement that language development takes place over a rather longer timescale than was originally claimed.

McNeill (1966) expresses the kind of view commonly held in the 1960s that 'in approximately thirty months [i.e. from 18 to 48 months] . . . language is acquired, at least that part of it having to do with syntax'. In contrast, Karmiloff-Smith (1979b) has argued that fundamental changes continue to take place in children's language beyond the age of 5 years and, as we have seen, Bruner (1975a;b) has argued that language has its earliest roots in the social interaction between young infants and their parents.

There are at least two main reasons why the development of language is now seen as taking place over a longer period of time. The first reason is that our concept of what the child has to acquire in order to become a fully competent adult language user has broadened beyond mere lexical and syntactic competence, to include such skills as the ability to understand and produce coherent discourse, (which involves being able to draw inferences as we discuss in Chapter 7), and to produce language which is appropriate for a particular listener and a particular situation (as we have seen in Section 3.5). Some of the abilities involved in these kinds of linguistic skills continue to develop well into adolescence. (See Brown and Yule, 1983; Kress, 1982; Stubbs, 1983.)

The second reason why language acquisition is seen as a more gradual process is that the development of more sophisticated experimental techniques has allowed researchers to investigate children's comprehension, as well as production. Such investigation has often revealed that a particular linguistic form is not fully understood when a child first uses it. We described in Section 3.3.1 how understanding of the passive develops from a stage when there is no understanding, through a stage of partial understanding involving specific strategies, to complete understanding of all types of passive. Karmiloff-Smith's (1979a) has shown a similar pattern in French children's interpretation of determiners like *les* and *mes* which goes through three distinct stages. Full comprehension is often not achieved until 12 years of age. This contrasts strongly with the picture presented by production, since children use these determiners apparently correctly as early as 3 years of age.

The other change in the picture of language development is that, in contrast to earlier searches for the existence of *linguistic universals* across cultures, there has been an increasing tendency to see the pattern of development as not necessarily identical for all children even within a single culture. We discussed some examples of individual differences in Section 3.3.2. Such individual differences are consistent with a move away from the view that language acquisition is essentially pre-programmed in the way Chomsky proposed in 1965. This is not to deny that there might be an essential innate component in language development, but it seems inevitable that explanations of the child's acquisition of language will become increasingly complex, as we attempt to take account of the wide range of linguistic and nonlinguistic information (both in the world, and in the child's current representation of the world) which could have an influence on the way in which children develop hypotheses about language.

4 Learning to read

4.1 Introduction

In the previous two chapters we considered how a child might learn to use and understand spoken language. We concentrated particularly on those aspects of language development which take place over the first five years of life, while recognising that many aspects of language acquisition do not take place until well after the child has entered school. However, once children start attending school developments in their spoken language tend to be overshadowed by development of another linguistic skill, namely learning to read.

For most children, the process of learning to read is very different from the acquisition of spoken language. As we saw in the previous chapters, learning to talk is a gradual process which has its roots in the earliest patterns of communication between child and adult. Children are seldom actually *taught* how to speak their native tongue, which is normally acquired in a gradual manner with children having the opportunity to learn at their own speed. In contrast, reading is almost always explicitly taught and the pace and sequence of learning is typically dictated by the person who is teaching the child to read. In spite of this, the process of learning to read has only recently begun to be understood and in this chapter we will describe some of the many experiments which have been carried out on children's reading. We will concentrate particularly on studies which have attempted to discover *how* children learn to read.

4.2 Alternative procedures for reading

Imagine a child who is at the very earliest stage of learning to read
– a child who can read aloud just a handful of words. Suppose that
the word *cat* is one of these: that is, the child, shown this printed
word, can say 'cat'.

How is this done? That is, what are the mental processes used by
the child to transform the orthographic representation *cat* into the
phonological representation 'cat'? This question is usually
approached by arguing that there are at least two different mental
procedures which the child might be using to read aloud, either of
which would be sufficient to produce successful reading aloud of a
word like *cat*.

The first of these general procedures, which in the context of
discussions of learning to read is usually called the **whole-word
procedure**, but which we will call the **direct procedure**, depends
upon the child having previously learned a direct correspondence
between the letter string *cat* and the spoken representation 'cat'. If
this is how our imaginary child is reading the small set of words
that he or she can read, then the child has learned a small set of
direct correspondences between the printed forms of a few words
and their spoken forms. A child who is just beginning to learn to
read will be familiar with the *spoken* forms of a large number of
words, of course, because reading normally begins at a point when
the child has already acquired a large vocabulary of words in
spontaneous speech. Access to this large set of spoken word forms
from print will, however, be severely limited at this stage of
learning to read. It is only for a small set of words that the child
has developed learned correspondences which allow the particular
word to be found in a store of spoken words which corresponds to
the printed form the child is looking at.

An alternative possibility for explaining how our child can read
cat aloud is to propose that the child can use a system of spelling-
to-sound rules: a **phonics procedure**. Perhaps the child knows
that *c* is pronounced /k/, *a* is pronounced /ae/ and *t* is pronounced
/t/, and by applying these three rules to the letter string *cat*, the
child can transform it into the spoken form 'cat'. This is an indirect
procedure in the sense that the child links print to pronunciation
via an intermediate step (the use of spelling-to-sound rules) rather
than using previously learned direct correspondences between

individual printed words and their spoken forms.

Because the child would succeed in reading *cat* aloud using either procedure, the observation that *cat* has been successfully read aloud provides us with no evidence concerning which of these two procedures the child actually used. Hence much research on learning to read takes the form of attempting to investigate the relative contributions made by these two general procedures in the early stages of reading: and this will be a basic theme of our chapter.

It is not only learning to read which is frequently discussed within this two-procedure framework. As will be seen in Chapter 6, most current models of skilled adult reading are 'dual-route' models, i.e. they postulate that the skilled reader has at his disposal at least two different procedures for converting print to speech (procedures which correspond to the direct and phonics procedures, although they are more often called the **lexical** and **non-lexical** procedures when skilled reading is being discussed). Furthermore, attempts to understand the various distinct ways in which reading can break down after brain damage are also often based upon the two-procedure idea, as we will see in Chapter 9. For example, one kind of reading disorder described in that chapter, the disorder known as **phonological dyslexia**, arises when a person can still use the direct procedure to read but finds it difficult or impossible to use the phonics procedure; and another kind of reading disorder, **surface dyslexia**, is the reverse – the use of the direct procedure to read has been impaired by brain damage with the phonics procedure remaining usable.

The relative importance of the direct and phonics procedures for the early stages of learning to read is a subject which has been debated for at least two centuries. Many strong views have been expressed, with each procedure having its advocates, who have pointed out the obstacles to learning to read which are inherent in the other procedure. There is no doubt that a child learning to read solely by using the direct procedure would have to deal with a set of problems arising because of the nature of that procedure. There is also no doubt that a different set of problems will arise for any child learning to read solely by using the phonics procedure.

The major difficulty for the direct procedure is that the knowledge of reading that a child accumulates using this procedure is not general knowledge, but word-specific knowledge, and is of no use when the child is trying to read a new word. A child who has learned to read *cat* and *hot* using the direct procedure will not thereby be assisted when he tries to learn *hat*: the fact that *hat* has some letters and some sounds in common with *cat* and *hot* will not be relevant, because the child is not learning about the relationships of letters to sounds.

A related disadvantage of using the direct procedure in learning to read is that it does not allow the process of learning to read to be parasitic upon a skill already possessed by the child, namely, understanding speech. What we mean by this is that, if a child knew something about letter-sound rules, he could take a completely new letter string and convert it into spoken form despite having never seen it before. If this novel letter string is one of the many words which are in the child's spoken vocabulary (i.e. is one of the words which the child can understand when it is heard) but not in the child's written vocabulary (i.e. has never been seen before), then the child, having converted the word from print to speech, will be able to understand it using the already well-developed ability to understand spoken words. A child reading via the direct procedure could not make this kind of use of existing knowledge of spoken language, because the child could not convert an unfamiliar letter string to its spoken form, even if this spoken form is a familiar word to the child.

These difficulties for the direct procedure are, of course, advantages of the phonics procedure, which *does* allow generalisation to new words (if the letter-sound rules needed to read *cot* and *hat* have been mastered, this allows correct reading of the words *hot* and *cat* without any new learning being needed) and which *does* allow reading comprehension to be parasitic upon speech comprehension.

However, the phonics procedure has its own problems. One is that the learning of correspondences between letters and sounds is a much more abstract task for a young child than the learning of correspondences between a whole printed word and its spoken form. In the former case, the units being dealt with (letters, sounds) are meaningless, whereas in the latter case they are meaningful, since they are words. A second problem is that, for a number of the elementary sounds of English, one cannot teach the letter-sound rules in any explicit way, because one cannot pronounce the sounds of certain letters. The sounds of the stop consonants *p t k b d* and *g* cannot be pronounced in isolation. They must be followed by a vowel, even if it is only the 'neutral' vowel as in 'puh', 'tuh', etc. Therefore one cannot teach a child that the letter *p* corresponds to the sound /p/ by showing the child the letter and saying the sound, because the sound cannot be said. What is usually done is to teach that *p* corresponds to 'puh': but now when the child comes to use this rule he will fail unless he can strip away the vowel 'uh' and treat the rule as *p* →/p/. The difficulties young children have in carrying out this phonological stripping can be heard in any classroom in which phonics teaching methods are used, and these difficulties are not encountered if a direct procedure is being used when a child is reading.

A final difficulty for the phonics procedure is the irregularity of English spelling. A child who was perfect at employing the phonics procedure (that is, at reading aloud using letter-sound rules) would not thereby read perfectly: errors would be made with all those words of English (a substantial proportion) whose spellings do not conform to standard letter-sound rules (words like *sew*, *yacht* and *pint*, for example). Once again, this would not be a problem for users of the direct procedure, since when this procedure is used correspondences between letters and sounds are irrelevant.

Considerations of this kind indicate that both procedures present problems when used during learning to read. Nevertheless, the skilled reader is someone who can use both procedures, as we will see in Chapter 6. Therefore, at *some* stage in learning to read, anyone who is going to become a normally skilled reader will have to learn to use the direct procedure, and at some stage will have to learn to use the phonics procedure. Hence we wish to discuss learning to read in terms of the acquisition of, and the relative importance of, these two procedures.

The sketch of how reading is acquired which we will discuss is based upon ideas proposed by Marsh, Friedman, Welch and Desberg (1981), Seymour and McGregor (1984), Frith (1985) and Seymour and Elder (1985), although we differ from these authors on various matters of detail. Some of these ideas are well supported by experimental evidence; others are somewhat more speculative and anecdotal, because for these there is not yet any relevant experimental evidence available.

The basic view we will propose is that children normally proceed through four broad phases as they progress from being entirely unable to read to possessing a normal adult level of skilled reading. The first phase we will call the **sight-vocabulary phase**; the second the **discrimination-net phase**; the third the **phonological-recoding phase**; and the fourth the **orthographic phase**.

4.3 Four phases in learning to read English

4.3.1 The sight-vocabulary phase

For any child in this first phase of learning to read, which emerges when children are perhaps 4 or 5 years of age, there exists a small set of words – a **sight vocabulary** – which the child can read aloud; the child uses the **direct procedure** to read these words. The ability to read this small group of words may have been acquired through teaching (a common practice amongst reading teachers is to teach children to read a small group of words, using whole-word methods, before attempting to begin to teach them to read using phonic methods) or acquired 'spontaneously': some children appear to learn to read individual words aloud without teaching, simply through their own observations of pairings of particular printed words and particular pronunciations (on television, for example). Even very young children can master this phase of reading: there are case studies (e.g. Fowler, 1962) of children as young as 2 years of age who had established sight vocabularies of some hundreds of words.

Both teachers and parents frequently affirm the existence of this sight-vocabulary phase as a very early stage of reading, a stage which may even be attained by a child before any explicit teaching of reading has begun. But very little is known about this phase of reading, because it has not been systematically studied. Some of the ways in which it could be investigated are, however, fairly obvious. This will be illustrated by discussing some informal studies of a 4-year-old child, Alice, who was, when studied, in the sight-vocabulary phase of reading.

She could read about thirty words; some of these (her name, her parents' first names) she had been taught to read, whilst others had simply been 'picked up'. However, unfamiliar words and non-words could not be read aloud at all. One example of a word which had been learned without being taught was the name 'Harrods', which Alice could and did read aloud from the sides of buses and from the store's shopping bags. This was a useful item for investigating the nature of Alice's whole-word reading, because one could be fairly certain that on every encounter the word would have the same visual format, namely that shown in Figure 5.

On the assumption that Alice had never seen this word in any other visual format, one can use the word to learn something more about the details of how word reading is actually achieved during the sight-vocabulary phase. A popular proposal has been that children in the sight-vocabulary phase recognise words in terms of their overall shape. This is plausible: if words are not being read by letter-sound rules, perhaps the fact that they are made up of letters is completely ignored, and they are treated as indivisible visual wholes, as single visual patterns.

This could be tested with Alice, by asking her to read this stimulus:

hArRoDs

Here is a word-shape, a visual pattern, which Alice had certainly never seen before. If her direct procedure for reading was based on recognising words as visual wholes, she would be unable to read this word, since it was entirely unfamiliar as a visual whole. This is not what happened. She read the word promptly as 'Harrods'.

In spite of the very small number of words in Alice's sight-vocabulary, it was possible to replicate this 'experiment' with a different word, because amongst the words Alice could read at this stage was the one shown in Figure 6. Since she had only read this word from the fronts and backs of cars, one can be sure that she had only seen it in this particular visual format. When she was presented, however, with the completely novel visual format:

fIaT

Alice was able to read it correctly.

These examples show that the direct procedure for reading used during the sight-vocabulary phase (a procedure which does not rely on letter-sound rules) does not necessarily depend on recognising words as wholes (by their overall shapes, for example), because giving a word a completely different and novel overall shape does not prevent a child from reading the word by the direct procedure. If the observations made with Alice are generally true of children in the sight-vocabulary phase, then the direct procedure

FIGURE 5   Harrods

FIGURE 6   Fiat

appears to operate by recognising words as *particular sequences of letters*, even though the procedure does *not* involve translating these letters into sounds. If this is true, the direct procedure involves analysing words into their constituent letters in order that the words be recognised, and hence it would be misleading to refer to the procedure as being one of 'whole-word' recognition.

One might propose that Alice recognised words by identifying only some – perhaps even one – of their letters. Perhaps she would read *any* word beginning with h or H as 'Harrods'? This was briefly tested as follows. Amongst the words she could read was *Max*, and the first time she saw this in the unfamiliar form *mAx* she read it correctly. To determine whether she was simply responding to one of the letters in the word, she was shown

mAx

rAx

mOx

mAv

and asked to indicate which of these four words was 'Max'. She succeeded, and her success in doing this suggested that she was using all three of the letters in the word *Max* to recognise it. If she were not she would not have been able to distinguish *Max* from all three of the other items in the list.

4.3.2   *The discrimination-net phase*

We have just considered, and rejected, the idea that the way Alice identified those few words she could read when she was 4 was by using fragmentary cues (the initial letter, for example) from each word. It turns out, however, that in the next phase of reading development it is precisely this kind of use of fragmentary cues which is responsible for increases in the number of words which the child can read aloud.

What is most characteristic of reading behaviour in this second phase, as demonstrated by Marsh et al. (1981) and by Seymour and Elder (1985), is that when a child is asked to read single words or non-words aloud, the response produced is virtually always a choice from amongst the set of words which have been used in the child's reading lessons. Thus in this phase reading aloud takes the form of selecting, from amongst the set of words that the child knows that he or she has learned to read, the one that most closely matches the letter string that has been presented for reading aloud.

The term 'discrimination-net phase' is used to describe this phase of reading acquisition for the following reason. The child behaves as if the task of reading single words is the task of deciding which of the words in the child's reading vocabulary is the item which has been presented. Of course, the item presented might be a word outside this vocabulary, or even a non-word, but the child behaves as if these possibilities are to be ignored. The job is to collect just enough information from the printed stimulus to discriminate sufficiently between all the words in the reading vocabulary so as to decide which word in this set should be produced as a response.

When the child has just entered the discrimination-net phase and has a rather small reading vocabulary, the quantity of information from the printed stimulus that is used to select an item from the reading vocabulary can be very small. For example, the child may simply use word length: one of the children studied by Seymour and Elder (1985) read *television* as 'children', and when asked why said that he knew the word was 'children' because children is a long word. Or the child may use single letters: other children studied by Seymour and Elder read any letter-string containing a *k* (e.g. *likes*, *bkacl* or *pjoek*) as 'black'. The child who read *smaller* as 'yellow', when asked why, said 'It's "yellow" because it has two sticks'.

This description of the discrimination-net phase of learning to read – that in this phase reading aloud is selection, often on minimal cues, from the set of words the child knows to be the words that have been used in reading lessons – obviously assumes that children know which, of the spoken words that are familiar to them, are the ones they have been taught and which are the ones they have not. This assumption is implausible. However, it appears to be true. Seymour and Elder (1985) presented their child subjects with thirty-six spoken words, *all within every child's spoken vocabulary*. Of these words, nine had been used in reading instruction in the first term of schooling, nine in the third term, and eighteen not at all. The children were asked for each word 'Is this one of your reading words?' They were remarkably accurate at this task, averaging about 90 per cent correct in deciding whether or not a word was one that had been used in their reading lessons.

If it is the case that, in this reading phase, features such as number of letters or the presence of particular critical letters (such as the *k* used to identify *black*) are the basis of word identification, then reading aloud should not be much impaired by gross distortions of the overall visual forms of words – by, for example, presenting them in zigzag or vertical form, as in Figure 7.

```
yellow          y   l   o           y
                  e   l   w         e
                                    l
                                    l
                                    o
                                    w
   NORMAL         ZIGZAG          VERTICAL
```

FIGURE 7   Presentation of the word yellow used by Seymour and
          Elder (1975)

On the other hand, if words are being treated as visual wholes in this phase of reading acquisition and identified when their overall visual forms are familiar, then zigzag or vertical presentation (which destroy visual familiarity) should have catastrophic effects on reading. So Seymour and Elder gave their children words to read in the three formats shown in Figure 7. Reading accuracy was 66.3 per cent for Normal presentation, 60.4 per cent for Zigzag presentation, and 49.7 per cent for Vertical presentation. Format distortion thus had rather minor effects on reading accuracy, supporting the view that fragmentary features of words were the main basis of word identification, and that overall word shape was unimportant as a means of word identification.

In sum, then, evidence provided by Seymour and Elder (1985) and also by Marsh et al. (1981) strongly supports the view that children of 5 or 6 years of age, at the end of their first year of reading tuition, read single words aloud by using salient features of presented letter strings to select the most plausible response from amongst a specific set of words, this set being the collection of words they know they have been taught to read.

4.3.3   *The phonological-recoding phase*

As the child's reading vocabulary expands, reading in the discrimination-net phase will become more and more complicated and cumbersome. The child will find it more and more difficult to identify fragmentary features of a word which distinguish it from all the other words in the reading vocabulary, simply because the number of items in this vocabulary is growing large. This difficulty is the stimulus which prompts a move into the next phase of reading development: the phonological-recoding phase.

Before this third phase is entered, the child is completely unable to read aloud printed non-words such as *vib* or *vud*, because, of course, responses are chosen from amongst those words which are in the child's reading vocabulary; the child does not use information about mappings from individual letters to individual sounds when reading aloud. Eventually, however, signs of the use of letter-sound rules begin to emerge. The child begins to exhibit some ability to read non-words aloud. His or her *responses* are no longer selected only from the reading vocabulary, but may be words which have never been used in reading instruction, or may even be non-words. There is a rapid expansion in the total number of words which can be correctly read aloud. Such behaviour indicates a transition from the discrimination-net phase to the phonological-recoding phase. In the phonological-recoding phase, children apply the phonics procedure, as we defined it earlier, in addition to a direct procedure for reading. Indeed, in this phase of learning to read the phonics procedure appears to be the dominant one.

Evidence in favour of this view is provided by Doctor and Coltheart (1980). The task they set their subjects who were young normal readers at five age levels (6 to 10 years), was to decide whether short sequences of words were or were not meaningful English sentences. Half of the sentences shown to a child were meaningful (e.g. *I have no time*) and the remaining half were not (e.g. *I have blue time*). The main point of the experiment concerned the meaningless pseudosentences. Half of these were constructed so that, if they were read using a phonics procedure, they became meaningful (e.g. *Tell me wear he went*) whereas the remaining half of the pseudosentences were meaningless even when phonically recoded (e.g. *Tell me new he went*). Now, the correct response to both types of pseudosentence is 'No', since both types are not meaningful. A child making use of a phonics procedure for reading, however, would have difficulty in determining that a pseudo-sentence like *Tell me wear he went* is meaningless, but no difficulty with a pseudosentence like *Tell me new he went*. In contrast, a child relying on a direct (non-phonic) procedure for reading would not behave any differently with the two types of pseudosentence: the fact that the former type *sounds* meaningful would not be relevant, because the child is not comprehending printed words via their sounds.

One can therefore index the degree to which the children used a phonic procedure to read the sentences and pseudosentences in this reading comprehension task by the difference in error rates found with the two types of pseudosentence. This is what Doctor and Coltheart (1980) did; and they found that 6-year-old children responded correctly to 91.7 per cent of those pseudosentences which sounded meaningless, but were correct with only 29.2 per cent of the pseudosentences which sounded meaningful. This suggests that these 6-year-olds were relying to a very large extent upon a phonics procedure when they were reading.

There are various other lines of evidence in support of the view that in the phase of learning to read that follows the initial acquisition of a small sight-vocabulary, and the subsequent use of fragmentary visual features to select from items in the reading vocabulary, the child relies very heavily on a phonics procedure. We will discuss just two of these additional lines of evidence: the work of Firth (1972) and the work of Bradley and Bryant (1983).

Firth studied a group of 8-year-old children, and began by administering a standardised test of reading ability to all of them, the result being, of course, that the children showed a range of scores on this test. This allowed Firth to divide the children into two groups in terms of their reading scores. Let us call these groups Group A (the above-average readers) and Group B (the below-average readers). The question Firth then asked was: what cognitive ability determined whether a child achieved membership of Group A rather than Group B?

Let us suppose for the moment that the direct procedure is the important one for learning to read in children of this age. If this is so, then the Group A children must be those who are good at using the direct procedure, and the Group B children will be those who are poor at using this procedure. In order to determine whether the two groups really did differ in this way, Firth invented a task which would seem to measure directly a child's ability to use the direct procedure, even though the task itself did not involve reading.

The stimuli for this task were composed of 'pseudoletters': visual patterns which are not letters of the Roman alphabet but look as though they could be. Each stimulus was a row of such pseudoletters, and the children's task was to learn to associate a different spoken English word with each of these unfamiliar but worldlike visual stimuli.

If it is accepted that this task is an appropriate measure of the ability to use the direct procedure – since it involved rote learning of direct correspondences between wordlike visual stimuli and verbal responses – then Firth's results imply that this procedure is not important for 8-year-old children when they are learning to read, since Firth found that children who were good at using the direct procedure were not learning to read more successfully than children who were bad at using this procedure.

Firth's work, then, implies that the direct procedure is not important for reading acquisition in 8-year-old children. What about the phonics procedure?

Using the same form of argument as we have already discussed, let us suppose for the moment that the phonics procedure is of crucial importance for progress in learning to read in children of this age. If this is so, the Group A children (the above-average readers) must be children who are good at using the phonics procedure, and the Group B children (the below-average readers) must be children who are poor at using the phonics procedure. In order to discover whether the groups really did differ in this way, Firth used a task which directly measures a child's ability to use the phonics procedure – namely, the ability to read aloud pronounceable non-words such as *bef* or *cal*. The children in Groups A and B were given 150 non-words to read aloud. There was an extremely large difference between the two groups in their ability to perform this task. The Group A children averaged 131 non-words correctly read aloud; the Group B children averaged 29.

The two tests carried out by Firth thus suggest that, at least amongst children in the age range he studied, reading ability is closely related to ability to use the phonics procedure, but is not related to ability to use the direct procedure. His results therefore provide substantial evidence in support of the view that there exists a phase of reading acquisition in which the dominant procedure used for reading is the phonics procedure, and that children of 8 years are generally at this particular phase.

As we have seen, the results of Doctor and Coltheart (1980) also support this view; and so do the results of the third of the investigations we discuss, that of Bradley and Bryant (1983). Their basic idea was that if the phonics procedure – that is, learning rules of correspondence between particular letters and particular sounds – is to be used during the course of learning to read, a child will first have to know that a spoken word is made up of particular sounds – that 'cot', for example, is not just one sound but three, each of which corresponds to a particular letter. Consequently children who are aware that a word like 'cot' is made up of three separate sounds should have more success in learning to read than children who are not aware of this.

Bradley and Bryant tested children's ability to analyse syllables into their constituent sounds by saying to a child sets of three one-syllable words (such as 'hill', 'pig', and 'pin'), and asking the child to say which word in each set was the odd one out. The correct answer here is 'hill' (it is the only word not containing the sound 'p'). Because the odd word out was always the only word not containing a particular sound, the child needs to be able to analyse syllables into their constituent sounds to perform this task successfully.

Four-year-old and 5-year-old children were tested on this task before they could read at all. The children then went to school and were given reading instruction in the usual way by their teachers.

Three years later the children's reading was tested, and it was found that the children who had been good at analysing words into their constituent sounds before they had learned anything about reading were better readers three years later than were the children who had been bad at analysing words into individual sounds.

Bradley and Bryant also carried out a training study. They took a group of pre-reading children who were poor at the sound-analysing task and trained some of them to analyse words into sounds so that they were now good at this task; other children in this group were trained to categorise words in terms of their meanings, not their sounds. Three years later, the reading abilities of these two groups were tested. The group who had been trained in breaking words into sounds consistently scored more highly on tests of reading and spelling than the groups whose training was unrelated to the sounds of words (though these differences did not reach statistical significance). When sound training had been augmented by the use of plastic letters to teach the children that individual sounds can be represented by letters, there were subsequent highly significant improvements in reading and spelling in comparison to children who did not receive this kind of training.

These results suggest that the success a child will encounter in learning to read will be greater if, before the beginning of learning to read, the child understands that the spoken forms of words can be broken down into individual sounds, and that each sound can be represented by a letter. We suggest that this knowledge assists learning to read because it helps the child to learn how to use the phonics procedure, a procedure which is the basis of the phonological-recoding phase of learning to read.

This perhaps an appropriate point at which to consider the general question of the relationships between the phases of reading through which a child progresses and the types of teaching programmes to which the child is exposed. The children studied by Seymour and Elder (1985) were taught almost entirely by a whole-word approach, with only a limited introduction to phonics in the last few months of their first year of reading instruction. If their reading instruction had been phonically-based from the very beginning, what would have happened? Would they still have entered the discrimination-net phase? We do not know. Studies by Barr (1974/75) and Cohen (1974/75) are relevant here. They showed that even children taught by whole-word methods transferred from the discrimination-net to the phonological-recoding procedure, but that children taught by phonics methods exhibited this transfer at an earlier age. Much more work needs to be done on the effects of teaching programmes upon the progress through the kinds of reading phases we have been discussing.

4.3.4 *The orthographic phase*

Whilst the use of the phonics procedure has obvious advantages (it allows completely novel words to be read, and allows the child to make use of an already-established ability, speech comprehension, when he or she is trying to understand printed language) it has its disadvantages too.

The first of these is that many homophonic words exist in English, and a reader who relied upon phonological recording could not discriminate between one homophone and its mate – between *sail* and *sale*, for example – since the two words have identical phonological representations. The second disadvantage is that, although one may speak casually of learning 'procedures for converting unfamiliar print to speech', in fact, as we mentioned earlier in this chapter, no procedures exist which can perform this conversion correctly for all the words of English. At best, there are procedures which do the job correctly for a majority of English words ('regular words') but yield incorrect phonological representations for the remaining words ('exception words'). Thus a reader who relied upon phonological recoding to cope with words she had never seen in print but knew in speech would be severely handicapped in dealing with homophones and exception words.

For these two reasons, reliance upon the phonics procedure may be an appropriate way to *acquire* reading, but cannot be sufficient as a way of becoming skilled in reading, since skilled reading is only achieved if the reader can deal adequately with homophones and with exception words. Doctor and Coltheart (1980) proposed that progress from being an effective beginning reader towards being a skilled reader involves a progressive increase in reliance upon orthographic ('visual') recoding. Their evidence for this was as follows. When children were asked to judge whether a printed sentence such as *Tell me wear he went* was meaningful or not, the 6-year-olds incorrectly responded 'Yes' 70.8 per cent of the time, whilst the 10-year-olds incorrectly responded 'Yes' 20.8 per cent of the time. Incorrect 'Yes' responses to such sentences are an indication of the use of phonological recoding in reading. Hence the use of phonological recoding decreases as age increases, from 6 years to 10 years.

Even the 10-year-old readers in this experiment were still making *some* use of phonological recoding, however, because they were more accurate at rejecting printed sentences which sounded incorrect (*Tell me new he went*) than those which sounded correct (*Tell me wear he went*), the percentages correct being 97.9 and 79.2 respectively.

Since all of these children were being taught to read by a mixture of various methods, and there certainly was no strong emphasis upon phonic instruction for them, we take these findings to be a reflection not so much of what the children are taught but rather of what they learn; and we suggest that over the period from

6 years of age to 10 years of age there is normally a transition from a phonological-recoding phase to an orthographic phase, a phase in which it is the way words are *spelled* rather than the way they *sound* which is the dominant representation used for reading. In other words, the direct rather than the phonics procedure is becoming dominant. In adult skilled reading, at least at the single word level, it appears that the phonics procedure has become irrelevant and that reading depends entirely on the direct procedure (Coltheart, 1980b).

4.3.5 Summary

We have discussed learning to read English in terms of four phases. In the first, the sight-word phase, the child has learned by rote association to read a small number of words using the direct procedure, and does not use the phonics procedure at all. This phase has not been extensively studied, and many questions about it remain unanswered. One question concerns what kind of visual information is used for recognising words in this phase: our incidental observations of Alice, if they are representative of children in general, suggest that in this phase word shapes are not important, and that recognising words depends upon recognising some or all of their component letters.

In the second phase, the discrimination-net phase, children use fragmentary or very general features of the printed stimulus to select, from amongst the set of words that constitutes their reading vocabulary, the word they believe the stimulus to be. Children in this phase cannot read aloud novel words or unfamiliar words, and they rarely produce as a reading response a word which has not been used in their reading lessons, no matter how familiar to them its spoken form is.

The third phase, the phonological-recoding phase, is one where the child makes extensive use of letter-sound correspondence rules to read words via phonological recoding, enabling words which have never been seen before nevertheless to be read aloud.

Since skilled reading of individual words does not depend upon this kind of phonological recoding (Coltheart, 1980b), this third phase cannot be the ultimate one. Skilled reading requires a transition from the phonological-recoding phase to an orthographic phase in which words are always recognised directly in terms of their spellings, never indirectly in terms of their pronunciations.

4.4   Learning to read in other languages

Although we have so far discussed only how English reading is acquired, the basic views we have expressed can be discussed in relation to learning to read in other languages. Considering now only the final two phases of learning to read that we have described, we want to argue that the existence of a phonological recoding phase, followed by a gradual transition to an orthographic phase, characterises learning to read not only for English but also for other languages, including languages with writing systems very different from those used by English.

It is of interest to explore these issues by, for example, investigating languages which are written in the Roman alphabet but for which the problems for phonological recoding are less severe than they are in English. As we discussed in Chapter 1, whilst there are other European languages for which letter-to-sound relationships are inconsistent, as they are in English (two examples are French and Danish), there are also European languages (for example, Finnish, Italian and Hungarian) in which letter-to-sound relationships are extremely regular. For such languages, one of the two disadvantages of using phonological recoding for reading – the problem of exception words – would not exist, because there are no exception words. The other disadvantage – inability to discriminate between homophones even when they are orthographically distinct – also does not exist because in these languages no words exist which are homophonous but spelled differently.[1] Thus, given the absence of exception words and the absence of dissimilarly-spelled homophones in languages such as Finnish, Italian and Hungarian, one might expect to find much more extensive use of phonological recoding in reading or learning to read in these two languages than in irregularly-spelled

---

[1] Of course, there are homophones which are not only identical in sound but also identical in spelling in these languages (for example, *voi* in Finnish means not only 'oh' but also 'butter'). Such 'homographic homophones', however, are not more efficiently read via orthographic recoding than via phonological recoding, so are irrelevant here.

languages such as English, French and Danish.

Whilst the success with which such phonological recoding can be achieved depends upon how uniform the correspondences are between letters and sounds, there is a further difficulty even for languages where these correspondences apply without exception. Because some phonemes (e.g. stop consonants) cannot be pronounced in isolation, the names of some letters must differ from the sounds which correspond to them. Thus letter names differ from 'letter sounds'; it is the letter names which are learned, but it is the letter sounds which are needed for the process of grapheme-phoneme conversion. This is often referred to as the problem of 'blending': a child who has learned that *p* is /pə/ and *a* is /æ/ must nevertheless recode *pa* as /pə/, not /pəæ/. The blending problem is unavoidable for alphabetic scripts. However, there is a different kind of writing system in which the problem does not arise: the syllabic script (see Chapter 1). In such scripts, each symbol of the script corresponds to a syllable, and hence the name of each symbol is also its pronunciation for the purposes of recoding from print to phonology.

Thus, if phonological recoding is of general importance for learning to read, syllabic scripts may have an advantage over alphabetic scripts. In contrast, ideographic scripts (as defined in Chapter 1) will be at a severe disadvantage, because it is impossible to determine the exact pronunciation of a word written in an ideographic script if the reader has not seen the word in its written form before. Learning to read therefore cannot be parasitic upon speech comprehension for readers of ideographic scripts, whereas such parasitism is possible for alphabetic scripts, and easy for syllabic scripts. Consequently, one way in which one might assess the general importance of phonological recoding for the acquisition of reading is to consider what learning to read is like with each of these kinds of writing systems. We do not suggest that it would be of interest directly to compare the rate at which children learn to read in Turku and in Shanghai, since cross-cultural investigations of this sort are subject to far too many methodological difficulties; but a number of interesting points nevertheless arise from considerations of the ways in which the reading of ideographic and syllabic writing systems is learned. We will consider two examples: Chinese and Japanese.

4.4.1   *Learning to read Chinese*

Chinese is written in an ideographic script. Although, as we discussed in Chapter 1, some Chinese characters include a component (the 'phonetic radical') which provides approximate information about the pronunciation of the character (see Wang, 1973, p. 54), this information would not be sufficient to enable a child to recode from an unfamiliar character to its phonology and to understand print in this way. For example, the phonetic component does not specify which of the four possible intonations of Chinese syllables is to be used, and these four intonations may correspond to four different meanings for the character. Furthermore, there are characters whose pronunciations, often for historical reasons, are quite different from that of their phonetic radicals. Thus, despite the existence of phonetic radicals for some characters, learning to access meaning from Chinese ideographs by intermediate phonological recoding is not a possibility.

What are the consequences of this for learning to read? There is no systematic research on learning to read in China, but the account by Leong (1973) of the teaching of reading in Hong Kong suggests that progress is not expected to be rapid: a set of reading books to be used over a six-year-period contains only 3,500 different words, and children in the fifth and sixth grades usually spend between one and one and a half hours *per day* after school on reading homework, as well as spending about a quarter of the time in school studying reading and other aspects of the Chinese language. The situation in China differs from that in Hong Kong in a significant way. In China, when children are first taught to read, they are *not* taught to read the ideographic script. Instead, they are taught to read their language written in the Roman alphabet (known as **pinyin**). According to Lehmann (1975, pp. 55–7), students are assumed to have mastered the reading and writing of *pinyin* by the end of primary school. It is only after students have had sufficient tuition in the reading of Chinese written alphabetically that learning to read the ideographic script is commenced. At the end of primary school, the student is expected to know about 3,000 ideographic characters, but he is still encouraged to use *pinyin* to write any words for which he does not know the ideographic characters.

Since the ability to read *pinyin* is of very little use to the adult

Chinese – indeed, Bonavia (1977, p. 76) claims that 'although Chinese schoolchildren learn (*pinyin*) they probably forget it in later life' – why is it taught to beginning readers? We suggest that it is because one can learn to identify words written in *pinyin* by using phonological recoding, whilst the Chinese ideographic script cannot be learned in this way, and that accelerated progress in learning to read depends upon being able to identify words via phonological recoding.

When ideographic characters are first introduced to children in China, each character is accompanied by its transcription in *pinyin*, which the children have already learned to read. Thus, despite the nature of the normal Chinese writing system, it can be argued that learning to read in China consists of an initial phase during which phonological recoding is relied upon (the *pinyin* phase) followed by a phase in which visual encoding is progressively emphasised (as ideographic characters are introduced).

4.4.2   *Learning to read Japanese*

As we described in Chapter 1, Japanese is written in a mixture of two scripts. One, **kanji**, is ideographic and is comparable to (and indeed derived from) the Chinese script. The other, **kana**, is syllabic. The existence of these two scripts, side by side, as it were, in a single culture, allows one to consider the relative ease with which the two types of script can be learned;[2] and it is quite clear that the advantage is with the syllabic script *kana*. It is common for Japanese children to be able to read and write the *kana* script by the time they first go to school; and initial tuition in reading is

---

[2] Perhaps Cherokee also provides another within-language comparison of the ease of learning to read in ideographic and syllabic scripts. Consider the following quotations: 'The Cherokee script was invented in 1821 by a native called Sequoia or Sikwaya, also John Gist or Guest or Guess . . . at first he created an ideographic script, but soon realised how cumbersome it was and invented the syllabary. After about ten years, this script was so widespread that nearly all the male members of the tribe could write and read' (Diringer, 1968, p. 128). 'It has been estimated that the Cherokee were 90 percent literate in their native language in the 1830's. By the 1880's the Western Cherokee had a higher English literacy level than the white population of either Texas or Arkansas . . . A Cherokee will say, for example, that it is easy to learn to read Cherokee, that he learned it in two days, in a day, or even in an afternoon' (Walker, cited by Halle, 1972, pp. 152–3).

confined to the teaching of *kana*. With fluency in the reading of *kana* established, there is a slow introduction to the reading of the ideographic script *kanji*. According to Sakamoto and Makita (1973), Japanese children are expected to learn 46 *kanji* characters in the first grade, 105 in the second, 187 in the third, 205 in the fourth, 194 in the fifth, and 144 in the sixth, making a total of 881 characters. In junior high school, an additional 969 characters are taught. Reading *kanji* is sometimes assisted by accompanying each *kanji* word with the same word in small *kana* characters, placed beside the *kanji* character, so that if the reader fails to recognise a *kanji* character he can use its *kana* representation to derive its phonology: this is known as **furigana**, and we presented an example in Chapter 1 (see Figure 4, p. 21).

There is thus a remarkable similarity between learning to read in China and in Japan, despite the differences in the writing systems of the two languages. In both cases, children are first taught to read using a system which permits phonological recoding of unfamiliar words. Next, there is a subsequent gradual introduction to an ideographic script. Ideographic characters can be accompanied by their transcriptions in a phonological script. The only difference is that in Chinese the phonological script (*pinyin*) is a recent introduction which is of little relevance to the skilled reader, whilst in Japanese the skilled reader uses both types of script.[3]

If it is so difficult to learn to read an ideographic script, why are such scripts used for Chinese and Japanese? Again, there is a parallel between the two here, since in both cases there have been

[3] The following objection may be made here: although the *kana* syllabary clearly provides an excellent medium for reading via phonological recoding, this does not mean that words written in *kana* are read via such recoding. Why could not a word written as a sequence of *kana* characters be read 'visually'? This is an interesting topic for Japanese research, and as yet the answer to this question is not known: but it does seem to be the case that 'visual' reading of words written in *kana* is difficult or impossible. In cases of deep dyslexia (see Chapter 8 for a discussion of this reading disorder), phonological recoding of unfamiliar words or non-words is impossible. This is true not only for English but also for Japanese (Sasanuma, 1980). 'Visual' reading is somewhat preserved in Japanese cases in the sense that many *kanji* characters can be read. It follows that if visual reading of *kana* is possible, Japanese deep dyslexics should show some preservation of *kana* reading as well as of *kanji* reading. This, however, is not so. Reading of *kana* is abolished (Sasanuma, 1980).

moves to abandon the ideographic script. Chairman Mao said in 1951: 'our written language should be reformed; it should take the direction of phoneticisation common to all of the languages in the world.'

The difficulty with phoneticisation of the Chinese writing system, however, is that at least eight major languages (often misleadingly termed 'dialects') are spoken in China. These differ from each other at least as much as the European Romance languages differ from each other: 'a man from Peking cannot be sure of being able to order dinner in a Cantonese restaurant' (Wang, 1973, p. 55). However, the man from Peking could communicate with the Cantonese waiter in writing, since the same writing system is used throughout China: but this could only be possible with an ideographic writing system, in which the pronunciations of words are not represented in their written forms. Phoneticisation of the script would mean that speakers of the different languages would no longer be able to communicate in writing. For this reason, it is now clear that script phoneticisation will not occur until a single standard *spoken* language (known as **Putonghua**) is used throughout China. Steps in this direction are being taken.

Shortly after World War II, the Japanese government issued a list of 1,850 *kanji* characters, the intention being that only these, rather than the tens of thousands of characters then in existence, would be used. This was meant as an interim step towards the complete abolition of *kanji*. Although popular newspapers today use only this limited set of characters, and it is this set which is taught in schools, many people know considerably more characters, and additional characters are still widely used; certainly, no moves towards using only *kana* have been made. Since every Japanese word can be written in *kana*, whilst many cannot be written in *kanji*, why has *kana* not prevailed? We suggest this is because of a problem endemic to phonological reading, a problem already mentioned: the discrimination of homophones. Homophones are even more prevalent in Japanese than in English: for example, amongst the meanings of the word *seika* are 'confectioner', 'shoemaker', 'greengrocer' and 'florist', and, amongst the 881 words whose *kanji* characters are learned in junior high school, 29 are pronounced 'ko' (Martin, 1972). That the degree of homophony is an obstacle to communication is indicated by the fact that, in conversation, the Japanese may disambiguate a spoken homophone by sketching its *kanji* in the air. Sketching its *kana* representation would, of course, be of no use: the four occupations called *seika* have different *kanji* characters but must be spelled identically in *kana* since they are pronounced identically. If writing were entirely in *kana*, the written language would be as seriously ambiguous as the spoken language is. It is only the use of *kanji* which makes written language less ambiguous than spoken language.

4.5   Overview

We have discussed the nature of the Chinese and Japanese writing systems, and how children learn them, in order to establish the basis for the following claim: although English, Chinese and Japanese are utterly different from each other as languages, and although the types of writing system they use also differ greatly, one can nevertheless provide a single description of the way children learn to read these disparate writing systems. Apart from the very earliest phases of reading, children begin by reading using phonological recoding, and subsequently they gradually develop a facility in using visual recoding.

During this introduction of visual recoding, all three languages use what might be called the *furigana* method – that is, symbols which are to be read 'visually' are accompanied by their equivalents in a phonological script, as a crutch if visual reading fails. A Chinese ideograph is accompanied by its transcription in *pinyin*, a *kanji* character is accompanied by its transcription in *kana*, and an alphabetic English word accompanies itself, as it were. The plausibility of this description, in the face of the dissimilarity of the writing systems, reinforces the basic point discussed in this chapter: that substantial advantages are to be gained by learning to read 'indirectly' rather than purely 'directly', whilst the attainment of full skill in reading depends upon moving from reliance upon an indirect procedure to the use of a direct non-phonological procedure for identifying printed words.

5 Developmental disorders of language

5.1 Introduction

In the three preceding chapters, we considered how normal children learn to use spoken and written language. As we saw, both learning to talk and learning to read involve the acquisition of a variety of complex skills. It is not surprising to discover that not all children acquire language to the normal degree. Children who acquire language more slowly or less completely than the majority are said to be exhibiting a **developmental** language disorder. As we will see in a later chapter, children who are slow to acquire language are different from adults who have acquired language normally, but then suffer some form of injury to the brain which makes them unable to use language normally. Language disorders which occur in this way are known as **acquired** disorders, and they are described in Chapter 9.

Before beginning our discussion of developmental disorders of language, we should clarify some terminology. There is a particular problem in choosing which labels to attach to the different types of disorder which children exhibit, since there is a wide range of different labels in use among those who investigate and treat developmental disorders of language. For the sake of simplicity, we will refer to three kinds of disorder namely, **developmental dysphasia** (impaired acquisition of spoken language), **developmental dyslexia** (impaired acquisition of reading) and **developmental dysgraphia** (impaired acquisition of writing and/or spelling). The term **developmental asphasia** is often used as an alternative to the first of these terms, but we prefer to reserve the term aphasia for referring to an acquired disorder. Another term which has been used recently in preference to developmental dysphasia is **specific language impairment**. However, we will use the earlier and more widely used term.

5.2 Developmental dysphasia

Children may be slow in learning to talk for a wide variety of reasons. One reason is that they may grow up in an environment which does not provide appropriate linguistic input. In extreme cases, children may be so deprived of an appropriate linguistic environment that they do not learn to produce *any* speech. One such extreme case of failure to develop language for environmental reasons is vividly described in the book *Genie* (Curtiss, 1977) which is the story of a girl who reached the age of 13 without learning to talk. She had an extremely deprived and isolated childhood, being tied to a chair by her father for long periods of time and deprived of any company. Consequently, Genie did not have sufficient experience of language to be able to acquire it. When Genie was finally taken away from her father's influence by her mother, the attempts to teach language to Genie were remarkably successful, although Genie learned to understand far more language than she learned to produce.

Fortunately, such cases of extreme deprivation are rare, but many more children experience less extreme forms of environmental disadvantage. This may also result in an unusually slow rate of language development because, as we saw in Chapter 2, the kind of linguistic experiences which young children have may affect the rate at which they develop language. Since particular patterns of adult-child communication may produce *accelerated* language development, it seems likely that other patterns might *retard* the rate of development. However, the precise role which environmental factors play in developmental language disorders has still to be discovered.

A better understood factor is hearing-impairment. Children will show severe retardation in language development if their hearing is very severely impaired; but they may also still have problems with language if they have a less severe hearing loss, for example, one which prevents them from hearing sounds of particular frequencies, or one which follows an infection of the middle ear. Hearing-loss of the latter kind can be particularly difficult to detect because its severity varies from day to day.

The term **developmental dysphasia** is reserved for a specific kind of language disorder which cannot be explained in terms of environmental or sensory deficits, or in terms of general intellectual retardation or emotional problems. Developmental dysphasia is, therefore, characterized by the late appearance or slow development of language in children of normal intelligence which cannot be explained in terms of environmental, sensory or emotional factors. Psychologists have been particularly interested in children who exhibit this disorder because their language can provide an insight into the processes which operate during the normal acquisition of language. One of the most frequent questions which researchers have asked is whether the language of dysphasics is actually *different* in kind from that of normal children (i.e. **deviant**) or whether it is like the language of younger normal children (i.e. **delayed**). However, one initial problem arises when we attempt to compare the language of dysphasic and normal children. Which normal children provide an appropriate comparison group?

One comparison which could be made is between dysphasic and normal children of the same *chronological* age. However, comparisons of this kind have merely revealed that dysphasic children are different from normals in virtually every aspect of language. This might mean either that dysphasics are like younger normal children in their use of language, or that they show a deviant pattern. A more useful comparison is the one between dysphasic children and normal children at a comparable linguistic level. Children can be matched for linguistic level either on the basis of their performance on a language test, or in terms of some measure of their level of spontaneous speech like the mean length of their utterances (MLU). If dysphasic children appear to be functioning exactly as young normals at a comparable linguistic level it is likely that dysphasia involves a delay in linguistic development. If, on the other hand, there are differences between the two groups this suggests that the language of the dysphasic children is deviant.

5.2.1 *Syntactic development*

Leonard (1979) has reviewed the results of several studies which have made comparisons between dysphasic and normal children. Many studies have been concerned with possible differences in syntactic development, and they show that dysphasic children have considerable difficulty with syntactic features. At first sight dysphasic children appear to be functioning like younger normal children because both groups use the same syntactic structures. However, when the relative frequencies with which dysphasics and normals use particular structures are compared some differences emerge.

Data from Johnston and Schery (1976) and Steckol and Leonard (1979) suggest that dysphasic children typically reach a higher MLU than normals before they begin to acquire their first grammatical morphemes, for example the 's' used to make regular nouns plural and the various tense markers which are added to verbs. Steckol and Leonard's study compared a group of normal children (aged between 2 and 4 years) with a group of older dysphasic children who were matched for MLU. The comparison revealed that the dysphasic children were using grammatical morphemes less frequently than the normal children. In other words, the dysphasic children were combining words to produce utterances which were the same length as those produced by the younger normal children, but they had not achieved a comparable level of complexity in their use of grammatical morphemes. To this extent the language of the dysphasic children appeared different from that of normal younger children. We will return to one possible interpretation of this finding later.

The two studies we have just considered were *observational*, that is, they analysed the spontaneous speech of dysphasic children. However some important insights into the syntactic abilities of dysphasics have emerged from experimental studies such as those carried out by Menyuk (1978). One of her studies compared dysphasic children's ability to imitate sentences with their ability to produce similar sentences spontaneously. Children with normal language are able to imitate some syntactic structures which they are not yet capable of producing spontaneously. However, in Menyuk's study the dysphasic children showed a reverse of the normal pattern and were *unable* to repeat some types of sentence which they had used in their spontaneous speech.

Another interesting finding was that dysphasic children were strongly affected by the structure of the sentences they were asked to repeat. Dysphasic children who had a vocabulary age of 6 years were very successful at repeating sentences of three words in length, as were normal children of the same vocabulary age. However, with four- and five-word sentences, while the normal children continued to find no difficulty with imitation, the dysphasic children found syntactic forms like negatives and questions very difficult. Analysis of the kinds of errors which the dysphasics made revealed that the dysphasic children preserved the meaning of the sentences they were attempting to imitate but made syntactic simplifications. Some examples of these simplifications are shown below:

Sentence	*Imitation*
He can't go home	He no go (home)
	He no can go
Where does he go?	Where he go?
	Where he do go?

Meaning constraints also had an influence on the dysphasic children's ability to imitate phonological sequences. Both dysphasics and normals were better at repeating phonological sequences which formed part of a word than they were at imitating the same sequences when they formed part of a nonsense syllable. The dysphasic children were also more likely to omit the final syllables of words when they were grammatical morphemes marking tense or number than when they were part of a word stem. For examples, *bees* might be incorrectly imitated as 'bee', while *nose* was correctly imitated and not reduced to 'no'. Within the dysphasic group the ability to preserve syntactic accuracy and the ability to preserve phonological accuracy were correlated. That is, those children who had the greatest difficulty with imitation of sentences also had the greatest difficulty in imitating phonological sequences within real words. Interestingly there were no correlations between ability to imitate sentences and ability to imitate strings of nonsense words, or between ability to imitate phonological sequences in real words and nonsense words. This supports the conclusion that meaningfulness is an important factor in the language processing of dysphasic children.

5.2.2   *Semantic development*

The semantic development of dysphasic children has been the subject of several studies. Semantic development is of course related to syntactic development because if a child has restricted syntactic skills he will also be restricted in his ability to express semantic forms, since semantic forms are usually expressed through syntax. However, as we saw in Chapter 3, children appear to be capable of expressing a variety of semantic relations before they have developed the appropriate syntax to express these relations. This early period of semantic development has been the subject of particular study in dysphasic children.

Leonard, Steckol and Schwartz (1978) compared the range of semantic relations expressed by a group of dysphasic and a group of younger normal children matched for MLU. Both groups were producing two and three word utterances. Leonard et al. found that although there were many similarities between the two groups there are also some interesting differences. In particular, the dysphasic children used early emerging semantic relations such as agent + object and action + object more frequently than the normal children, while using later forms such as experiencer + experience (e.g. baby see) less often. Similar findings emerged from an earlier study by Freedman and Carpenter (1976). The semantic development of dysphasic children therefore seems to be slow in comparison with that of younger normal children.

A related aspect of semantic development is early vocabulary development. There has not been a great deal of research into the vocabulary development of dysphasic children, but the studies reviewed by Leonard (1979) suggest that this appears to follow a similar pattern to that of normal children, although it takes place much more slowly. However, learning new vocabulary can be a particularly difficult problem for some dysphasic children. This has been highlighted in recent experiments by Haynes (1982) in which a group of dysphasic children was compared with two groups of normal children, one of the same chronological age (9 years) as the dysphasics and the other of the same verbal age (7 years). The children were read stories about two space creatures who had adventures involving a series of animals and objects each of which was illustrated by a picture. All the strange animals and objects had been given names which were legal non-words. One of the stories began as follows:

Pong took Ping into a school. In the classroom some children were doing their sums on a dʒænɪp. They put their sums in at one end, and the answer came out all by itself from the other end of the dʒænɪp.

After listening to the stories, the children were asked to recognise the unfamiliar names, each of which had occurred twice. Recognition was tested in a forced choice task in which the distractor items had varying degrees of similarity to the target name. The dysphasic children were much less successful at recognising the names they had heard in the story than normal children of the same verbal age. Not only did the dysphasics identify the correct name from the story much less frequently; they were just as likely to choose one of the distractors which was very different from the correct name as they were to choose one which was similar. In contrast, both groups of normal children showed a significant preference for distractor items which were similar to the target, suggesting that they had some partial knowledge of the correct name even when they could not identify it correctly. The dysphasic children did not appear to possess even this partial knowledge.

5.2.3 Pragmatic development

Before we consider how these findings might be explained by some of the theories of developmental dysphasia which have been put forward, we will turn to one final aspect of language development in dysphasic children. Pragmatics, the communicative function of language, is an aspect of development which has been receiving an increasing amount of attention in recent years. We considered one aspect of this in normal children when we discussed communicative competence in Chapter 3. One finding which emerged clearly was that normal children soon become adept at reformulating their speech in order to aid an uncomprehending listener, providing that they realise that such reformulation is appropriate. However, Gallagher and Darnton (1977) showed that dysphasic children find reformulating their speech extremely difficult even though they attempt to do this as frequently as normal children at the same verbal level. In Gallagher and Darnton's experiment the groups of dysphasic and normal children were equated for MLU. Both groups contained a range of linguistic ability (MLU 1.75–2.75). The more advanced normal children differed from the less advanced children in that they often altered the *structure* of what they had just said and rephrased their utterances, while the less advanced normal children relied on making *phonetic* changes. However, all the dysphasic children made phonetic changes rather than structural ones. Since structural changes are usually more effective than phonetic changes, it is reasonable to conclude that the older dysphasic children were not capable of making such changes. This conclusion is supported by Hoar (1977) who found that dysphasic children had difficulties with a paraphrasing task.

On other pragmatic measures, however, dysphasic children seem to use language very similarly to younger normal children. Leonard, Camarata, Rowan and Chapman (1982) investigated the early acquisition of communicative functions by a group of dysphasic children at the single-word stage of development who were aged between 2 years 8 months and 3 years 4 months. They were compared with a group of younger normal children (aged 2 years or under) who were at a comparable linguistic level. Both groups of children used single words for essentially similar communicative functions like naming, requesting, attracting attention and when giving or receiving objects. There were some differences in the frequencies with which particular functions were expressed. For example, the dysphasic children were less likely to name things spontaneously, but were more responsive to adult questions requiring yes/no answers. These differences were inter-related because the parents of the dysphasic children tended to ask them more questions because the children did not name things spontaneously. However, in general, the dysphasic children exhibited communicative behaviours which were generally consistent with their other linguistic skills, suggesting that developmental dysphasia does not involve a problem with acquiring linguistic functions, but rather a difficulty with acquiring linguistic forms.

As we have seen, the most striking features of the language of dysphasic children are the marked difficulty they have with syntax, particularly with *reproducing* syntax; their difficulty with both the recognition and reproduction of novel phoneme sequences; and their inability to reformulate sentences they have just produced. Another difficulty which is often reported by those who work with dysphasic children is one with the reproduction of rhythms. (See Tallal and Piercy, 1978, for a review.) These difficulties might appear to be wide-ranging. However, they do have one thing in common, namely a difficulty with the storage and reorganisation of complex auditory material. We will now examine some of the theories which have been put forward to account for developmental dysphasia.

5.2.4   Theories of developmental dysphasia

The first theory which we will discuss proposes that children with developmental dysphasia have a *general* deficit in their representational abilities. As Chapter 2 explained, Piaget has argued that the ability to use language is only one aspect of a more general ability to represent the world symbolically. One implication of this view is that children who have difficulties with language might also have difficulties with other tasks which involve symbolic representation. If they do, this suggests that developmental dysphasia is not a language-specific deficit, but one which arises from a more general deficit.

In a study of one 9-year-old dysphasic child, Inhelder (1963) found that the child was poor at performing tasks which involved the use of representational imagery. One such task involved describing what the level of water in a glass container would be like when the container was tilted. The child was unable to give the correct description, which involves realising that the level remains horizontal regardless of the inclination of the sides of the container. Since the child had impaired language, it is probably not surprising that he found giving appropriate descriptions difficult. However, other studies have suggested that dysphasic children have difficulties with representational imagery in tasks which do not involve verbal descriptions. These are reviewed by Leonard (1979), together with studies which suggest that dysphasic children might also show less symbolic play than normal children. Leonard ends his review by supporting the theory of a representational deficit.

The studies we have just considered could indeed be seen as support for the view that dysphasic children are suffering from a general deficit in their capacity for symbolic representation.

However, since the relationship between language and other symbolic skills is by no means clearly understood, this conclusion may be premature. While language is clearly influenced *by* cognitive development, language does have a crucial influence *upon* cognitive development, as Piaget recognised. Therefore it is impossible to be certain of the extent to which apparently nonlinguistic abilities might be affected by a more specific impairment.

Cromer (1978) has put forward a rather different view of developmental dysphasia in which he has argued that a satisfactory account of the disorder must take into account the nature of language processing. In order to gain a useful insight into the precise difficulty which dysphasic children have with language, Cromer compared the written language of profoundly deaf and dysphasic children. The deaf children were between 9 and 10 years of age, while the dysphasic children had a median age of 13 years. The children in both groups were presented with puppet shows and then wrote an account of what they had seen.

One of the most striking differences between the accounts written by the dysphasic children and those of the deaf children was one of sentence complexity. The sentences written by the dysphasic children were less complex than those written by the deaf children even though both groups used sentences of similar length. While the dysphasic children used mainly simple active affirmative sentences like *The wolf is taking his table tennis ball*, the profoundly deaf children used a variety of complex sentence forms which involved negatives, interrogatives and qualifying adjectives. None of the dysphasic children used any of these forms.

There were also clear differences on other measures of complexity. Far more of the sentences used by the deaf children involved the use of conjoining or embedding of simple structures. For example, one deaf child wrote *The wolf was very angry because the ball is gone* which contains two simple structures joined together by *because*. Of the sentences written by the deaf children 36 per cent involved the combination of two or more simple structures, whereas only 12 per cent of the sentences written by the dysphasic children involved such combination.

This tendency for dysphasic children to use short simple sentences and to avoid adjectives is supported by clinical observation of the spoken language of developmental dysphasics. It also fits in with the experimental finding, which we considered earlier, that dysphasic children find dealing with complex syntactic forms very difficult. Cromer suggests that the reason dysphasic children have such difficulty with complex sentences is that they have a **hierarchical structuring deficit**.

In order to understand what Cromer means by this term it is necessary to consider what additional factors are involved in the comprehension and production of complex sentences as compared with simple sentences. This is related to the way in which language is hierarchically organised at the sentence level. Sentences are considered to be hierarchically organised because individual sentences can be broken down into various components or constituents, and each constituent can in turn be broken down into its constituents. This is shown in the following example which illustrates the hierarchical constituents of one simple sentence. (For the sake of simplicity we have not given the traditional linguistic labels to each of the constituents. Readers who are interested in how linguists describe sentences constituents are referred to Smith and Wilson, 1979.)

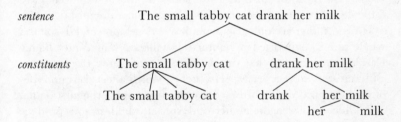

Spoken or written sentences can be thought of as being organised in *two* ways; in addition to their hierarchical organisation, written sentences are also organised in left-right sequence, and spoken sentences have a corresponding temporal sequence. In the particular example we have just considered, words which form part of the same constituent also occur next to one another. Words within the same constituent would also have been temporally close if this sentence had been spoken, rather than written. However, the words which make up particular constituents do not always occur next to one another when a sentence is spoken or written.

If we compare the sentence above with a more complex one such as *The cat that drank the milk was a small tabby*, we can see that the first two words form part of one constituent (*the cat was a small tabby*). However, before this constituent is completed, another constituent (*that drank the milk*) begins. Therefore, in order to produce or understand this sentence it is necessary to deal with more than one constituent at a time. In complex sentences like this, we cannot finish processing one constituent before proceeding to deal with the next one. (For a more detailed discussion of this point see Chapter 7.) Cromer's argument is that it is this aspect of language, which arises because language is hierarchically as well as sequentially structured, which causes particular difficulties for dysphasic children.

One implication of the claim that developmental dysphasia arises from a hierarchical structuring deficit is that dysphasic children should have difficulty with other tasks which involve processing of hierarchically structured constituents. We have already seen that dysphasic children find difficulty with the processing of rhythms. Since rhythms are hierarchically organised, this difficulty might provide support for Cromer's theory. There is also evidence from recent experiments carried out by Cromer (1983) which show that at least some dysphasic children have difficulty with other tasks involving hierarchical organisation.

However, there is a third explanation of developmental dysphasia which is also supported by empirical evidence. Tallal and Piercy (1978) have claimed that the problems encountered by dysphasic children stem from a very specific deficit which affects certain types of auditory processing. In a series of elegant experiments, Tallal and Piercy explored the ability of dysphasic children to reproduce sequences of tones. Many people have suggested that dysphasic children might have a sequencing problem; but Tallal and Piercy point out that most tasks which involve remembering sequences confound several different abilities, including memory for sequences and discrimination of items within a sequence. Their own task, therefore, involved reproducing two-tone sequences by making a series of panel presses in which one panel corresponded to one tone, and a second panel to the other tone.

Dysphasic children could do this task as well as normal children of the same age and nonverbal intelligence, providing the tones were separated by more than 150 milliseconds. However, when the time interval between tones was 150 milliseconds or less, the dysphasic children performed much worse than normal children. A similar pattern emerged in another task in which children listened to two sequences and had to indicate whether they were the same or different. Normal children could do this task when the tones in the sequences were separated by only 8 milliseconds, whereas the dysphasic children required a separation of 305 milliseconds before they could reliably distinguish two sequences. This difficulty was restricted to auditory stimuli because there were no differences on comparable tasks involving visual sequences.

Tallal and Piercy's results suggest that dysphasic children have difficulty in processing very rapidly presented auditory information. Under normal circumstances speech can be accurately perceived at a rate of 400 words/minute (or approximately 30 phonemes/second), which is extremely fast. If dysphasic children experience great difficulty with rapidly presented auditory information, this might explain their difficulty with language. A later experiment (also reported in Tallal and Piercy, 1978) highlighted a particular problem which might arise. This compared the ability of dysphasic children to discriminate between two synthesised *vowels* (/ɛ/ and /æ/) with their ability to discriminate two synthesised *stop consonants* (/ba/ and /da/), using the panel-pressing tasks described earlier. The main difference between these pairs is that the differences in frequency which distinguish one member of the pair from the other occur over significantly different lengths of time. Each of the vowels has three characteristic simultaneous pitch levels called **formants** which remain constant over the entire vowel (250 milliseconds in Tallal and Piercy's experiment). In contrast, the consonants are distinguished from one another by very rapid changes in two formants, which take place over about 50 milliseconds.

The dysphasic children could reproduce and discriminate between sequences involving the two synthesised vowels as well as normal children. However, they had great difficulty in dealing with sequences involving the two synthesised consonants /ba/ and /da/. In order to see whether it was the short duration of the critical formant transition which was affecting the dysphasic children, rather than the transition itself, Tallal and Piercy increased the length of the formant transitions from 40 to 80 milliseconds. This made an enormous difference to the dysphasic children's ability to discriminate /ba/ from /da/, and improved their performance to the level of normal children.

Tallal and Piercy argue that the inability to perceive rapid formant transitions could have wide-reaching effects, not only on the perception of particular phonemes, but also on the perception of the temporal order of sequences of phonemes in normal speech. Thus, what might initially appear to be a very narrow deficit, could have implications for many different levels of language processing.

This explanation of development dysphasia as an inability to perceive rapid formant transitions might appear to be completely different from Cromer's hypothesis of a hierarchical structuring deficit. However, one way of viewing both explanations is to see them as focusing on a difficulty with rapid auditory processing. We have already seen Tallal and Piercy's research in this light. Let us now consider one effect which the hierarchical organisation of language has on processing.

As we will see in Chapter 7, there is considerable evidence that sentences are processed constituent by constituent. If sequential and hierarchical organisation correspond it is possible to deal with one constituent before proceeding to the next. However, if one constituent begins before a previous one has ended, additional processing will be necessary in order to allocate subsequent words to their appropriate constituents. When we are understanding spoken language, there is only a fixed amount of time for us to carry out processing, because spoken language is arriving at a roughly constant rate. Therefore, the only way in which more processing can be done in a limited time is for processing speed to be increased. The difficulty which dysphasic children face in understanding complex sentences could be that they find it very difficult to carry out processing sufficiently fast to deal with complex sentences.

We should, however, end our discussion of developmental dysphasia with a note of caution. Although we were careful to define developmental dysphasia at the start of this chapter as a specific impairment of language occurring in children of normal intelligence, which cannot be explained in terms of environmental, sensory or emotional factors, it would be wrong to assume that all children who show specific impairment in the acquisition of language form one homogeneous group. One important distinction exists between those children whose language production lags far behind their language comprehension, and those who show very poor language comprehension as well as poor production. Most of the studies we have reviewed in this chapter have focused on the more common production difficulties which dysphasic children have. However, a smaller group of children show very severe comprehension (i.e. receptive) problems. In a recent paper, Bishop (1982) has suggested that the hierarchical nature of language presents particular problems for dysphasic children with **receptive** language difficulties. As we have seen, it is possible that some aspects of Cromer's theory may be applicable to dysphasic children whose problems lie mainly in language production. However, it is likely that there are also important differences between the underlying difficulties of children with production problems, and those with a receptive disorder. More research is needed before a clear picture emerges.

What is particularly needed are more studies characterising the different patterns of linguistic deficit shown by individual developmental dysphasics. It may be that some developmentally dysphasic children have difficulties only with syntax, some only with semantics, and some only with pragmatics. As we have already seen, one group of children who show particularly severe comprehension problems have already been identified (e.g. by Bishop, 1982). It seems likely that further detailed investigation of individual patterns of deficit may confirm the view, currently expressed by many therapists who work with developmental dysphasics, that it is misleading to think of developmental dysphasia as a clearly defined and unitary syndrome.

When we consider **acquired** disorders of language in Chapter 9, it will become clear that the recent rapid progress in understanding such disorders has come about largely from research in which attempts are made to describe in detail the patterns of preserved and impaired linguistic abilities exhibited by *individual* patients with language disorders. These individual patterns are then interpreted in relation to models of normal language processing. A similar approach may be fruitful in the study of developmental dysphasia, although it should be remembered that the picture which emerges from a study of a developmental disorder may well be rather different from that emerging from the study of an acquired disorder.

5.3   Developmental dyslexia

Considerably more research has been carried out on developmental dyslexia and dysgraphia than on developmental dysphasia. One reason for this is that developmental dyslexia and dysgraphia occur much more frequently than developmental dysphasia. It is by no means uncommon for a child of normal or above-normal intelligence, *and* normal or above-normal ability to produce and understand *spoken* language, to experience great difficulty in learning to read.

In order to discuss the difficulties which children may experience in this latter process, we need to reconsider the concepts of **delay** and **deviance** which we introduced earlier in the chapter. For any child who is not reading as well as one would expect given the particular child's age and intelligence, one can ask whether the way the child reads corresponds to the way that a *younger normal* child reads (in which case the dyslexia is a matter of delay) or whether the child's reading is quite unlike what one sees in any normal reader of whatever age (in which case the dyslexia is a matter of deviance).

In order even to *ask* such questions, one must first have information about how young normal readers read at various ages. Chapter 4 provides such information. In that chapter, we proposed that the normal course of reading acquisition involves a progression through four phases of reading behaviour. These were the sight-vocabulary phase, the discrimination-net phase, the phonological-recoding phase, and the orthographic phase. Very roughly speaking, children normally progress through the first and second phases during the first year or two of reading instruction, then spend several years during which there is a gradual transition from the phonological-recoding to the orthographic stage. Any child who is at an earlier phase than he or she should be for a given age and intelligence level is developmentally dyslexic in the **delayed** sense. Any child who is reading in a way that does not correspond to *any* of the phases is developmentally dyslexic in the **deviant** sense.

This is the way we propose to discuss developmental dyslexia. We will begin by describing the relationships between the patterns of reading behaviour seen in dyslexic children and the phases involved in the normal acquisition of reading.

5.3.1 The sight-vocabulary phase

In Chapter 4 we discussed the idea that, at the very beginning of reading acquisition, children can often read a small set of familiar words which they have learned to read in a rote fashion, involving one-to-one associations between particular orthographic patterns and their spoken equivalents.

How necessary is this phase for the normal acquisition of reading? If a child never passes through this phase, will reading acquisition be impaired – that is, will some form of developmental dyslexia occur? It is difficult to answer such questions because, as we mentioned in Chapter 4, the sight-vocabulary phase has only been very sketchily investigated so far. We do not even know whether or not all children who acquire reading abilities at a normal rate start off with this phase. If it were shown that some children acquired reading normally without passing through this phase, it would then of course follow that the phase was not necessary for normal learning to read. But even if it turns out that all children who learn to read normally *do* start off with the sight-vocabulary phase, this would not entitle one to claim that, for reading acquisition to develop normally, it is *required* that the child begin with this phase.

There are two lines of evidence which might be taken as indicating that normal learning to read does not depend crucially upon the sight-vocabulary phase. One of these comes from the work of Firth (1972). The other comes from studies of precocious readers (Lynn, 1963; Fowler, 1962).

As we discussed in Chapter 4, Firth found that whether a child is good or bad at rote-learning visual-to-word associations does not influence how rapidly progress has been made in learning to read by the age of 8 (what *does* matter, as we discussed when dealing with Firth's work in Chapter 4, is how good a child is at using rules relating letters to sounds). This conclusion is evidence against the view that the sight-vocabulary phase is one the child *must* pass through normally if reading acquisition is to proceed at a normal rate.

The second line of evidence against this view comes from studies of children who reached the sight-vocabulary phase at an abnormally early age. Lynn (1963) taught his daughter, by a whole-word association method, to read over 100 words aloud before she was 3 years old. However, this did not lead her on to the next phase of reading at an abnormally early age. On the contrary, she subsequently regressed in reading, and three months later could read only 34 of the 100 words. Fowler (1962) also taught his daughter by a look-and-say method to read single words before she was 3. As was the case with Lynn's daughter, this did not accelerate reading development: not only did she make little further progress in reading over the next two-and-a-half years, but she forgot most of the recognition vocabulary she had previously acquired.

These studies by Lynn and Fowler indicate that children can learn to read at the level of the sight-vocabulary phase at a very early age. If this phase is *necessarily* the initial stage in the normal course of learning to read, one might expect that children who master this phase at a very early age should go on to acquire further reading abilities earlier than children normally do. However, this did not happen with the children studied by Lynn and Fowler.

5.3.2   The discrimination-net phase

In this phase of reading acquisition, word recognition depends upon analysing out partial cues from the printed word and using these to discriminate between the various words which constitute the child's reading vocabulary. These partial cues can be individual letters or letter groups, or even minute features such as the presence of a dotted letter or of an initial letter having an ascender (t or f, for example). *Analytic* processing of this sort allows the child to extend his reading vocabulary and the more detailed the analysis the larger will be the number of different words which can be discriminated from each other.

Seymour and MacGregor (1984) report a case study of a reader in whom this kind of analytic processing appeared to be disturbed. Their subject, RO, was not a young reader at the time he was studied: he was aged 16 years. How well he had learned to read initially is not known, but at the age of 12 he had a reading age of about 12 years (a poorer score than would be expected given his superior intelligence, his IQ being 126) and a spelling age of only about 9 years. When his ability to read single words aloud, or to make judgments about their meaning, was tested at age 16, he was found to perform competently provided that words were presented in normal orientation, but to be abnormally slow when words were presented vertically or in zigzag format. Vertical or zigzag presentation is assumed to force the reader to process words analytically, rather than holistically as is possible with normal presentation (see Seymour and MacGregor's paper for detailed arguments about this). Hence it can be argued that, for RO, holistic processing of words was normal but the kind of analytic processing essential during the discrimination-net phase was impaired. The slightly backward reading and even more backward spelling present in RO at age 12 may have been a consequence of earlier difficulties during the discrimination-net phase of reading acquisition.

Of course, the only way to obtain really direct evidence concerning a possible variety of developmental dyslexia associated with difficulties during the discrimination-net phase is to study young children at an age when they ought to be in this phase. For example, if one could find a child in whom a small sight vocabulary had been established in the way characteristic of the first phase of reading, but who appeared to have a great deal of difficulty in using partial cues from printed words to establish a system for discriminating between a larger set of words and in expanding sight vocabulary by using more and more complex analyses of the features of printed words, then one would have very clear evidence for a form of developmental dyslexia linked to the discrimination-net phase. This form of investigation remains to be done.

It is evident that not much is yet known about possible varieties of developmental dyslexia associated with the first two phases of reading acquisition. Fortunately, the position is clearer in relation to the phonological and orthographic phases.

5.3.3 *The phonological-recoding phase*

In this phase, children make extensive use of rules relating letters to sounds, which allows them to read words which are visually unfamiliar to them. This provides children with a means of understanding any printed words which they have never seen before but whose spoken forms they can comprehend. A child who is poor at using letter-sound rules will experience reading difficulties at this stage even though he will have been able to negotiate the first and second phases of reading acquisition without any difficulty.

Temple (1984) and Temple and Marshall (1983) have described cases of developmental dyslexia which take this form. The most straightforward way of determining how well someone can apply letter-sound rules is to ask them to read aloud *non-words*. The cases described by Temple and by Temple and Marshall were particularly poor at this. For example, case HM, a 17-year-old girl with average IQ, was given 25 simple words and 25 simple non-words (for example, *foop, floon, boak* and *ede*) to read aloud. She read every word perfectly, but responded wrongly to 64 percent of the non-words, producing such errors as *cimy* – 'clammy', *streed* – 'stress', *fape* – 'fap' and *fime* – 'firm'. This very low level of performance in reading simple non-words, and these types of erroneous responses, demonstrate that cases like HM have a major impairment in the ability to use letter-sound rules for recoding printed letter strings into their correct phonological forms. Such an impairment would make it impossible to progress normally through the phonological-recoding phase of learning to read. The consequences of this for reading acquisition would seem to be quite severe. When HM was tested at age 17, her verbal IQ was average (105) but her reading and spelling were far below average for her age (single-word reading age 10 years 11 months; text-reading age 9 years 7 months; single-word spelling age 10 years 7 months).

As we will see in Chapter 9, this kind of selective difficulty in using letter-sound rules to read non-words can also be caused by injuries to the brain of a previously normal reader who before injury would have read the non-words easily. Beauvois and Derouesne (1979), the first to study this variety of *acquired* dyslexia, referred to it as 'phonological dyslexia'. Hence Temple, and Temple and Marshall, refer to the form of reading disorder their subjects showed as 'developmental phonological dyslexia'.

The same pattern, developmental phonological dyslexia, was shown by case JE, described by Temple (1984), whose ability to read non-words was, like HM's, very poor. JE was above average in intelligence (her IQ was 115) but at the age of 16 years she was very backward in reading (single-word reading age 12 years 4 months, text-reading age 9 years 2 months) and in spelling (single-word spelling age 10 years 7 months).

Seymour and MacGregor (1984) describe a similar case of selective difficulty in non-word reading. Once again, this case showed marked backwardness in reading and spelling, despite an above-average IQ. At the age of 17, her reading age was 11 years 2 months and her spelling age 11 years 6 months. Yet another case of this kind is described by Campbell and Butterworth (1985).

These observations are consistent with the view that a necessary preliminary to the attainment of fully skilled reading is a successful negotiation of the phonological-recoding phase. To enjoy the fruits of passing through this phase, one must be competent at using letter-sound rules for recoding from print to phonology. An impairment of the ability to use such rules makes it very difficult to progress from a reading age of 11 years or so on to a normal adult level of reading skill.

5.3.4 The orthographic phase

We pointed out in Chapter 4 that the strategies used by children in the phonological-recoding stage are particularly useful because they allow a child to comprehend many unfamiliar printed words, those that have been heard before but not seen before. We also pointed out that, at least for English, this phase cannot be the ultimate one as far as reading acquisition is concerned, because English contains substantial numbers of words which cannot be handled appropriately by the letter-to-sound rule strategy.

Two types of words produce problems for this strategy: exception words and homophones. If you apply letter-sound rules to exception words, you will obtain *incorrect* phonological codes (*pint* will be read as if it rhymed with *mint*). If you apply letter-sound rules to homophones, you will obtain *ambiguous* phonological codes (you will not know whether *sail* is about ships or shops).

Skilled readers of English do not make mistakes in reading exception words, and do not confuse homophones with each other. The only way to achieve these skills is to recognise words in terms of their orthographic representations – their specific spellings – rather than in terms of their pronunciations as yielded by application of letter-sound rules. In other words, the reader must pass from the phonological-recoding to the orthographic phase.

A child who has failed to make this final transition, and is still at the phonological-recoding phase when other children of the same age have moved on to the orthographic phase, will demonstrate this by having particular problems in reading those words for which the orthographic phase is necessary. Such children will, unlike their peers who have passed on to the orthographic phase, misread exception words, and confuse homophones.

As, again, we will see in Chapter 9, this kind of selective difficulty with exception words and homophones can also be caused by injuries to the brain of a previously normal reader who, before injury, would have dealt entirely correctly with such words. Marshall and Newcombe (1973), the first to describe this variety of *acquired* dyslexia in any detail, referred to it as 'surface dyslexia'. Hence an appropriate term to use for cases of developmental dyslexia in which the child has failed to move on from the phonological-recoding stage is **developmental surface dyslexia**.

Developmental surface dyslexia was first described by Holmes (1973), who studied four cases. Subsequently, studies of this variety of developmental dyslexia have been published by Coltheart, Masterson, Byng, Prior and Riddoch (1983), by Job, Sartori, Masterson and Coltheart (1984), and by Seymour and MacGregor (1984), who use the term 'developmental morphemic dyslexia'.

The case studied by Coltheart et al. (1983), CD, was a 16-year-old girl of average IQ and normal ability to understand and to produce *spoken* words. Her processing of *printed* words was, however, impaired. Her single-word reading age was 10 years 1 month, and her single-word spelling age was 9 years. Detailed tests of her reading showed that she did have specific difficulties with exception words and with homophones.

She was given a set of 39 exception words and a matched set of 39 regularly-spelled words to read aloud. She was significantly worse at reading the exception words (67 per cent correct) than the regular words (90 per cent correct). As we have explained, this is the pattern to be expected if someone is still at the phonological-recoding stage and so is relying extensively on letter-sound rules to read aloud, rather than being able to identify words directly as familiar orthographic patterns. If this interpretation is correct, then the errors made in reading exception words should frequently be 'regularisation errors' – that is, should take the form of applying letter-sound rules correctly (to words which disobey these rules). Such errors were common in CD's reading of exception words – for example, *bury* was read as if it rhymed with 'fury', *come* read as if it rhymed with 'home', *gauge* as 'gorge', *quay* as 'kway' and *break* as 'breek'.

Homophone reading was tested by giving CD single printed homophones such as *pane* or *bowled* and asking her to say what these words *mean*. She defined *pane* as 'something which hurts', *bowled* as 'fierce, big' and *soar* as 'to cut', and made numerous other such confusions between homophonic words. This type of error in reading comprehension tests must occur if the reader is at the phonological-recoding phase. Only by passing on to the orthographic phase will readers attain a strategy which will allow them to distinguish between words with the same pronunciation (i.e. the same phonological representation) and different spellings (i.e. different orthographic representations). Thus CD's susceptibility to homophone confusions is further evidence that she has failed to progress from the phonological-recoding phase to the orthographic phase.

5.4 Developmental dysgraphia

Spelling acquisition, like reading acquisition, appears to involve progress through a series of phases. Very young children cheerfully interpret the task of spelling as simply producing linked squiggles when asked to write words (for an example, see Margolin, 1984). It is conceivable that such behaviour, though it has little resemblance to spelling as we adults know it, may assist the child subsequently to begin writing in a more appropriate way. Some ideas about the subsequent course of spelling acquisition are provided by Frith (1980, 1984, 1985).

She suggests that, before anything resembling proper spelling will be generated by children, they need first to develop the ability of **phonological segmentation** – the ability to analyse spoken words into constituent sounds. Once this ability emerges, children can use sound-letter rules to write down words they hear. This might be referred to as the **phonological** phase of spelling acquisition. For English, this cannot be the ultimate phase of spelling, because English words cannot all be spelled correctly if one is only using sound-letter rules, the reason being that for most of the sounds of the English language there are several legal spellings. The word 'drain' *could* be spelled *drane, drayn, dreyn, drain,* etc., and if one spelled by sound-letter rules there would be no way of choosing the correct spelling.

Hence there follows a second phase in which spelling is accomplished, not by rule, but by retrieving word-specific orthographic information from a store of learned spellings of words. This we might refer to as the **orthographic** phase of spelling acquisition.

One can determine that a child is at the phonological phase of spelling acquisition by inspecting the spelling errors of the child: in this phase, the errors will be phonologically correct even if orthographically incorrect. For example, Alice, whose early reading we discussed in Chapter 4, is currently in this spelling phase, and so produces such spellings as *boilay* for 'beaujolais' and *chardnay* for 'chardonnay'.[1] If a child is poor at the processes required in this phase, spelling errors which are phonologically *in*correct will characterise the child's developmental dysgraphia – e.g. 'capacity' – *capisdy*, 'cough' – *couge*, or 'resource' – *recorse* (Frith, 1980). The child will also be particularly poor at spelling non-words to dictation, since here the use of sound-spelling rules is particularly crucial. This type of dysgraphia could be described as 'developmental phonological dysgraphia'. The term is appropriate because the term 'phonological dysgraphia' has been used to refer to cases of acquired dysgraphia in which damage to the brain has selectively impaired the previously-normal speller's ability to use sound-letter rules to spell (see Chapter 9).

When a child stops making phonological spelling errors and can generally produce correct spellings, the orthographic phase has been reached. If a child is poor at the processes required for this orthographic phase, then phonological spelling errors will persist well beyond the age at which they ought to have disappeared. This kind of dysgraphia may be referred to as 'developmental surface dysgraphia', again because it corresponds to a form of acquired

---

[1] The use of a single letter to write a syllable which is that letter's name (*r* for the *ar* in chardonnay) or which is that letter's sound (*d* for the *do* in chardonnay) is very common in this phase.

dysgraphia, surface dysgraphia, in which the previously-normal speller now makes numerous phonological spelling errors; this is discussed in Chapter 9.

The developmental surface dyslexic CD we discussed earlier also exhibited developmental surface dysgraphia. Amongst her errors in writing to dictation were 'search' – *surch*, 'anniversary' – *anerversary*, and 'else' – *elce* (see Coltheart et al., 1983). Another case of developmental surface dysgraphia is described by Frith (1984): amongst the errors in his writing to dictation were 'suitable' – *soutable* and 'opposite' – *oppersite*.

5.5 Overview

In this chapter we have discussed a variety of ways in which the path of language acquisition may fail to run smoothly. We have emphasised that developmental language disorder is not a single entity. Children who acquire *spoken* language entirely normally may nevertheless have great difficulty in acquiring *written* language. Even developmental difficulty in acquiring written language is not a single condition – we distinguished developmental dyslexia from developmental dysgraphia, and then went further by describing different kinds of developmental dysgraphia. What enabled us to do this was a fairly detailed model, set out in Chapter 4, of the various phases through which children normally progress as they acquire reading and writing.

Much less is at present known about developmental disorders of spoken language simply because very little has been done relating patterns of difficulty which can occur in acquiring spoken language to what is known (and discussed in Chapters 2 and 3) about normal language acquisition. Nevertheless, it is becoming quite clear that developmental disorders of spoken language occur, and that different developmentally dysphasic children can have quite different forms of difficulty in the processing of spoken language.

Part III

Language processing in adults

6 Understanding language: recognising words

6.1 The mental lexicon

In the first chapter of this book we explained that language is an **arbitrary** communication system. Among other things, this means that we have to learn to recognise the sounds, spellings and meanings of individual words, and to store this information in such a way that we can call upon it when we encounter spoken or written words. Since dictionaries also contain information about the orthography (i.e. spelling), phonology (i.e. pronunciation) and semantics (i.e. meaning) of words, terms such as 'mental dictionary', 'internal lexicon' or 'mental lexicon' have been used to refer to the internalised system of knowledge we use when we perceive or produce words. We will use the term **mental lexicon**, and we will assume that there is a single mental lexicon that is used for both the perception and production of both written *and* spoken language. This simplifying assumption may turn out to be incorrect – future psycholinguistic research may provide evidence that different lexicons are involved in the perception and production of language, or that different lexicons are involved in the processing of spoken and written language – but at present there are no good reasons for rejecting the simplifying assumption of a single mental lexicon.

The representation of a word in the mental lexicon is referred to as that word's **lexical entry**: this entry contains semantic, phonological and orthographic information about the word. In order to understand a word, the reader or hearer must gain access to the semantic information contained in the word's lexical entry. This process is known as **lexical access**. In reading, lexical access

135

involves using information from a printed word to gain access to that word's entry in the mental lexicon. In understanding spoken language, lexical access is achieved by using information from the acoustic representation of a word.

The mental lexicon is also involved in the **production** of written or spoken language. In this case, speakers or writers start out with a semantic representation of what they want to say or write, and search for the corresponding phonological information (enabling one to say a word) or orthographical information (enabling one to write a word.

Although we will assume that the same mental lexicon is used whether we are reading, writing, spelling, speaking or under-standing speech, we will introduce several complications. We have seen that a mental lexicon must contain semantic, phonological and orthographic information about words. However, we wish to reject the view that there is a *single* lexical entry for each word, containing all three kinds of information. We will instead provide reasons for believing that the mental lexicon consists of separate sub-systems: one containing semantic information, another contain-ing phonological information, and a third orthographic information.

We will also argue that it is probably necessary to make another distinction within the mental lexicon, and to think of there being separate sub-systems for input and output. What we mean by this is that the lexical sub-system we use for recognising printed words in reading may be different from the sub-system we use for producing printed words in writing. In other words there may be two separate orthographic sub-systems: an input lexicon (used in reading) and an output lexicon (used in writing and spelling). Similarly, there may also be two phonological sub-systems: an input lexicon used for recognising speech and an output lexicon for producing speech.

If the mental lexicon does consist of a number of separate sub-systems, then we need to explain how these sub-systems can communicate with each other, since such communication is obviously essential. For example, if we ask you 'What is large, grey and has a trunk?', your ability to answer will depend on communication from the phonological input lexicon (used to understand the words we say to you) to the semantic component of the lexicon (containing information about the meaning of the words). Having understood the question, you then have to produce an answer. This will involve communication from the relevant semantic entry to the phonological output lexicon, which enables you to produce the appropriate spoken form corresponding to the semantic entry, i.e. to say 'elephant' (unless what we asked you to do was write the answer down, in which case what is needed is communication from semantics to the orthographic output lexicon).

6.2 Theories about the structure of the mental lexicon

As we will see in Chapter 9, one way in which the organisation of the mental lexicon is being investigated is by studying the kinds of language disorders which adults suffer as a result of certain kinds of brain damage. However, although neuropsychological studies of patients are of great value, the information such studies yield must be considered in relation to studies of normal subjects. Fortunately, various purely psychological methods have been devised for studying the organisation of the mental lexicon in normal subjects, and some of these will be discussed in this chapter. What one hopes, of course, is to find that one comes to the same conclusions from using the neuropsychological method as from using psychological methods of investigation: and, as we will show in Chapter 9, such agreements between conclusions do actually occur.

The concepts **mental lexicon**, **lexical entry** and **lexical access** provide a vocabulary which we can use when discussing how words are perceived and produced. However, these concepts do not constitute a *theory* of word perception or production: they are names for structures and processes whose nature is to be explained by any theory of word perception or production. A variety of such theories has been proposed. Some of these theories concern a rather narrow aspect of the use of the mental lexicon; others are broad in scope, and attempt to say at least something about all the linguistic activities which depend upon using the mental lexicon.

In order to illustrate ways in which the concept of mental lexicon may be made more specific and applied to such activities as reading, spelling, speaking and understanding speech, we will discuss the most ambitious and most influential model of the mental lexicon yet developed, the logogen model, originated by Morton (1968, 1969).

6.2.1   *The logogen model: first version*

We write 'first version' because this model has recently undergone drastic revision, and a second and rather different version now exists. We discuss this later version in the next section, but we begin with the first (and now obsolete) version of the logogen model since the evolution of the second version from the first is instructive.

The original version of the model is depicted in Figure 8. The component labelled **logogen system** is a collection of logogens, one logogen for each word known to the person whose logogen system this is. A logogen is a mechanism for collecting evidence; each logogen is specialised for collecting evidence concerning the presence of the word to which this logogen corresponds. Logogens have thresholds: whenever the total amount of evidence exceeds this threshold level, the logogen 'fires'. This has two effects. First, information about the *meaning* of the word in the component labelled **cognitive system** is accessed, since there is a pathway of communication from entries in the logogen system to semantic information in the cognitive system. Secondly, information enabling the word to be *produced* (spoken or written) is transmitted to the component labelled **response buffer**, from which a spoken or written response can be generated.

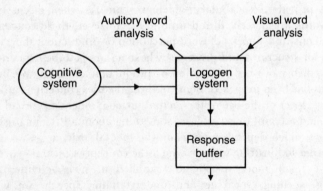

FIGURE 8   The essential parts of the original version of the logogen model

Any logogen accepts three types of evidence: **visual** (contributed by the visual analysis of visual input), **acoustic** (contributed by acoustic analysis of acoustic input) and **semantic** (contributed from the cognitive system). This latter kind of evidence is usually a consequence of the prior occurrence of a context. For example, if one reads *bread and*, the logogen for *butter* will receive some input (collect some evidence) from the cognitive system even before the word *butter* is actually seen.

Although there are three sources of input to the logogen system, there is only one set of logogens, and any word has only a single logogen. Therefore the logogen for *cat* is used for all the following tasks:

(a) reading *cat* aloud
(b) understanding the spoken word *cat*
(c) naming a picture of a cat, or a real cat
(d) naming the source of a heard miaow
(e) answering the question 'What drinks milk and catches mice?'

Any input will contribute evidence to more than one logogen. If the printed word *cat* is presented, '. . . the output from the visual analysis might include the attributes ‹three-letter word›, ‹tall letter at the end›, ‹initial c›, ‹final t›, and so on' (Morton, 1970, p. 206). All of these pieces of evidence are relevant to *cat*, and so would increment the level of evidence in the logogen for *cat*: but they are relevant to other words too. Detection of the attribute ‹three-letter word› would excite the logogens for all three-letter words, not just the logogen for *cat*. The logogens for three-letter words ending with *t* would be even more excited. The consequence of presenting any printed word, then, will be that a number of logogens will receive varying degrees of evidence – these logogens will be *activated* to different levels. This is why thresholds are needed: when *cat* is presented, numerous logogens will be excited, but in every case the excitation will not be high enough for the threshold level to be reached – except for the logogen for *cat*, which will receive so much evidence that its threshold *will* be reached.

It is necessary to assume that, once a logogen has reached threshold, its activation level must decay away rapidly. If not, the identification of subsequent words would be hindered. For example, imagine that you have just seen *cat*, and the appropriate logogen has reached threshold, and activation of that logogen remains high. Then you see a visually similar word like *cot* which increases the activation of *cat* as well as the activation of *cot* (because of the many features shared by these two words). This additional activation of *cat* might cause the logogen for *cat* to be more highly activated than the correct logogen for *cot*: *cot* would be incorrectly identified as *cat*. Morton (1968) therefore proposed that logogen activation '. . . decays very rapidly with time, reaching its original value in something of the order of 1 second.' However, it is not the case that presentation of a word is assumed to leave *no* trace behind in the logogen system after a second or more has elapsed. It is assumed instead that, each time a logogen reaches its threshold, the value of that threshold is lowered; and this value then slowly drifts up towards what it had been, but never quite reaches the previous level. In the long run, the obvious consequence of this is that the more frequently a word occurs the lower the threshold of its logogen will be, and hence the less activation of the logogen needed for it to reach threshold. Hence common words will be more rapidly identified or produced than uncommon words, and also a word which has been presented previously will be more rapidly identified than one which has not. This is because (other things being equal) the prior presentation of that word will have slightly reduced the threshold of its logogen.

We have said that when a logogen reaches threshold 'a response is available'; but since there are two output routes from the logogen system (to the cognitive system and to the response buffer) this term is ambiguous. In fact Morton proposed (e.g. in Morton, 1970, p. 215) that each logogen has *two* thresholds, one governing communication to the cognitive system and one governing communication to the response buffer. One reason for this proposal is that, when people read aloud, they make errors which are caused by the preceding *and following* semantic and syntactic context around the incorrectly read word. This means that (during reading aloud) before a word reaches the response buffer, *subsequent* words must have reached the cognitive system – this being the only way that their semantic and syntactic features could come into play. Information can then be fed back from the cognitive system to the logogen system to influence the response of this system to the word which is going to be misread. If the thresholds from logogen system to cognitive system were sometimes or always lower than the thresholds from logogen system to cognitive system, one could then explain **subception** (gaining access to the meaning of a word without being able to report the word) and also semantic errors which occur in the condition known as **deep dyslexia** in which single printed words are often incorrectly read as semantically related words, e.g. reading *storm* as *thunder*. (For an account of deep dyslexia see Chapter 9.)

One important theoretical characteristic of logogens which has stimulated a great deal of experimentation is that they mediate priming effects in word recognition, i.e. the faster recognition of a word following previous recent exposure to that word. As we mentioned earlier, once a logogen reaches threshold, its activation level does not immediately return to its normal resting level; it decays over a period of a second or so. If the word is re-presented within that period, it will be recognised unusually rapidly, because its logogen will still be relatively strongly activated, and hence very little evidence need be collected for threshold level to be reached. This kind of short-term priming effect (occurring over inter-presentation periods of a second or so) is not the only form of priming, however. In many of Morton's experiments, priming effects of much longer duration were observed: there can be as much as half an hour between the primer and primed, or sometimes a day or more (Scarborough, Cortese and Scarborough, 1977).

These long-term priming effects are explained, within the logogen model, by assuming that after threshold has been reached activation dies down rapidly at first over a period of a second or so, but does not quite reach the normal resting level: there follows a long period during which there is very slow decay of residual activation – a period measured in hours or even days.

On this account of long-term priming, the priming effect can be experimentally generated in a number of ways. The detectability of a tachistoscopically presented target word (let us say the word *fork*) should be improved by any of the following:

(a) having seen the word *fork* previously
(b) having heard the word *fork* previously
(c) having named a picture of a fork previously
(d) having answered the question 'What eating utensil has prongs?' previously.

This is because, if there is only one logogen for *fork*, all these different tasks will involve activation of the same logogen.

This prediction from the original version of the logogen model turns out to be wrong. Winnick and Daniel (1970) showed that, whilst tachistoscopic recognition of a printed word was facilitated by prior reading aloud of that word, there was no facilitation by prior picture naming, or by prior production of that word in response to a definition – tasks (c) and (d) above. This failure to find cross-modal priming was confirmed by Clarke and Morton (1983) and by Morton (1979), who failed to find facilitation of visual word identification by prior auditory presentation.

If priming effects are to be attributed to residual activation of logogens, the absence of cross-modal priming effects means that one must abandon the view that a single logogen system is used for visual and auditory word recognition, picture naming, and responding to definitions. A revised version of the logogen model – a multicomponent version containing several different logogen systems – was therefore proposed (Morton, 1978).

6.2.2   *The logogen model: second version*

There are several ways in which one might explain why priming effects are not cross-modal. For example, one might propose that the mental lexicon is divided into a semantic and a phonological system, rather than being a unified whole, and that priming occurs in only one of these systems. On this view, however, it cannot be the phonological system in which priming occurs, because both reading aloud and answering definitions by an oral response use the phonological system (since both culminate in the subject saying a word); yet these two activities do not prime each other. Hence, if the mental lexicon consists of a semantic system and a phonological system, priming effects must be attributed to the semantic system. However, as you have probably realised, this will not work either. Since reading aloud primes subsequent tachistoscopic recognition, the semantic system (if it is indeed the locus of priming effects) must be playing a part in tachistoscopic recognition; from which it follows that prior use of that system in responding to a definition should also prime tachistoscopic recognition. Yet, as we have already seen, priming of this kind does not occur. Therefore, one cannot locate the priming effect in a semantic sub-system of the mental lexicon, nor in a phonological sub-system, and hence a model of the mental lexicon involving just these two sub-systems is untenable.

What other kind of lexical sub-system might be accessed when one reads a word aloud? An obvious candidate is a *visual* recognition system. Suppose then that we divide the mental lexicon into a semantic system, a phonological system and a visual recognition system (used for the visual recognition of words). If priming effects arise because of residual logogen activation in the visual recognition system, then one can explain why priming occurs as it does. The only way in which visual recognition of a word can be primed is by previously *seeing* the word. Thus hearing a word, or producing it in response to an incomplete definition, will not prime visual word recognition.

The priming experiments can tell us something more specific about the visual recognition system used for identifying words. First, they allow us to ask whether there is a *general* visual recognition system, or whether there are separate recognition systems for visually presented words and pictures. If there is one general visual recognition system then visual word recognition should be primed by prior picture presentation; since this is not so, it can be inferred that visually presented words are recognised by a system specific to words – a **visual word-recognition system**.

A second question we can ask is whether the visual word-recognition system treats the uppercase, lowercase and handwritten version of a word as different (which would happen if the system operated at a relatively concrete level). An alternative possibility is that these three versions of a word are treated as the same (which would happen if the visual word-recognition system operates at a relatively abstract level). If the former, *tree* will not prime TREE; if the latter, the extent of priming will not depend on the typographical similarity of primer and target. What is found in studies of this question is that priming is *not* reduced when the primer is handwritten and the target printed (Morton, 1978) or when the primer is in one case and the target is in another (Scarborough, Cortese and Scarborough, 1977). As we will explain in the next section, the results of priming experiments like these mean that any model of the visual word-recognition system must incorporate a level of *abstract* letter recognition.

If long-term priming of visually presented words arises within a visual word-recognition system, not within a semantic or phonological component of the mental lexicon, then of course one needs to postulate not only a **visual word-recognition system**, but also an **auditory word-recognition system**, since hearing a word primes subsequent auditory recognition of that word.

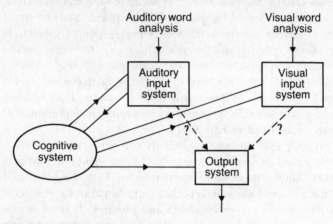

FIGURE 9   The revised logogen model

Thus we arrive at the second version of the logogen model, as described by Morton (1978); it is depicted in Figure 9. In this model, there are separate input logogens for recognising printed words and for recognising spoken words, a cognitive system (responsible for processing semantic information, generating context effects, and other complex linguistic manoeuvres), and an output logogen system, responsible for the production of spoken words. The two direct connections from input logogens (visual or auditory) to output logogens are dotted and accompanied by question marks because no evidence relevant to whether or not they existed was available when this model was first described.

Although this second version of the logogen model is considerably more elaborate than the first, it is still seriously incomplete. As Morton (1978) pointed out, a third input system (for recognising pictures) is needed: this kind of picture recognition system, which one might call the pictogen system (or, more strictly, the input pictogen system) was first discussed by Seymour (1973). Figure 9 is also incomplete on the output side: it has a system to mediate spoken output, but nothing to mediate written output or drawn output. So to be complete the model should have three input systems and three output systems, plus a central (semantic/cognitive) system.

A further and very different way in which Figure 9 is incomplete is that it deals only with the processing of words and has nothing to say about the processing of non-words. Any system which is exhaustively described by Figure 9 would be incapable of repeating nonsense words or reading them aloud or writing them to dictation. This is because the output logogen system is solely for producing *words*, and the input logogen systems can only recognise *words* – a spoken or printed non-word would not cause an input logogen to respond, and hence non-words cannot enter the mental lexicon at all.

This may seem an unimportant omission: we are rarely called upon to deal with spoken or written non-words in the course of day-to-day linguistic activities. For a variety of reasons, however, the failure to include mechanisms for dealing with non-words in one's model of the mental lexicon is not unimportant. One reason has to do with learning to read. As we discussed in Chapter 4, most 5-year-old children just beginning to learn to read already have a substantial auditory-recognition vocabulary. It is often argued that if a child learned how to recode unfamiliar letter strings – printed words not previously encountered – into a phonological form, this would permit reading to be parasitic on an already established ability to access the semantics of a word from its phonology. Learning how to translate unfamiliar letter strings into phonological form is just like learning to read non-words aloud, of course: and so a procedure for reading non-words aloud may be a crucial aspect of learning to read. This procedure would play a central role in the phonological-recoding phase of learning to read, described in Chapter 4; and one of the varieties of developmental dyslexia described in Chapter 5 appears to be a consequence of difficulties in using this procedure when learning to read.

It may also be necessary to include mechanisms for the identification of non-words in order to explain skilled reading. According to some views (e.g., Gough, 1972) skilled reading involves translating a word from its visual to its phonological representation prior to recognising it, and such translation would require the use of a mechanism which could also translate printed non-words into phonological form. (This is because, on this kind of view, the fact that words are familiar affects their recognition only *after* their phonological representation has been derived.) Any model of skilled reading which incorporates this view can only be properly tested if the mechanism by which unfamiliar printed letter strings are translated into phonological form is described in adequate detail.

Yet another reason for the theoretical importance of considering how non-words are dealt with is that, according to some authors (e.g., Marcel, 1980; Shallice, 1981b), the visual recognition of letter strings uses the same recognition system regardless of whether the letter string is a word or non-word. If studies of non-word reading support such a view, then any model in which the visual recognition of words is accomplished by a system which is unable to process non-words could not be correct: and, of course, the logogen model is one such model.

For reasons like these, it would seem a dangerous policy to ignore the processing of non-words entirely in one's theorising about the organisation of the mental lexicon; hence we must consider now what the mechanisms might be that people use when processing non-lexical verbal stimuli (spoken or written non-words).

The non-lexical task most intensively studied is reading non-words aloud, and the most commonly advocated view has been that this task is accomplished by using a system of *rules* relating spellings to sounds. Sometimes these are referred to as 'letter-sound rules', but this term cannot be a correct one, because of certain aspects of the nature of the writing system used for English. Take the non-word CHOOPH, for example. This contains six letters but only three individual sounds (phonemes). Thus if the rules really were letter-sound rules, they could not be used successfully with such non-words, because there are not single letters corresponding to each of the sounds in the non-word. Here we need the concept **grapheme**. What we mean by a grapheme is the written representation of a single phoneme – so, for example, the PH in CHOOPH, is a single grapheme because it represents a single phoneme. In fact, CHOOPH is made up of three graphemes – CH, OO, and PH. Thus the spelling unit which maps onto the phoneme is not the letter, but the *grapheme*, and the term we should be using is 'grapheme-phoneme rules' (not letter-sound rules). Such considerations lead to the idea that the way non-words are read is by first dividing them up into their graphemes (CHOOPH –

CH + OO + PH or SLOATCH − S + L + OA + TCH) and then using a table of grapheme-phoneme correspondence rules to find the appropriate phoneme for each grapheme. According to this theory (see e.g. Coltheart, 1978, 1984), there are just two different kinds of unit for reading aloud, the whole word (the unit used when reading aloud via the lexicon) and the grapheme (the unit used when reading aloud non-lexically).

The claim that no spelling unit smaller than the word but bigger than the grapheme is used when we read non-words aloud can be tested with non-words like *gean, geak,* and *gead.* In English, all words ending *-ean* have the 'ee' pronunciation for the grapheme *ea.* Most words ending *-eak* also have this pronunciation, but not all (e.g. *break*). Most words ending *-ead* do *not* have the 'ee' pronunciation for *ea.* These fact will be irrelevant if no unit larger than the grapheme is used to read aloud, because a standard rule *ea* − 'ee' will be applied to *ea* regardless of what other graphemes exist in the non-word. If some unit *larger* than the grapheme is used, such as a (vowel + consonant) unit, one might expect *gead* to be pronounced to rhyme with *bread,* because the most common pronunciation for *-ead* is the one used for *bread.* Kay and Lesser (1985) gave non-words like these to twelve skilled adult readers. They found that the 'ee' pronunciation was given 96 per cent of the time with items like *gean,* 92 per cent of the time with items like *geak,* and 79 per cent of the time with items like *gead.* The finding that 'ee' occurred significantly less often in the *gead* condition than in the other two conditions shows that it is not only the single grapheme that is used as a unit in reading non-words aloud. The grapheme is the *dominant* unit (since, although most *-ead* words do *not* have 'ee' pronunciation, a large majority of the subjects gave this pronunciation) but not the only one. Larger units play some role too. So one cannot say that grapheme-phoneme conversion is *the* way non-words are read aloud. Instead, we will use the term 'subword-level orthographic-to-phonological conversion' to stress the fact that the unit used is smaller than the whole word but not invariably as small as the grapheme.

Exactly the same issues arise in relation to the task of spelling non-words to dictation, and here again it appears that this not done solely by phoneme-grapheme rules, but that some role is played by units larger than the grapheme (Campbell, 1983). Hence we refer to the process used for writing non-words to dictation as 'subword-level phonological-to-orthographic conversion'.

Our discussion of the evolution of the logogen model has led us to the following view of the organisation of the mental lexicon. We wish to distinguish between lexical input systems, lexical output systems, and a semantic system. At the input-system level, we wish to distinguish between a visual word-recognition system and an auditory word-recognition system (and also a picture-recognition system, not relevant when stimuli are words). At the output-system level, we wish to distinguish between a system for producing spoken output and a system for producing printed output (and also a system for producing drawn output, not relevant when what is to be produced is a word). In addition, we need a procedure for subword-level orthographic-to-phonological conversion and a procedure for subword-level phonological-to-orthographic conversion.

Ths entire processing apparatus is depicted in Figure 10. This figure contains all the separate information-processing components which seem to be needed to explain how we do all the things we can do with verbal stimuli, plus arrows indicating pathways of communication between these components.

In the remaining sections of this chapter we will concentrate on two of these components: the visual word-recognition system and the auditory word-recognition system. We have chosen these because, for the moment, we want to consider only language comprehension. We will discuss language production in Chapter 8. Since there has been such extensive research on both systems we have had to be selective: we have therefore confined ourselves to discussing just one line of work in connection with each.

6.3   The visual word-recognition system

The function of a visual word-recognition system is to accept, as input, information gathered from a printed or written word, and to produce, as output, an abstract identification of that word. What we mean by **abstract** identification is that semantic and phonological properties of the word are not specified by the output of the visual word-recognition system. One way of thinking about abstract identification is to think of the output as being a statement like 'This is word number 538'. Such a statement tells you nothing about the meaning of the word – to discover the meaning you have

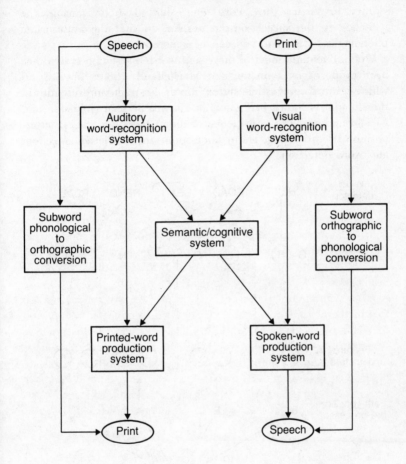

FIGURE 10 An information processing model of language

to transmit code 538 to the semantic system. Similarly, if you wanted to *pronounce* the word you would have to transmit the 538-code to the speech output system, so that the appropriate phonological representation can be generated.

One influential model of the visual word-recognition system has been proposed by Johnston and McClelland (1980). The way in which printed input is translated into an abstract word-identity in their model is shown in Figure 11. As will be seen, Johnston and McClelland propose a sequence of four processing stages: letter-position preprocessing, feature detection, abstract letter detection, and word detection.

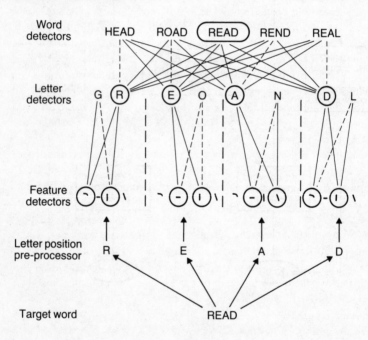

FIGURE 11   The Johnston-McClelland model

In the first stage, **letter-position preprocessing**, each letter in a word is simply segregated from its background, and its ordinal position noted. The outcome is that the word has been encoded as a sequence of unanalysed visual blobs, each labelled with its ordinal position (first, second, third, etc.) in the sequence of blobs.

In the next stage – **feature detection** – each blob is subjected to feature analysis. In the example given in Figure 11, the feature analysis system detects the features *curve at the top*, *vertical contour*, and *oblique contour* in the first blob, while not detecting such features as *horizontal contour* or *curve at the bottom*, since the first blob does not contain these features.

At the next stage – **abstract letter detection** – all twenty-six letters of the alphabet are represented by individual letter detectors. Every feature detector in the feature-detection stage is linked to every letter detector in the letter-detector stage. If there are, say, 20 different feature detectors, then there are $20 \times 26 = 520$ connections between the two levels. Each of these connections is either excitatory (indicated by a solid line in Figure 11) or inhibitory (indicated by a broken line). Any feature detector has excitatory links to all the letter detectors for letters having that feature, and inhibitory links to all other letter detectors. Thus, for example, if the feature *curve at the top* is detected, this will excite the letter detectors for all letters with that feature (such as G, R or O), and inhibit all letter detectors for letters without that feature (such as H, E or J).

The letter detector for any letter (let us say R) is used to identify that letter regardless of its precise visual form: for example, uppercase, lowercase and handwritten forms of the letter R are all identified by the same letter detector. This is why the letter detectors are referred to as **abstract**: they do not provide information about specific visual form. It follows from this that a reader who has just identified a particular letter will not be able to tell whether it was in upper or lower case on the basis of the information from the letter detector level. Concrete information of this sort must be supplied in some other way (e.g. by the feature detector level).

Experiments show that when words or letters are presented very briefly, subjects are in fact sometimes able to report what letter or word they have seen but not whether it was upper or lowercase (Coltheart and Freeman, 1974; McClelland, 1976; Adams, 1979; Friedman, 1980). These experiments provide strong evidence for the existence of a system of **abstract** letter detectors. However, it is difficult to see precisely how the feature detection and abstract letter detection levels could be linked together in such a way that a letter can be detected regardless of its case of presentation. The problem is that for some letters the majority of features which occur in upper and lowercase forms (like E and e) are different. So if, for example, a feature like *straight line at the top* has excitatory connections with the letter detector for E, and *curve at the top* has inhibitory connections, how can the E-detector be excited by the stimulus e?

This problem has not yet been considered in relation to the Johnston-McClelland model, where it is of particular importance because in this model, **inhibition is absolutely decisive**. No matter how many excitatory inputs a letter detector receives from feature detectors, if it receives even just one inhibitory input, it is switched off completely. The letter detectors for P and R would both receive excitatory inputs from the *vertical contour* and *curve at the side* feature detectors if an R was presented. However, the P-detector would be switched-off by the inhibitory link from the feature detector *oblique contour*. It follows from this view of inhibitory input that activation at the letter detection level will be all-or-none: when a letter is presented, the detector for this letter is fully activated, and the detectors for all other letters are completely silent.

One could relax the postulate of decisiveness of inhibition, and propose instead that the activation of letter detectors was more-or-less rather than all-or-none. This would happen if the total amount of activation in a detector were determined by the amount of excitation minus the amount of inhibition. Thus, the stimulus R would excite the R-detector most, the P-detector and the B-detector to a considerable degree, and other letter detectors less. This alternative has been adopted in the model of word-recognition proposed by Rumelhart and McClelland (1982) and McClelland and Rumelhart (1981). As we will see, however, the all-or-none conception of activation leads to some very powerful predictions, including some which are counterintuitive yet supported by experimental results. Thus at present there are good reasons to retain the Johnston and McClelland assumption that inhibition is decisive.

We now come to the final stage in the Johnston and McClelland model – **abstract word detection**. All the twenty-six letters of the alphabet have links to all the words at the word detector level. Each link is either excitatory or inhibitory, and, again inhibition is decisive: a single inhibitory input is sufficient to prevent a word detector from being activated, no matter how many excitatory inputs it receives. Thus, in the example shown in Figure 11, all detectors for words beginning with an R will receive excitatory inputs from the letter detector level, while detectors for all other words will be completely switched off by inhibition. The detector for a word like REAP will also be switched off, despite its similarity to READ, because it will receive an inhibitory input from the letter detector for D-in-the-fourth-position. Thus only one word detector – the one for READ – will be activated.

One point about this model which is unclear is this: what is it that prevents words like READY or READJUST from activating the word detector for READ? There are various possible ways of dealing with this problem. One way would be for the letter detector for, say, Y-in-the-fifth-position to have inhibitory links not only to the word detectors for words which have any other letter in that position, but also to those detectors for words which have no fifth letter. This would cause READY to inhibit words with four letters or less, like READ. However, this does not explain how READ could inhibit READY, or any other word of more than four letters beginning with the sequence READ. This kind of inhibition could perhaps be achieved by including, amongst the letter detectors, a space detector, activated by the absence of input from the feature level. The activation of this space detector would inhibit all detectors for all words containing more letters than the target. This kind of end-of-word detector is discussed by Humphreys, Quinlan and Evett (1983).

The Johnston-McClelland model may seem very complicated, with its many levels, many detectors at each level, and very many interconnections between levels. However, this model is simple enough for one to be able to make numerous predictions from it, and hence it has been easy to submit the model to experimental tests. The model has emerged honourably from these tests; and we will now describe some of them.

In order to understand how predictions are derived from the model, one must first consider the phenomenon of **backward visual masking**, since the logic of the experiments depends upon using masking. When a target word is briefly presented in a tachistoscope, and the subject's task is to report the word, the ability to do so is reduced if the word is followed by another stimulus (a **backward mask**) rather than simply darkness. There are two different kinds of backward masking – **brightness masking** and **pattern masking** (Turvey, 1973). In **brightness masking**, a homogeneous bright field is used after the target word. The field behaves as if it had been presented simultaneously with the target display, and so reduces the contrast between target contours and their background (that is, the target contours will look grey rather than black). If the brightness backward mask follows soon enough after the target and is bright enough, it will reduce contrast in the target display so much that the target contours will not be discriminable from their background, and so the target will not be identifiable. Brightness masking can be thought of as operating primarily at the feature detector level in Figure 11; by reducing the discriminability of target features, it makes feature detection difficult (or imposible, if the mask is bright enough). In other words, the result of brightness masking is *feature shortage* (Johnston, 1981).

In **pattern masking**, the stimulus which follows the briefly presented target is not a homogeneous field, but itself contains contours, for example, a randomly arranged collection of fragments of straight lines and curves. A pattern mask will impair the detection of the target not by causing feature shortage, but by causing *time shortage*. Suppose the target is a letter. Its features will be detected at the feature detector level, and these will cause the letter detector for the target letter to be activated. If the subject's task is to report the letter, however, further work needs to be done: the abstract code for the letter must be generated and transmitted to the appropriate lexical output system. Now, suppose that a pattern mask is presented during the time interval between the activation of the target's letter detector, and the transmission of the code from the letter detector level to the appropriate output system. Since the mask is patterned, it will contain features which will be detected by feature detectors. It is extremely likely that some of these detected features will *not* be present in the target, and so the detection of these non-target features in the mask will, via the inhibitory links from feature to letter level, *turn off the activation in the target letter's detector*. Since the target's code has not yet been transferred to a lexical output system, there will no longer be any representation of the target anywhere. In this way a pattern mask limits the time for which a target letter is represented in the system, and if the time limitation is severe enough to prevent the target's code from reaching a lexical output system, then the subject will fail to report the target, *even though the target was identified in the sense that its detector in the lexical input system was activated.*

This account of the difference between brightness masking and pattern masking is supported by the introspections of subjects in masking experiments. With brightness masking, subjects report that although the target appeared to be present for a reasonably long period it was too vaguely defined – its contrast was too low – for it to be identifiable. In contrast, with pattern masking, subjects report seeing a crisp, clear high-contrast target for an extremely short period of time, too short for the target to be reportable.

We have described the properties of brightness and pattern masking in order to be able to show how studies of letter and word recognition in backward masking experiments provide strong support for the model shown in Figure 11. We will now go on to describe three of the experimental findings which provide such support.

(i) masking and the word-superiority effect

Reicher (1969) and Wheeler (1970) found that words of four letters are more accurately reported than single letters under tachistoscopic conditions, even when a forced choice technique is used to equate the chances of guessing. This **word-superiority effect** is clearly important for models of word recognition: any model would have to offer an account of why, even though a word target has four times as many letters as a single letter target, the word is easier to perceive. The effect, however, turned out to be a somewhat elusive one in subsequent research, until the conditions under which it can be obtained were elucidated by Johnston and McClelland (1973).

In their experiment, the stimulus was a brief visual presentation of a four letter word (e.g. COIN). This was followed by two alternatives, the word itself and another differing by one letter (e.g. COIN and JOIN). The subject's task was to decide which of these two alternatives had been presented. In a second condition, the target was a single letter (e.g. C) and the alternatives were single letters (e.g. C and J). The chances of guessing correctly were therefore the same in both conditions.

Johnston and McClelland used both of the types of backward mask which we have described. With a brightness mask, no word-superiority effect was obtained: performance was equivalent for word and single-letter targets. With a pattern mask, however, performance was very much better when the target was a word than when it was a single letter.

The model of Figure 11 may be used to explain this pattern of results as follows. Consider the pattern mask condition first. When the target is a *letter*, it activates one unit at the letter-detector level but none at the word-detector level (*all* word detectors will be inhibited). This letter detector remains active for some brief period of time, until the pattern mask is presented. The mask activates a variety of features, at least some of which will not be features of the target letter. Activity in the target letter's detector will therefore be inhibited (switched off). In contrast, when the target is a *word*, both letter and word detectors will be activated. The mask will then arrive and terminate activity in the letter-detector level – *but it will not affect activity in the word-detector level.* This is because termination of word-detector activity can only be produced by inhibition from active letter detectors, and the mask does not activate any letter detectors: on the contrary, the mask *terminates* the activity of letter detectors. Thus a pattern mask will greatly reduce the time available for a letter detector to generate and transmit a code to the lexical output systems, but will not affect the time available to a word detector. Therefore, words will be reported better than single letters, i.e. there will be a word-superiority effect.

In the case of brightness masking, however, the situation will be completely different because, since a brightness mask has no features, it will not cause any feature-detectors to respond. Rather, it will make *both* single letters *and* words more difficult to discriminate by its action at the feature-detector level, and so will have an equal effect on both types of stimuli. Therefore, with a brightness mask there will be no word-superiority effect.

(ii)   word masks v. feature masks

So far we have only considered pattern masks which consist of a random jumble of fragments of letters. These are called **feature masks**, and, as we have seen, they will stimulate feature detectors, and hence affect letter detectors, but they will not penetrate to the word detector level. Another kind of pattern mask is a **word mask**, in which the backward-masking stimulus is itself an actual word. A mask of this kind will cause activation of detectors at the feature, letter and word levels. It will, therefore, be capable of cutting short the period of time available for an activated word detector to generate and transmit a code to the lexical output systems. This means that a word mask should reduce the word-superiority effect in comparison with a feature mask; and Johnston and McClelland (1980) showed that this was the case.

You might be wondering why a word mask merely reduces rather than eliminates the word-superiority effect, since it effectively short-circuits the operation of the target word's detector. Presumably, the reason is that even with a word mask, word targets are represented at two levels (word detector and letter detector) while letter targets are represented at only one. Even if the time for which these representations are available is very brief (because of the word mask) two representations will still be better than one.

(iii) word masks and non-word masks
We hope that it has not escaped the reader that the predictions concerning the different effects of word and feature masks do not depend on the mask being a *word*; they depend only on the mask being composed of *letters*. It is the detection of letters in the mask whose occurrence is inconsistent with the current activation of the detector for the target word which inhibits the activation of the target-word detector.

The Johnston and McClelland model therefore predicts that the advantage of word targets over letter targets will be the same with a backward mask which is a word, as with as backward mask consisting of a random sequence of letters. In other words, it will make no difference to the word-superiority effect whether the mask is a word or a non-word. This prediction was confirmed by Johnston and McClelland (1980).

These and other findings discussed by Johnston and McClelland (1980) not only provide evidence in favour of their model of visual word-recognition, but also evidence against other types of model. This is an essential aspect of theory testing, of course: results which are consistent with all models cannot count as evidence for any of them. We will therefore end this discussion of the Johnston-McClelland model by briefly considering one further example of empirical evidence which supports this model, but does not support alternatives.

All the inhibitory and excitatory connections in the Johnston-McClelland model operate *vertically* (between one level and another) but not *horizontally* (within a level). However, some theories of visual word-recognition propose that there are horizontal excitatory links at the letter detection level, since these could potentially serve to speed the identification of words. This is because, in English, only certain combinations of letters are allowed in the formation of words. For example, if we saw the sequence PQZT, we would know that it could not possibly be an English word. So, if we knew that P was the first letter of a word we would know that the second letter could only come from a small group, and that A, E, I, O, and U are the most likely candidates, H and S are less likely but possible, and F and N very unlikely, but not impossible. (Other letters like B, C, D etc. are impossible.) It is therefore legitimate to ask whether these intra-word letter constraints are used in visual word-recognition, or whether the identification of each letter in a word is carried out independently.

Gibson and Levin (1975) proposed that information about letter constraints reduces uncertainty and facilitates the reading of words. However, a variety of experiments have revealed that both tachistoscopic recognition (Johnston, 1978; McClelland and Johnston, 1977; Manelis, 1974) and lexical decision time (Coltheart, Davelaar, Jonasson and Besner, 1977) are unaffected by inter-letter constraints.

There are also good reasons for rejecting the proposal of Rumelhart and McClelland (1982) and McClelland and Rumelhart (1981) that there are horizontal inhibitory connections between *word* detectors. If word detectors inhibit each other, a backward mask which is a word will inhibit the word detector for a target, whilst a non-word mask will not. In other words, superiority of word targets over letter targets should be smaller with word masks than with non-word masks if there is horizontal inhibition at the word detector level. However, as we noted earlier, Johnston and McClelland (1980) showed that this was not so: the nature of a backward mask (word or non-word) made no difference to the size of the word-superiority effect.

Because numerous theoretical approaches to visual word-recognition postulate horizontal interconnections between detectors, evidence suggesting that such interconnections do not exist serves a vital function in adjudicating between theories. This evidence suggests that, whatever one's model of visual word-recognition is, the model should share one of the basic characteristics of the

Johnston-McClelland model, namely, that excitatory and inhibitory connections may be vertical (between-level) but not horizontal (within-level).

We have chosen to describe this model in detail because in our view it is both more complete, and better able to offer explanations of many more findings, than other existing models of visual word-recognition. We have noted some unresolved problems for the model, however. In addition, the model provides no account of how pronounceable non-words are read aloud, nor of how context influences word identification. Presumably, the letter detector level is used equally when non-words or words are presented. If so, there must be a second output route from this level to a system that converts letter information to pronunciation without going via the word level. As for context effects, we will consider these after having discussed the auditory word-recognition system.

6.4 The auditory word-recognition system

We will again concentrate our discussion on one particular model; and we have selected the one which is probably the most fully worked-out. This is the so called **cohort model**, due to Marslen-Wilson, Tyler and co-workers (see, for example, Marslen-Wilson and Welsh, 1978; Marslen-Wilson and Tyler, 1980). This model proposes that there exists a set of auditory word detectors, closely analogous to the visual word detectors in the Johnston-McClelland model. The way in which these detectors are used to identify spoken words, however, differs considerably from the way in which identification is achieved in the Johnston-McClelland model.

The auditory word detectors are activated by input from a spoken word, and an essential aspect of the model is that this activation begins as soon as the first sounds in the word are heard. An alternative to this view is that identification does not begin until an entire word has been heard, so that only *one* word detector is activated for each word. According to the cohort model, however, as soon as the first part of the word has been heard, *all* the detectors for words beginning with this initial sound are activated. This set of words is called the **word-initial cohort**, since it is a set of words all having the same initial sound.

In the cohort model all words are initially potential candidates for recognition, i.e. all word detectors are equally activated before a spoken word actually begins. As soon as any information from a spoken stimulus reaches the word detectors, however, a process of candidate elimination begins. For example, if the first phoneme of the word is /p/, all detectors for words not beginning with /p/ are switched off, leaving only detectors for the word-initial cohort activated. If the next phoneme is /r/, then all detectors for words beginning with /p/ followed by some sound other than /r/ will be switched off.

At any point while the word is being spoken, the set of detectors which remain activated is known as the **cohort**. As more and more of the presented word is heard, the size of this cohort will shrink, until eventually only one word detector remains activated. This detector must, of course, be the detector corresponding to the word actually presented.

A system like this could be very efficient, since it could identify words even before they have been completely spoken. Consider the word *trespass*, for example. No English word except *trespass* (and its derivations and inflections such as *trespasser* and *trespasses*) begins with the phoneme sequence *tresp*. Therefore, as soon as the phoneme /p/ is heard, the cohort will have only one member left, and the word can be identified as *trespass*, even though its final phonemes have not yet been heard.

In fact, a system like this is optimally efficient. Identifying the word as *trespass* sooner, that is *before* the /p/ is heard, would be inefficient because mistakes could be made (for example, choosing *trespass* when you have only heard *tres* could be wrong – the word could be *trestle* or *tress*.) However, waiting for further phonemes after the /p/ would also be inefficient because this increases recognition time without increasing accuracy, since the additional phonemes do not provide any necessary information. The most efficient point at which to identify a word is thus after hearing the phoneme at which the word first differs from every other word in English. This is known as the word's **recognition point**; and in the case of the word *trespasses* it is the phoneme /p/. In terms of the Marslen-Wilson model, the recognition point of a word is the phoneme whose input to the word detectors shrinks the cohort down to a single word.

It is also possible to define the recognition point of a non-word: it is that phoneme at which the stimulus no longer corresponds to any English word. For example, the recognition point of VLEESIDENCE is very early because no English word begins VL. In contrast, the recognition point of THOUSIDING is comparatively late – until the first I is heard the stimulus could be the word *thousand*.

If the subject's task is auditory lexical decision – that is, to decide whether a *spoken* item is a real word or a pronounceable non-word – monitoring the size of the cohort would allow this decision to be made. Whenever the cohort reaches zero (i.e. whenever no word detectors remain activated), the decision NO can be made. An obvious prediction, then, is that non-words with *late* recognition points (like THOUSIDING) will take longer to reject as words than non-words with *early* recognition points (like VLEESIDENCE). Marslen-Wilson (1978) has shown this to be true. He has also shown that, as the model predicts, the lexical decision time for non-words with early and late decision points is identical if reaction time is measured *from the decision point*.

One wants evidence from the processing of *words*, of course, if one is investigating a model of word recognition, and this is provided by the second experiment described by Marslen-Wilson (1978). Here all stimuli were spoken words, and the subject's task was to listen to each word and press a button as quickly as possible on hearing the sound /t/ – a task known as **phoneme monitoring**. The subject's reaction time was measured *from the time at which the target phoneme occurred* (not from the onset of the word containing the target). Bearing this in mind, the results are perhaps surprising because they showed that when the target came early in a word, reaction times were long; but when the target came late in a word, reaction times were short.

In order to explain this Marslen-Wilson proposed that his subjects were first identifying each word they heard and then searching their phonological representations of that word for the presence of a /t/. In other words, they were not directly listening for the sound /t/ in the speech as it came in, but rather determining that a word contains a /t/ after actually identifying the word. Thus, the time taken to identify a /t/ will be directly related to the time taken to identify the word in which it occurs; and, as we have seen, this time depends on the word's recognition point. When a target occurs *late* in a word, it is likely to occur *after* the recognition point. Consequently, the word will often have been identified before the target has even occurred, and so reaction times will be short. In contrast, when a target occurs *early* in a word, it is likely to occur *before* the recognition point. Consequently, such a word can be identified only after the subject has heard phonemes occurring later than the target phoneme, and so reaction times will be long.

If this is what was happening in Marslen-Wilson's experiment, the really important variable should be where the target occurred relative to the recognition point, rather than where the target occurred within the word. Reaction times should be fast if the target phoneme occurred after the recognition point, and slow when it occurred before the recognition point. More generally, if reaction time is plotted against the time interval between target and recognition point, the result should be a function which increases linearly. This is the pattern which emerged from Marslen-Wilson's (1978) data.

These data are of interest not only because of the support they provide for the cohort model, but also because of a more general point they make about cognition, namely, that we must make a clear distinction between the sequence of processing stages and the accessibility of these stages for consciousness, or for the control of responses. Analysis of the word-superiority effect in terms of the Johnston-McClelland model led to the conclusion that although word identification depends upon and occurs after letter identification, tasks requiring responses to words may neverthless be performed more accurately, and indeed more quickly, than tasks requiring responses to letters. The same kind of conclusion is suggested by Marslen-Wilson's phoneme monitoring data. A /t/ which occurs before the recognition point must be used for the purposes of recognising the spoken word: but it appears not to be used for making phoneme-monitoring decisions, since monitoring latencies are related to the word's recognition point, not to the point at which the target occurred.

The two experiments we have just described, one on auditory lexical decision and the other on phoneme monitoring, support the view of auditory word recognition as a process by which an initially large cohort of candidate word detectors shrinks rapidly in size as information from the speech signal flows in, until eventually the cohort is reduced to a single candidate. At this moment (which occurs when a word's recognition point is reached), the word can be identified, even if much more of the speech signal has yet to reach the word-recognition system.

6.5   Context effects on word recognition

6.5.1   *Context effects on auditory word recognition*

Our discussion of the cohort model is incomplete as yet, however, because we have not discussed context effects. As a rule, people do not hear single isolated words, and in the great majority of cases any word we hear is preceded by a context which could in principle be used to assist word recognition. For example, we noted earlier that if we hear *tres . . .*, the cohort will include *trestle, tress* and *trespass*, and so the recognition point will not have been reached. Suppose, however, that when we heard *tres* it was preceded by *Forgive us our. . . .* If the recognition of spoken words is affected by preceding context then we would expect that this highly familiar context should be sufficient to rule out *trestle* and *tress* as possible candidates, despite their consistency with the partial word *tres. . . .*

The effect of preceding context on auditory word recognition was investigated by Marslen-Wilson and Welsh (1978) using a speech-shadowing task in which the subject listened to continuous speech through headphones and repeated it aloud with as little delay as possible. The speech input contained occasional deliberate mis-pronunciations – for example, *tragedy* mispronounced as *trachedy*. Very often these mispronunciations were corrected when the subject repeated the speech, and in about 50 per cent of cases the correct pronunciation was restored with no disruption of the fluency of shadowing. Such cases are known as **fluent restorations**.

If we return to our example, we can see that if a subject hears *Forgive us our tres . . .* and a decision has been made at this point that the incomplete word is *trespasses*, the subject can begin to say *trespasses* and ignore the rest of the word. In doing this the subject will fail to detect that it was not *trespasses* that was presented, but the mispronunciation *tresbasses*. The frequency of fluent restorations is thus an indication of whether mispronunciations occurred before or after the recognition point of a word, and thus an indication of where in a word the recognition point actually occurred. By comparing the frequency of fluent restorations in different conditions, it is possible to see whether preceding context affects the recognition point of a word. If it does, fluent restorations should be more frequent when there is an appropriate context than when there is not. Marslen-Wilson (1975) found that fluent restorations occurred far more often during the shadowing of normal prose than when the mispronounced word was semantically or syntactically incongruent with respect to the sentence containing it.

If context affects the recognition point of a word, as this result suggests, then it should be possible to show that a context which makes a word very predictable will have a greater effect on fluent restorations than a context which makes a word only fairly predictable. Marslen-Wilson and Welsh (1978) found that fluent restorations occurred more frequently when the word was very predictable (e.g. in *Still he wanted to smoke a **cikarette***) than when it was only moderately predictable (e.g., in *It was his **mizfortune** that they were stationary*). Such results indicate that the recognition point of a word depends on the preceding context. In terms of the cohort model this means that the size of a cohort at any given moment will depend not only on how much of a current word has been analysed, but also on information from the preceding context. A very predictable word has a smaller context-produced cohort than a moderately predictable word, so less of the word itself will need to be analysed to reduce the cohort to a single candidate. There is, thus, a higher probability that the mispronunciation will be in the unanalysed segment of the word and so will escape detection.

A similar rationale lies behind a somewhat different experimental task – **word monitoring** – used in the work of Marslen-Wilson and Tyler (1980). Subjects are given a particular word – let us say the word *lead* – and then they listen to a pair of sentences and press a button as soon as they hear the target word. The sentences heard were either normal prose (e.g. *Some thieves stole most of the **lead** off the roof*) or syntactic prose (e.g. *No buns puzzle some in the **lead** off the text*) which was syntactically correct but semantically anomalous. In a third condition the 'sentences' were randomly arranged strings of words (e.g. *some the no puzzle buns in lead the text off*) which were neither syntactically correct nor meaningful.

Mean reaction time for detecting the target word in normal prose was 273 milliseconds, measured from the onset of the target word. Since, on average, the target word actually took 369 milliseconds to say on the recording subjects were listening to, this means that subjects had often pressed the button before they had heard all of the target word. In fact, assuming that the time elapsing between a subject's decision to respond and the actual pressing of the button was about 75 milliseconds, subjects on average identified the target after having heard only the first 200 milliseconds of it. Now, the first 200 milliseconds of a word rarely identify the word exactly, and in fact analysis of the 81 different target words used by Marslen-Wilson and Tyler showed that these first 200 milliseconds were consistent with an average of 29 different words for each target. Put another way, this means that after only 200 milliseconds the target word cohort would have contained an average of 29 words if the word was being identified independently of any context. However, since subjects could make accurate identifications of a word at this point, it follows that the cohort did not contain 29 items but only 1. The only possibility is that information from the context was used to eliminate from the cohort items which were inconsistent with the preceding context.

This explanation is consistent with the finding that monitoring latencies were considerably slower in the two conditions where preceding words were of considerably less help in predicting target words. In the syntactic prose condition the mean latency was 331 milliseconds and in the random condition the mean latency of 358 milliseconds was even longer. (Remember that the mean latency in the normal prose condition was 273 milliseconds.)

A similar pattern emerged from a second kind of monitoring – **rhyme monitoring** – in which subjects were given an instruction like *Press the button whenever you hear a word rhyming with 'bread'*. As we saw in our discussion of phoneme monitoring, phonological information (needed to decide whether a word rhymes with a target) is accessed after the word has been identified. This means that rhyme monitoring should take longer than word monitoring because it involves an additional stage. However, since rhyme monitoring involves word identification it will also show the same context effects as word monitoring.

The results of the two monitoring tasks in the three context conditions are shown in Figure 12. It will be seen that there is a constant difference (about 140 milliseconds) between the word monitoring and rhyme monitoring conditions. This suggests that subjects always identified a word first and *then* decided whether or

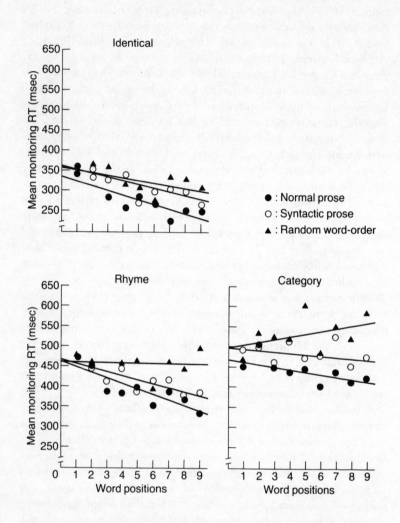

FIGURE 12   Raw word position means for each combination of prose contexts and monitoring tasks

not it rhymed; and that the rhyme decision took about 140 milliseconds to make after the word had been identified.

Further information about the operation of context effects in auditory word recognition can be obtained by examining the relationship between detection latencies and the position of the word in the context. With normal prose there was a strong relationship – the later the target occurred in the context, the faster the response. With syntactic prose, this relationship was present but less strongly. In the random words condition, reaction time was unrelated to target position.

We can explain this pattern if we remember that in the normal prose condition subjects were receiving both a syntactic and semantic context. This allowed the initial size of the cohort for target words to be reduced both on syntactic and semantic grounds. The greater the number of preceding words making up the context, the more specific the syntactic and semantic constraints would be, and thus the greater the number of words that could be eliminated from the target word's cohort. In the syntactic prose condition there were, of course, no semantic constraints available to reduce the size of the target word's cohort. However, there were syntactic constraints, and it is these which are responsible for the weak link between monitoring latency and target position.

Given that cohort size is reduced both by syntactic and semantic context and by incoming sensory information, it is necessary to decide how these two influences are co-ordinated in time. There are two possibilities: either, that contextual information is used to reduce the size of the cohort before *any* sensory information is received, or else contextual factors reduce the size of the cohort only after some sensory information has been received. Marslen-Wilson and Tyler adopt the second view, proposing that: 'the system . . . does not allow . . . contextual factors to pre-select some class of likely words even before any of the relevant sensory information has been received.' The main reason that Marslen-Wilson and Tyler give for rejecting the idea that context can operate before *any* sensory information is received is one which has been used by many other theorists, including Fodor (1983). The crux of the argument is that, since language users are essentially unpredictable, if we use contextual information very early on in the process of word identification, we will often be misled, since successive words in an utterance are only rarely fully predictable from their prior context. In other words, the example of *Forgive us our . . .* is not typical of the majority of speech in suggesting only one likely candidate for the identify of the next word. In most cases, the kind of predictions about successive words which are possible from the preceding context are much less specific and would select a very large class of words, which would be of little help in discriminating between possible candidates. On some occasions, however, contextual information might actually be unhelpful in that it might *exclude* the correct item. If *Forgive us our . . .* had been followed by *sins* (as it is in some modern versions of the Lord's Prayer), inappropriate contextual information could slow down word identification if used too early.

What Marslen-Wilson and Tyler propose is that at the onset of a word no reduction of the cohort by context has occurred, and that initial reduction of cohort size depends solely upon sensory input, not context. In the first stage of word recognition, cohort reduction occurs as early sensory information defines the word-initial cohort. Only after this cohort has been defined can context come into play; words which are members of the word-initial cohort but are inconsistent with the prior context are discarded from the cohort. At the same time, sensory information is continuing to arrive as more of the word is heard, and this is also serving to reduce the cohort.

We might ask how much of a word needs to be heard in order to define the word-initial cohort. This is not considered in much detail by Marslen-Wilson and Tyler (1980); however, they do suggest that the acoustic-phonetic information needed to define the word-initial cohort must include the first vowel of the word.

6.5.2   *Context effects on visual word recognition*

Before we conclude our discussion of context effects on word recognition, we will briefly mention two experiments which show that context effects also exist in visual word recognition. Fischler and Bloom (1979) presented subjects with a lexical decision task in which the target item was either preceded by an incomplete sentence, or by a row of Xs. The relationship between the sentence context and the target word varied. In one condition, the target word was highly predictable from the context. In a second condition it was an unlikely completion of the sentence, while remaining both syntactically and semantically consistent with the context. In a third condition, the target word was semantically anomalous with respect to the context. For example, with the context *She cleaned the dirt from her*, the targets were *shoes* (in the highly predictable condition), *hands* (in the unlikely condition) and *terms* (in the anomalous condition).

Results showed that the relationship between the target and context had a strong effect on performance; words which were highly predictable were responded to more quickly than words which were unlikely, while anomalous words produced the slowest response times of all. These results could have occurred either through *facilitation* of responses following a predictable context, or through *inhibition* of anomalous responses. Close inspection of the data showed that the context effects were due to inhibition: when preceded by an anomalous context, words took an average of 110 milliseconds longer to identify than when preceded by a row of Xs. Furthermore, the anomalous condition produced the greatest number of incorrect lexical decisions (i.e. NO responses to real words).

Fischler and Bloom conclude from these results that in visual word recognition the effect of context is essentially inhibitory rather than facilitatory. However, before we discuss the difference between this finding and that of Marslen-Wilson's demonstration of *facilitatory* effects of context in auditory word-recognition, we should note that another experiment carried out by Fischler and Bloom (1979) showed that some facilitation did occur with words which were *very* predictable from their context. (These were words which could be accurately predicted by 90 per cent of subjects in a sentence completion task.) In comparison with the inhibition effect, however, this facilitation only occurred when the subject was given a relatively long time to read the context. With a different method of presentation, in which the subject was forced to read each word of the context very rapidly (Fischler and Bloom, 1980), only inhibition effects occurred. If we accept the claim of Fischler and Bloom that this latter task produces effects which are more typical of those which operate in normal visual word recognition during reading, we might ask why context effects appear to operate differently in visual and auditory word recognition?

As we saw in our discussion of Marslen-Wilson and Tyler (1980), there are good reasons why word identification cannot be a largely top-down process. Prediction from context is not normally very efficient since language is essentially unpredictable. However, since in auditory word recognition we hear the different sounds of a word in sequence, it is possible to make use of contextual information after we have heard part of the word – in which case such information can be used effectively. In contrast, visual word recognition does not proceed by analysing part of the stimulus. We can have access to *all* of a written word at the same time, and so there is no advantage in having a visual word-recognition system which uses context to help identify words after they have been only partially processed. However, there is an advantage in having a system which can check word identification to see if the word which we have identified is consistent with context, and it is this checking procedure which Fischler and Bloom claim is causing the inhibition effects which they have demonstrated. In other words, in visual word recognition, preceding context is not used to predict what word is coming next, but, rather, to see whether the latest word to be identified is semantically coherent with what has gone before. Detection of a semantic anomaly is highly informative because it indicates that an error may have been made either in understanding the context, or in perceiving the new unit. Thus detection of a semantic anomaly forces a check to be made on the identification of a word, and this checking increases lexical decision time.

6.6   Overview

In this chapter we have discussed the recognition of spoken and printed words. We began by considering the concept of a 'mental lexicon' and we described the evolution of the Logogen Model of word recognition. We then went on to describe the Johnston-McClelland model of visual word recognition and the Cohort model of auditory word recognition. In doing so we have argued that the processes involved in word recognition are rather different for spoken and printed words. In particular, we have shown that the effect of context on word identification is different. In the case of *spoken* words, context is used to speed up recognition by reducing the number of possible candidates in the cohort. Thus, in spoken word identification, context plays a part *before* identification has been achieved. However, when words are identified in *reading*, context appears to influence word identification only *after* a word has been identified.

Presumably, what we might term this 'post word identification' effect of context is also present in the perception and comprehension of *spoken* language as well as *written* language. However, in order to understand the many ways in which context affects language processing we need to move away from a consideration of single-word recognition to a consideration of how sentences are processed. It is important to realise, however, that what we have discussed in this chapter is relevant to the next chapter, since if we want to know how language is understood we have to be aware of the large number of different levels of processing which are involved.

7 Understanding language: interpreting sentences

7.1 Introduction

In the previous chapter we discussed some of the factors which might be involved in the identification of written and spoken words. However, as we saw in the final sections of that chapter, a consideration of single word identification leads naturally to a consideration of the larger linguistic units in which words normally occur; and hence we concluded the previous chapter with a discussion of contextual effects on visual and auditory word recognition. As we saw, experiments by Marslen-Wilson and Tyler (1980) on auditory word recognition showed that a word can be identified more rapidly if it is *predictable*, that is, if there are syntactic and/or semantic constraints on the number of possible words which might occupy that particular position in a sentence. We also saw that context can have an effect on the speed of visual word recognition, although experiments by Fischler and Bloom (1979; 1980) suggest that the effect is inhibitory rather than facilitatory, with a word taking longer to identify when preceded by a context which makes it semantically anomalous.

In this chapter we want to examine some of the factors which are involved in the stages of language understanding which occur beyond the stage of word recognition. Traditionally, these aspects of processing have concentrated on an analysis of the way in which people understand and produce *sentences*. However, there are good reasons for not limiting a discussion of language processing to sentences, since in many ways the sentence is not the most appropriate *psychological* unit – and, indeed, some authors have argued that it is not the most appropriate unit for *linguistic* analysis.

(See Taylor, 1984, for a discussion of the case against sentence-based syntax.)

Since this claim requires some justification, we will briefly discuss two of the main arguments against concentrating exclusively on sentence processing. The first is that many important aspects of language processing occur in units that are larger than the single sentence. Understanding what is written or spoken does not merely involve understanding the meaning of individual words plus their syntactic and semantic relationship within a sentence. Language understanding also involves being able to relate the information in *successive* sentences, which is why psycholinguists have turned their attention to **discourse interpretation**, that is, to the comprehension of whole passages rather than single sentences. We will describe some of the experiments on discourse interpretation in this chapter. However, we have chosen to discuss experiments on discourse and experiments on sentence comprehension in a single chapter because we see them as being closely related. Furthermore, there are good grounds for assuming that the distinction between sentence processing and discourse processing is by no means a clear one. This is because while the sentence is an important unit in *written* language (where the boundaries of a sentence are clearly defined by the use of punctuation), it is less obviously a unit in *spoken* language. This difference between spoken and written language usually becomes apparent when researchers attempt to transcribe spontaneous speech.

The single most important difference between written and spoken language is that spoken language contains many incomplete sentences, and is often simply a sequence of phrases or clauses. As the following extract illustrates, breaking a transcription of spoken language into sentences often proves to be impossible (the + in the transcript indicates where the speaker made a short pause):

> well it starts off + um + an owl + comes into his shop + and
> there's + just the counter + with a till and + a few + bottles
> an' um + pots of jam on it + an' he um + inspects the counter
> + an' + sort of 'tut-tut's 'cos it's + dusty + an' goes off to get
> um + a small + sweeping brush an' sort of + cleans it up + an'
> then decides to move + um + the display over from + one side
> + over to the other. . . .
> (undergraduate student describing events in a puppet film)

It is perhaps ironical that the differences between spoken and written language are typically much smaller for researchers working on language than for the majority of the population. This is because the spoken language of those who theorise about language has typically been influenced by long and constant immersion in written forms of language. As Brown and Yule (1983, p. 14) point out,

> . . . the speech of, say, an academic, particularly if he is saying something he has said or thought about before, may have a great deal in common with written language forms. For the majority of the population, even of a 'literate' country, spoken language will have very much less in common with the written language.

It may be this unusually close relationship between spoken and written forms which has led psycholinguists to concentrate on the processing of single grammatical sentences, with the tacit assumption that the sentence is an important processing unit. However, as transcripts of spontaneous speech like the one above illustrate, the listener who is attempting to understand spoken language is often being confronted with something other than a string of sentences. (Such transcripts can also reveal a great deal about the processes which might be involved in language production, as we will see in Chapter 8.)

We are not suggesting, of course, that it is not legitimate to study the comprehension of sentences, or of passages which consist of discrete sentences. Many illuminating results have been obtained from experiments which study single sentences and sententially-structured passages – indeed, the experiments which we report in this chapter have done just this. However, we want to argue in favour of thinking in terms of something other than a sentence as being the major psychological processing unit; and, as we will see, a more appropriate processing unit is probably the clause. We will, therefore, continue this chapter by examining some of the evidence concerning the units of language used in processing beyond the level of single word identification. We will consider two distinct but related issues: the units involved in the perception of speech and in reading, and the units involved in the storage of written and spoken language in memory.

7.2   Units in language processing

7.2.1   *The perception of spoken language*

The first experimental investigations of the linguistic units involved in sentence perception were carried out using the **click paradigm**. This involves presenting subjects with sentences which are accompanied by bursts of noise – 'clicks' – and asking the subjects to report the apparent location of the noise. This may appear to be a rather strange task to use. However, the rationale for using this paradigm as a way of investigating perceptual units was established by Ladefoged and Broadbent (1960) who showed that the position of clicks is not reported accurately, because they are heard as displaced from their original position to the boundaries of perceptual units. Therefore, the apparent position of a click within a sentence is an indication of what the perceptual units of that sentence are. Garrett, Bever and Fodor (1966) showed that clicks were perceptually localised at clause boundaries, and hence concluded that the clause is the main perceptual unit.

However this study, and the many others which followed it, were criticised on the grounds that subjects' reporting of the position of a click might not be a perceptual effect, but the result of memory or response bias. A modification of the original click paradigm was therefore devised which removed the possibility of click displacement being due to these two latter influences. This modified technique, involving the measuring of *reaction time* to clicks, was used by Holmes and Forster (1970) who showed that subjects were able to detect the presence of a click more rapidly when it occurred at a major constituent boundary than when it did not. Holmes and Forster interpreted this pattern as indicating that a listener's processing load is least at clause boundaries, since reaction time should be shortest when a subject has the smallest processing load. This interpretation has proved to be compatible with other results, including the finding that a click located near the *end* of a clause tends to elicit longer reaction times than a click located at the *beginning* of a clause (Abrams and Bever, 1969). This suggests that processing load tends to *increase* near the end of a clause.

A similar conclusion emerges from a study by Caplan (1972) using another reaction time technique in which subjects had to decide whether a target word presented after a two-clause sentence had occurred in that sentence. Reaction time was faster when the target word occurred at the beginning of a clause, than when it was at the end of a clause. For example, the time to decide that the target word *snow* had occurred was faster for sentence (a) than for sentence (b):

(a) Because the weather is cold and damp, *snow* storms are expected.
(b) Although we still have not had any *snow*, storms are expected.

Before we consider why processing load might be greater at the end of a clause than at the beginning, we will discuss some experiments which have been carried out on reading, from which a similar pattern has emerged.

7.2.2   Processing units in written language

The click paradigm can, of course, only be used for investigating the perception of spoken language. However, it is possible to discover something about the relationship between clause structure and the processing of written language by using a **subject-paced reading task**. In this task subjects read a passage in which only one word (Aaronson and Scarborough, 1976), or a small group of words (Mitchell and Green, 1978), are presented at any one time. Subjects press a button as soon as they have read the currently available word or words, and this makes the next word or words available. Since subjects are instructed to read *and understand* the passage, the varying times which elapse between presentation of one part of a passage and the subject's pressing of the button give an indication of the amount of time needed to comprehend that part of the passage.

In Experiment I reported by Mitchell and Green (1978), subjects read extracts from Tolstoy's *War and Peace* three words at a time. All words were printed in uppercase and the end of each sentence was indicated with a full stop; but no other punctuation was used. Results showed that the amount of time subjects spent reading each group of three words varied as a function of clause and sentence boundaries. Subjects spent longer reading words when they occurred at the end of a clause or a sentence.

Mitchell and Green point out that these pauses could have occurred for several different reasons. Subjects might pause out of habit at points where it would be appropriate for them to pause when reading aloud. Alternatively, they might pause in order to connect the material they have just read to material they had read earlier in the text. Finally, the additional time taken to read words occurring at the end of clauses and sentences might reflect the time taken to carry out syntactic processing of that particular clause or sentence. Mitchell and Green (1978, Experiment IV) attempted to distinguish these explanations by presenting subjects with an extract from Pirsig's novel *Zen and the Art of Motorcycle Maintenance*, which began and ended with a simple concrete description of the countryside. The middle of the passage was, however, rather different since it concerned a motorcyclist's deliberations about the nature of empiricism, and it was considerably more difficult to understand.

The general pattern of pausing in this experiment proved to be very similar to that found in the earlier experiment; subjects tended to pause at clause boundaries. However, these pauses were considerably longer for the philosophical section of the passage than for the description of the countryside. For the latter, the additional time spent on reading words occurring at clause boundaries (in comparison with words not occurring at boundaries) was 73 milliseconds. For the philosophical passage, the additional time was 228 milliseconds.

The finding that the length of pauses occurring in the subject-paced reading task is related to the difficulty of the material being read suggests that pause length is an indication of processing demands of some kind. Further analysis of the relationship between pause length and syntactic complexity suggested that the additional reading time was not caused by greater syntactic complexity. Therefore, Mitchell and Green concluded, the additional reading time must reflect the additional difficulty of relating the information currently being obtained to information presented earlier in the passage.

As we will see later in this chapter, there is evidence that relating new information to earlier information is an important aspect of language comprehension. For the moment, however, we want to consider what might be involved in the processing of an individual clause, and we will suggest that the additional processing load at the end of clauses arises because of several different processes, some concerned with understanding the syntax and semantics of the clause which has just been read, and others with the relating of information in this clause to earlier information in the passage.

7.2.3   Memory for written and spoken language

In order to continue our discussion of the linguistic units involved in language comprehension, we will now review some of the experiments which have investigated the storage of spoken and written language in memory. Like the experiments we have discussed in the two previous sections, these, too, lead to the conclusion that each sentence in discourse is processed clause by clause.

We will begin by briefly mentioning one of the first experiments to investigate memory for prose passages, as distinct from single sentences. This was carried out by Sachs (1967) and it compared recall of sentences which had just been heard with recall of sentences which had been heard earlier in a passage. Sachs argued that since only a limited amount of information can be stored verbatim in memory, normally only the most recently heard sentence is remembered word for word. For earlier sentences, only meaning will be retained. It follows from this that in a recognition test subjects will find it extremely difficult to distinguish one of the early sentences in a passage from similar sentences which mean the same. However, if a sentence has only just been heard, subjects should be able to tell the difference between that sentence and all other sentences – even sentences which mean the same.

Sachs tested this prediction by presenting subjects with passages containing a target sentence in various positions. As an important control, this sentence was neutral with respect to the rest of the passage, so that subjects would be unable to reconstruct it from what they remembered of other sentences in the passage. Subjects were told that after they had heard the passage one sentence from it would be repeated, either exactly, or with some small change, and that their task was to say whether the sentence had been in the passage or not. If we think of *He sent a letter about it to Galileo the great Italian scientist* as the target sentence, the kinds of changes which

Sachs introduced when the sentence was repeated were either **semantic** – *Galileo the great Italian scientist sent him a letter about it* or **syntactic** – *A letter about it was sent to Galileo the great Italian scientist/He sent Galileo the great Italian scientist a letter about it.*

Sachs compared subjects' performance with a variety of target sentence positions varying from 0 syllables delay (for a sentence which had been heard immediately before the recognition test) to 160 syllables delay (for a sentence occurring relatively early in the passage). As expected, she found that subjects were very accurate at distinguishing a sentence they had only just heard from similar sentences with semantic or syntactic changes. However, when subjects had heard several sentences after the target sentence, they were only able to distinction reliably between the target and a similar sentence involving a *semantic* change; sentences with syntactic changes were confused with the target. Sachs therefore concluded that the syntax of sentences is held for only a short time, after which only their meaning is retained.

Sachs experiment was concerned with memory for *sentences*. However, an experiment by Jarvella (1971) suggests that similar arguments can be made about memory for *clauses*. Jarvella presented subjects with prose passages which were interrupted at intervals for testing of immediate recall. The passages were constructed so that they contained a target clause which in one version of a passage formed a sentence on its own and in another version was part of a longer sentence. For example, the third clause in the following extract (a) is part of a longer sentence: (1) *The tone of the document was threatening.* (2) *Having failed to disprove the charges* (3) **Taylor was later fired by the president**. Compare this version with the following (b) in which the same final clause forms a complete sentence: (1) *The document also blamed him* (2) *for having failed to disprove the charges.* (3) **Taylor was later fired by the president**.

Jarvella was interested in comparing the accuracy of recall for clauses in these two conditions. He found that the clause which had been heard immediately before testing was usually recalled completely accurately. (On average recall scores were 96 per cent.) However, recall of the preceding clause (clause 2) varied depending on whether or not that clause formed part of the same sentence as the most recent clause. When it did not (as in version (b)), recall scores dropped to 50 per cent. However, when the preceding clause and the last-heard clause formed part of the same sentence (as in version (a)), recall scores for the preceding clause were 81 per cent.

Since Jarvella instructed his subjects to recall as much as they could remember *word for word*, and he scored for accuracy of verbatim recall, these results suggest not only that the last-heard clause has the highest verbatim recall but also that the amount of syntactic information which is being retained about a preceding clause depends on whether or not that clause forms part of a larger linguistic unit which also includes the most recent clause. If the last two clauses heard are syntactically related to one another then sufficient syntactic information about the penultimate clause needs to be retained in order for the larger linguistic unit they form to be understood. If we return to the example, we can see that clause (2), *having failed to disprove the charges*, cannot be fully understood in version (a) until clause (3) has also been heard. However, in version (b) this same clause *completes* a larger unit, and so information about its syntactic structure need not be retained.

With this explanation in mind, it is interesting to look at the accuracy of recall of clause (1) in the two conditions. We might expect that in condition B, where clauses (1) and (2) are syntactically related, verbatim recall of these clauses should be similar. In contrast, in condition A, where clause (1) forms a complete sentence on its own, this should not be the case. Jarvella's results show this pattern: in condition B the average recall of the first two clauses was almost the same (47 per cent for clause (1), 50 per cent for clause (2)), whereas in condition A recall of the first clause was only 29 per cent, compared with 81 per cent for the second clause.

7.2.4   The 'clausal hypothesis'

The results of Jarvella's (1971) experiment, and those which we described in sections 7.2.1 and 7.2.2 have led several authors to propose a **clausal hypothesis** in order to explain sentence and discourse comprehension. This hypothesis (originally proposed by Carroll and Bever, 1976 and Fodor, Bever and Garrett, 1974, and more recently discussed by Marslen-Wilson, Tyler and Seidenberg, 1978 and Flores d'Arcais and Schreuder, 1983) has two main aspects. First, it proposes that clauses are the primary units of normal speech perception in that incoming material is organised in working memory clause by clause, with the listener or reader accumulating evidence until the end of a clause. Second, it proposes that once the end of a clause has been reached, working memory is cleared of information about the syntactic structure of the clause and the content of the clause is represented in a more abstract form.

We will consider the second claim of the clausal hypothesis first, since it relates to some of the findings which we have just been discussing. The claim is that working memory is cleared as each clause is completed, and the results of initial processing are re-coded for storage in long-term memory, with the effect that syntactic information is lost. However, as we saw in Jarvella's (1971) experiment, this is an over-simplification. The amount of information about the syntactic structure of a clause which is retained depends on what kind of clause we are dealing with. For clauses which form a complete unit on their own, or which complete a larger linguistic unit, syntactic information may well be cleared from working memory once the clause has been analysed. However, for clauses which are not 'complete', such purging of syntactic information is not appropriate.

Flores d'Arcais and Schreuder (1983) propose that the kind of processing carried out at the end of clauses depends on their degree of 'completeness'. Evidence from several studies supports this view. For example, in a study by Flores d'Arcais (1978) subjects were asked to detect sudden changes in which ear they were receiving a spoken message. It was found that detection latencies were generally longer when the change in ear of presentation took place during presentation of a subordinate clause than during a main clause. However, latencies were faster for subordinate clauses when they occurred in sentence final position rather than sentence initial position. This pattern of latencies can be explained if we assume that when a subordinate clause appears before its main clause syntactic information about the subordinate clause needs to be retained until the main clause has been heard. This requirement increases the listener's processing load, and leads to increased response latencies on the localisation task. However, when a subordinate clause *follows* a main clause this additional processing load does not occur.

Results reported by Marslen-Wilson, Tyler and Seidenberg (1978) using monitoring tasks also show that the completeness of information in a clause has an important influence on its processing. In their experiment, subjects listened to sentences and pushed a button as soon as they heard a target word. The target words occurred in sentences with two clauses, but the clauses varied in the extent to which the first clause could be fully interpreted without information from the second clause. For example, in sentence (1a) the information in the first clause is relatively complete in comparison with the first clause of sentence (1b):

(1a) Even though they are quite small *cats*, they need a lot of living space.
(1b) Even though they are quite small, *cats* need a lot of living space.

This is because in sentence (1a) the referent for the pronoun *they* is provided within the first clause, whereas it does not become available until the beginning of the second clause in sentence (1b). This means that, for both sentences, it is only the arrival of the word *cats* which allows the listener to complete interpretation of the first clause. Therefore, if the completion of (what we will call for the moment) a 'unit of information' is important in sentence processing, rather than the completion of a clause, monitoring latencies for the word *cat* should not be significantly different in sentences (1a) and (1b). However, in sentences like (2a) and (2b) where the clause boundary and the unit of information boundary do coincide, the monitoring latency for *trout* should be significantly different depending on whether it completes a clause (as in 2a) or begins a new clause (as in 2b):

(2a) Although Mary very rarely cooks *trout*, when she does so it tastes delicious.
(2b) Although Mary very rarely cooks, *trout* is one of the things she prepares well.

In order to compare processing of sentences in these two conditions, Marslen-Wilson et al. used two different monitoring tasks. In one task – **rhyme monitoring** – subjects were asked to listen out for a word which rhymed with a cue word given in advance (e.g. *doubt*). In the other task – **category monitoring** – subjects were asked to listen out for a word belonging to a particular semantic category (e.g. *fish*). The pattern of results obtained by Marslen-Wilson et al. was similar for both tasks. With sentences like (2a) and (2b) in which clause boundary and information unit boundary coincided, monitoring latencies were *slower* when target words occurred after the clause boundary than when target words occurred before the clause boundary. (As we explained in Chapter 6, this is because a word which is highly predictable from the syntactic and semantic context can be detected more quickly than a word which is less predictable.) However, there were no differences in monitoring latencies for words occurring before and after the clause boundary in sentences like (1a) and (1b) where clause and information boundary do not coincide. These findings support the view that it is not the boundary of clauses *per se* but the boundary of units of information which is a major determinant of the units involved in language comprehension.

In the light of experiments like the two we have just described, Flores d'Arcais and Schreuder (1983) propose a modification to the clausal hypothesis, which is that, after a clause has been presented, the continued presence of information about the syntactic structure of that clause in working memory will depend on whether such information is needed for further processing. When syntactic information is not needed for further processing, it may be cleared from the short-term store.

As we have seen, there are good reasons for accepting this proposal. We want to suggest, however, that clause-to-clause processing demands are not the only constraints on the storage of information about the syntactic structure of clauses and sentences. The amount of syntactic information which is retained also depends on relations between syntactic and semantic form and pragmatic aspects of what was being communicated. An interesting illustration of this comes from a series of experiments by Kintsch, Bates and co-workers (Kintsch and Bates, 1977; Bates, Kintsch, Fletcher and Giuliani, 1980) in which recognition memory for real-life speech was tested.

Kintsch and Bates (1977) tested students on their memory for classroom lectures several days after the lecture, when the students were not expecting such a test. Kintsch and Bates used a similar procedure to Sachs (1967) (see section 7.2.3), asking the students to distinguish between original sentences and paraphrases. Surprisingly, after 48 hours, there was a significant ability to discriminate paraphrases from originals for all types of lecture material tested (topic statements, details, jokes and asides). Even after 5 days, students could still discriminate original forms of jokes and asides.

At first sight it is difficult to reconcile this finding with those of Sachs (1967) and Garrod and Trabasso (1973) that recognition memory for the surface form of sentences disappears within 40–60 syllables of input. However, the difference between performance can be explained if we consider the relation between surface form and pragmatic distinctions. In normal spoken language there are often clear pragmatic constraints on the choice of particular syntactic forms. For example, the choice of a passive rather than an active is influenced both by whether the things referred to are animate or inanimate and by what the basic theme of the speaker's current discourse currently is (Harris, 1977; 1978). However, as Bates, Kintsch, Fletcher and Giuliani (1980) point out, the relation between syntactic form and pragmatic constraints is often ignored in the kinds of discourse which subjects are typically asked to process in psycholinguistic experiments. Bates et al. therefore investigated recognition memory for conversation in a 'soap opera' and found that the surface form of an utterance *was* remembered if it carried some pragmatic meaning. For example, subjects were able to remember whether a character had been referred to by name or by pronominal reference (as in, **He** *won't leave Rachel's* *room*/**Mac** *won't leave Rachel's room*) and whether an utterance had contained a full clausal unit or an abbreviated elliptical clause (as in *You mean that Jamie doesn't know that his mother is in the hospital yet?*/*You mean that Jamie doesn't know that yet?*).

This suggests that the claim that *all* information about the surface form of an utterance is lost when it is purged from working memory needs to be modified to distinguish between surface structure which reflects underlying pragmatic distinctions, and surface structure which does not. Surface structure which does carry pragmatic significance may well be retained. (See Keenan, MacWhinney and Mayhew (1977) for a further discussion of this point.)

Another possible modification to the clausal hypothesis concerns the claim it makes about clause interpretation. As Marslen-Wilson et al. (1978) have pointed out, in its *strong* form, the clausal hypothesis is that interpretation of a clause does not begin until the last word in the clause has been heard or read. In its *weak* form, the clausal hypothesis is that some partial and preliminary hypotheses about the meaning of a clause will be developed as information about the clause is being taken in, although the definitive decision about clausal meaning could only be taken once the clause had been fully perceived. The issue here is conceptually the same as the one which we considered in the previous chapter (section 6.4), when we discussed whether the identification of spoken words begins after only *part* of a word has been heard, or whether identification begins only when the *whole* word has been heard.

Aspects of the work of Marslen-Wilson and Tyler (1980) which we discussed in Chapter 6 (see section 6.5.1) strongly suggest that clause interpretation begins as soon as a listener hears the first part of the clause. This is because both syntactic and semantic constraints affect the speed of word recognition even fairly early on in a clause, and, for this to happen, a listener must be building up an analysis of both aspects while proceeding through the clause. If this were not so, contextual facilitation of auditory word recognition would occur only for words at the end of clauses. It therefore seems sensible to reject a strong form of the clausal hypothesis as inconsistent with what we know about the way in which the syntax and semantics of clauses is analysed. Instead, there are good grounds for believing that the listener constructs a syntactic and semantic interpretation of the input word-by-word, and that this information is used to guide the processing of subsequent words.

Marslen-Wilson, Tyler and Seidenberg (1978) take the view that this *on-line* view of language processing is not necessarily inconsistent with a weak form of the clausal hypothesis, in that once a complete information unit (which may not always coincide with clause boundaries) has been interpreted, other processing which results in the freeing of working memory then takes place. However, as Flores d'Arcais and Schreuder (1983) point out, the relationship between these different kinds of processing remains to be investigated.

7.3   Syntactic and semantic processing

We have just shown that there is good evidence for believing that in the comprehension of spoken language syntactic and semantic analysis is continually being carried out. So far, we have not said anything about how these two kinds of analysis might be related. Before we do so, however, it is important to note that the issues about the point in a clause at which processing begins, and whether such processing is both syntactic and semantic, are independent. We point this out because in order to consider the latter issue we will discuss experiments using both written and spoken presentation, even though we restricted our discussion of *when* processing begins to spoken language, where a relatively clear picture has emerged.

The relationship between syntactic and semantic processing has been a central concern of psycholinguistics for the last two decades. The main question which was posed was whether semantic (and pragmatic) constraints could affect the amount of syntactic processing which was carried out in sentence comprehension. Experiments by Slobin (1966), Johnson-Laird (1968), Herriot (1969), Greene (1970b) and Steedman and Johnson-Laird (1977) showed that the relative processing difficulty arising from complex syntactic forms was significantly *reduced* by semantic and pragmatic constraints. For example, Herriot (1969) found that in passive sentences like *The sister was hated by the brother* it took longer to name the actor and acted-upon than in corresponding active sentences (*The brother hated the sister*). However, when there were pragmatic constraints on which of two people was likely to be the actor and which the acted-upon, there was no difference in response times to active and passive forms, and a sentence like *The bather was rescued by the lifeguard* was responded to just as quickly as *The lifeguard rescued the bather*. These, and the results of other similar experiments, were taken as evidence that pragmatic and semantic constraints can over-ride syntactic analysis, information from which is only used if there are no other cues to interpretation.

There are two possible ways in which syntactic analysis might be over-ridden by semantic and pragmatic factors. One way is that semantic and/or pragmatic factors might affect the syntactic analysis of a clause or sentence; that is, these different kinds of processing are **interactive**. The other is that syntactic analysis might proceed independently of semantic or pragmatic factors, but that the results of this analysis might be ignored because a plausible interpretation is derived using semantic and pragmatic information. In this interpretation, syntactic analysis is **autonomous**. We will consider evidence for these two views in the next sections.

7.3.1 *'Autonomous' versus 'interactive' models of processing*

The view that syntactic analysis is autonomous has been put forward most consistently by Forster and his co-workers (Forster and Ryder, 1971; Forster and Olbrei, 1974; Forster 1979). For example, Forster and Olbrei (1974, p. 320) propose that: 'syntactic processing is relatively independent of semantic processing, in the sense that the time required to analyze the syntactic structure of a sentence is constant, despite variations in the meaning of the sentence.' This may seem a surprising claim in view of the earlier experiments we mentioned above (e.g. Herriot, 1969) which support an opposite conclusion; so we will consider the experimental results on which Forster and Olbrei base this claim with some care.

The subject's task in Forster and Olbrei (1974: Experiment 1) was to decide whether or not a given sequence of words formed a meaningful sentence. Sentences and non-sentences were both seven words long. The non-sentences consisted of a sequence of words in which the initial words formed a coherent unit (e.g. *The chorus of winning loud the lions.*) This was to ensure that the sequences could not be rejected as sentences merely by reading the first words. The sentences varied in syntactic complexity and were either plausible or implausible. For example, the following sentences are plausible: *The officials were given a warm reception/The dress that Pam wore looked ugly.* The equivalent implausible sentences – equivalent in the sense that they have a comparable syntactic structure – were *The aborigines were shown a rusty invention* and *The aunt that Jim ate tasted foul.* The stimuli were presented visually and the subject responded by pressing a button if the sequence of words was meaningful.

Forster and Olbrei found that there was a significant correlation (.65) between the time taken to respond to a plausible sentence and its implausible equivalent, and hence concluded that the time taken to analyse a syntactic structure was approximately constant, and independent of semantic constraints. As the authors themselves point out, this finding does not provide definitive evidence against an interactive view of syntactic and semantic analysis. Nevertheless, they claim that if syntactic analysis is guided by semantic cues then the relative difficulty of different syntactic forms should not be constant. It should be pointed out, however, that the results of the Forster and Olbrei experiment do *not* provide evidence for a constant effect of syntactic analysis since a correlation coefficient of .65 accounts for less than 40 per cent of the variance in processing times.

Another experiment carried out by Forster and Olbrei (1974: Experiment 5) used a rapid serial visual presentation (RSVP) in which each word of a sentence is presented successively at an extremely rapid rate (16 words/second). The subject's task was to report as many words as possible. Forster and Olbrei presented active and passive sentences which were either logically reversible (e.g. *The girl kissed the nurse*) or non-reversible (e.g. *The girl kissed the photo*). In contrast to the findings of Slobin (1966) and Herriot (1969), they found that the difference in performance with actives and passives was identical for reversible and non-reversible sentences. In other words, differences in processing times arising from the greater syntactic complexity of the passive were not reduced by semantic constraints.

Forster and Olbrei conclude from this that syntactic analysis is autonomous, and suggest that the difference between their results and those of Slobin (1966) and Herriot (1969) could be explained by viewing the earlier results as an artefact of the tasks used. (Slobin used a verification task in which subjects had to decide whether a sentence is a true description of a subsequently presented picture, and Herriot asked subjects to name the actor and acted-upon.) However, it seems more justifiable to claim that the RSVP technique is not testing the normal comprehension of sentences. Where subjects are asked to perform tasks which *do* involve comprehension, consistent evidence for the interaction of syntactic processing with other kinds of processing has emerged.

We have already seen that the work of Marslen-Wilson and Tyler (1980) supports an **interactive** view of processing in which different levels – phonological, syntactic, semantic and pragmatic – actively communicate with each other. Experiments by Flores d'Arcais (1978), Greene (1970) and Steedman and Johnson-Laird (1977) also support this view. A recent study has been carried out by Warman (reported by Johnson-Laird, 1983). In his experiments, subjects were presented with an informative sentence on a screen for 4 seconds, and then presented with a question about the content of the sentences. Subjects had to respond 'Yes' or 'No' to the question, and latencies were recorded. Warman compared response latencies for different kinds of questions in which syntactic and semantic variables were systematically varied.

Results showed that whereas increased syntactic complexity of the question increased response latencies, the effects of such complexity could be removed by the presence of both semantic and pragmatic cues. For example, one informative sentence used by Warman was *In the park, the man saw the boy who waved at him.* Subjects took longer to answer a subsequent question like *Did the boy that the man saw wave?* than one like *Did the boy the man saw wave?* This is because there are no semantic cues as to who is waving at whom, and so a syntactic analysis of the question is necessary and this is more difficult in the second version where the relative pronoun (*that*) has been deleted. However, for comparable pairs of questions in which there were semantic constraints on the identity of actor and acted-upon, complete syntactic analysis was not necessary; and here the presence or absence of a relative pronoun did not affect processing time. Thus the time taken to respond to a question like *Did the dog that the bus hit die?* did not increase when the relative pronoun was removed (*Did the dog the bus hit die?*).

The results of Warman's experiments strongly suggest that in normal language comprehension syntactic processing is not autonomous, in the sense that the time taken to understand a sentence does not depend solely on the amount of syntactic analysis required. However, there is another sense in which syntactic analysis might be independent of semantic and pragmatic analysis, and it is this which we discuss in the next section.

7.3.2 *'Obligatory' versus 'optional' syntactic analysis*

Although there seems to be fairly clear evidence in favour of an interactional view of sentence comprehension, there remains the question of whether syntactic analysis is **optional** or **obligatory**.

What we mean by this is whether a syntactic analysis is carried out even when it is rendered unnecessary for sentence comprehension by the presence of semantic or pragmatic factors. This is obviously an important issue for psycholinguistic models of sentence and discourse comprehension, but so far evidence has been very difficult to obtain.

Recently, experiments have been carried out by Flores d'Arcais (1982) in which subjects' eye fixations were recorded as they read sentences containing a syntactic, a semantic, or a spelling error. The subjects were required to understand the sentences and report any errors they noticed. What was interesting in this study was that subjects' eye movements showed that they looked longer and more frequently at syntactic errors *even when they did not actually report the errors*. This could be seen as evidence that there is a level of automatic syntactic processing which is not always used in sentence comprehension.

Flores d'Arcais and Schreuder (1983) take the view that syntactic computation seems to take place automatically, but that the extent to which the results of such computations are used in normal comprehension depends on whether or not pragmatic or semantic cues are available to aid interpretation. In other words, syntactic analysis is always carried out but it may not be used in the interpretaton of any particular sentence. Unfortunately, it is difficult to demonstrate that an analysis which does not have an influence on interpretation has actually been carried out. It will require the devising of yet more ingenious techniques to provide conclusive evidence for or against the view of obligatory syntactic analysis.

7.4   Context effects in processing

We have already seen that the comprehension of individual clauses and sentences in written and spoken language can be influenced by information that is not contained within the sentence or clause itself, that is, information that is *extra-sentential*. For example, in Herriot's (1969) experiment, the interpretation of a sentence was influenced by general knowledge about the likely connection between two people, such as a lifeguard and a bather. In Chapter 3, we saw that children's comprehension of difficult sentences is similarly influenced by their knowledge of what kinds of events are likely, and we suggested that this kind of non-linguistic knowledge plays an important role in language acquisition. We also noted that children's interpretation of sentences can be improved by presenting a preceding context which serves to inform the child about the kind of meaning that a sentence will contain. Dewart (1975) showed that young children's comprehension of a sentence like *The duck is bitten by the monkey* was facilitated by the provision of an appropriate context (*poor duck*), in comparison with their level of performance when the co..text was inappropriate (*poor monkey*).

We can therefore think of there being two somewhat different extra-sentential effects of context in language comprehension. One effect comes from the use of general knowledge about the world – we will call this a **general context effect**. The other comes from the information which has been derived from earlier parts of a discourse, and which is specific to that discourse – we will call this a **specific context effect**. As we will see, the distinction between these kinds of effects is often difficult to make in practice, since processing of earlier sentences will often have involved the use of more general knowledge.

7.4.1 *Specific context effects*

We will begin by discussing an experiment by Dooling (1971) which looked at the effect of having a specific prior context on the speed of sentence comprehension. Dooling argued that if an individual sentence is comprehended as part of a larger semantic unit, part of the meaning of the sentence is likely to be redundant. He predicted that this redundancy would facilitate comprehension. Surprisingly, however, he found that sentences took *longer* to understand when they were preceded by a context than when they were not preceded by a context. Dooling argued that this was because a context can affect sentence comprehension in two different ways. First, the presence of a context can speed up comprehension because it has prepared the listener or reader for some or all of the information contained in the sentence. Second, a context may *increase* comprehension time by introducing additional processing demands, namely, the integration of the meaning of the sentence with the preceding context.

In order to distinguish these two aspects of context Dooling (1972) presented subjects with two tasks. In one, subjects had to make a judgment about whether or not the sentence was meaningful. In the other task, subjects had to judge whether or not a sentence followed appropriately from the preceding context. Obviously, it is not legitimate to compare the time taken for these two different tasks, so Dooling used two different types of context for each task. One type of context consisted of a single word and the other of a sentence. For example, with the target sentence *The baby vomited the milk* one single word context was *baby* and one sentence context was *A baby was given sour milk before her nap*. The rationale for the use of these two types of context is that they provide different amounts of prior information. Dooling predicted that when subjects had to decide whether the target sentence was meaningful, a sentence context should make this task easier than a word context since the former provides more advance information about the likely meaning of the target sentence. However, when subjects had to decide whether the target sentence followed appropriately from the context, a sentence context should be more difficult than a word context since it presents the subject with a more complex piece of information. The results of the experiment supported Dooling's predictions. In the task involving a meaningfulness judgment, performance was better with a sentence context, but when subjects had to judge whether the target sentence followed on from the context, performance was better with the word context.

In terms of natural discourse interpretation, Dooling's sentence context condition is much closer to what normally occurs than is the word context condition. So we can assume that analysis of prior linguistic units has two effects on subsequent processing. First, prior analysis facilitates current analysis by reducing the amount of processing needing to be done in order to determine the literal meaning of a clause or sentence. Second, a prior context imposes an additional processing load (and hence an increase in processing time in Dooling's experiment) when a current sentence has to be integrated with information presented earlier in the discourse.

One of the main ways in which the integration of information presented in successive sentences of a discourse has been investigated is by looking at *memory* for discourse. Many experiments have been concerned to show that information from successive sentences is integrated into an organised whole; and that efficient memory for a discourse depends on such organisation being possible.

Evidence for the way in which information from successive units is integrated into an organised whole has been derived from experiments on **semantic integration**. One of the best known experiments was carried out by Bransford and Franks (1971) who tested recognition memory for sets of related sentences. One set concerned some ants going into a kitchen where there was jelly on the table. The jelly was sweet and the ants ate it. These ideas could either be expressed by four simple sentences (each containing one piece of information), or by a smaller number of complex sentences (each containing two, three or four pieces of information). Subjects heard sentences from four different sets, in random order, and after a distractor task, were given a forced-choice recognition test in which they were given both sentences they had originally heard and new sentences which were constructed either by combining information from within a set, or combining information from different sets.

Bransford and Franks found that only sentences which contained one piece of information, or information from different sets, could be reliably identified as not having been heard before. New sentences containing more than one piece of information from the same set could not reliably be distinguished from sentences which had been heard before. Sentences containing all four pieces of information from a set were most frequently identified as having been heard before even when they had not, suggesting that the information from a related set of sentences had been integrated into one complex whole which was closest in form to a four-idea sentence.

One problem with this experiment is that it presented subjects with a very artificial task and, not surprisingly, various criticisms have been made by authors such as Hupet and Le Boudec (1977) and Schultz and Kamil (1979). However, there are good reasons for believing that the interpretation of discourse in more natural situations does involve the integration of related pieces of information in memory. More specifically, it has been proposed that the related ideas expressed in a discourse are organised into a coherent whole or **schema** – to use the concept first developed by Bartlett (1932). The effect of schematic organisation in memory was studied in a series of experiments, such as those carried out by Dooling and Lachman (1971), Dooling and Mullett (1973) and Bransford and Johnson (1972). As we will see, some of these experiments used visual presentation and some used auditory presentation. However, it is reasonable to assume that interpretation of all discourse, whether written or spoken, involves the integration of successive ideas into an organised whole.

We will begin with one of the earliest experiments, that of Dooling and Lachman (1971). It is interesting to compare the methodology of this experiment with that of recent studies which have used more natural discourse. Dooling and Lachman tested memory for passages which were vague and metaphorical and consequently very difficult to interpret on one reading, particularly when the overall theme of the passage was unknown. If you have not read it before, try and understand the following passage used by Dooling and Lachman:

> with hocked gems financing him/ our hero bravely defied all
> scornful laughter/ that tried to prevent his scheme/ your eyes
> deceive/ he had said/ an egg/ not a table/ correctly typifies this
> unexplored planet/ now three sturdy sisters sought proof/ forging
> along sometimes through calm vastness/ yet more often over
> turbulent peaks and valleys/ days became weeks/ as many
> doubters spread fearful rumours about the edge/ at last/ from
> nowhere/ welcome winged creatures appeared/ signifying
> momentous success

You probably found the passage difficult, and it would have been even more difficult presented one word at a time as it was in the Dooling and Lachman experiment. However, your comprehension of the passage would doubtless have been improved if you had known that it was about '*Christopher Columbus discovering America*'. Half the subjects were given this information in advance but the other half were not told anything about the subject matter of the passage. In addition, there were three conditions of presentation. Words were either presented in the correct order (shown above), or in a completely random order. In a third condition, words were presented in randomly ordered phrases, so that the sequence of words within a phrase (marked by / above) was maintained but the sequence of phrases within the passage was disrupted.

Recall of the passage was measured by counting the number of words correctly recalled. (This is not, of course, a direct measure of how well the passage had been *understood* and, as we will see later, subsequent experiments have used more sophisticated measures of recall.) Knowing or not knowing the title of the passage had a significant effect on recall, as did word order. The fewest words were recalled with the random word order and the greatest number with correct word order. However, within each word order condition subjects recalled more words from the passage when they had been informed of its title. This difference cannot be attributed to more enlightened guessing when subjects knew the title because recall of words closely related to the title and of words not closely related to the title was equally improved. Dooling and Lachman argue that the better performance of the subjects who were told the title of the passage reflects their greater ability to organise the words in the passage in memory. Their results also show that this effect is independent of syntactic constraints, since there was no interaction between word order and knowledge of the title.

In a later experiment, Dooling and Mullett (1973) attempted to determine the locus of the thematic title effect. They argued that the higher recall scores in the earlier experiment could have occurred because of more efficient storage of the passage at input, or because of better reconstruction of the material at recall. They, therefore, introduced a third condition in which subjects were given the title of the passage *after* having read it. In this new condition subjects had the benefit of knowing the thematic title at recall but not at the stage of encoding.

The results showed that knowing about the theme of the passage only at recall did not improve performance. There was no significant difference between the number of words recalled in this condition and the number recalled by subjects who were not given any information about the theme of the passage. As in the previous experiment, significantly more words were recalled when the title was presented *before* the passage.

A similar finding emerged from an experiment by Bransford and Johnson (1972). This differed from the two experiments we have just described in several ways. Subjects listened to the passage, which was read with normal intonation in order to provide information about sentence and clause boundaries. (In the Dooling experiments no punctuation was supplied so this information was not available.) The passage itself was less metaphorical and the contextual information which Bransford and Johnson supplied was a picture rather than a title. In spite of these differences the passage was still difficult to understand without knowing in advance what it was about, as you can judge from the following extract:

> If the balloons popped the sound would not be able to carry since everything would be too far away from the correct floor. A closed window would also prevent the sound from carrying since most buildings tend to be well insulated. Since the whole operation depends on a steady flow of electricity a break in the middle of the wire would also cause problems. Of course the fellow could shout, but the human voice is not loud enough to carry that far.

Subjects were given varying amounts of contextual information. Some received none. Others were presented with a picture depicting the strange juxtaposition of events in the passage *before* hearing the passage, while others were presented with the picture *after* hearing the passage. Another group received partial information about the events described in the passage. The complete context picture depicted a young man standing in the street, serenading his girlfriend who is looking out of the window at the top of a tall block of flats. In order to make his song heard the young man is singing into a microphone wired to a loudspeaker. This is supported in the air, level with the girl, by several balloons. The partial context picture showed the young man, the girl, balloons, microphone, loudspeaker and the block of flats but not their unique relation in the story.

Subjects were asked to rate the passage for comprehensibility and to recall as much of it as they could. Recall was scored in terms of the number of ideas expressed in the passage which a subject was able to remember. (This is obviously a better way of measuring recall than merely counting the number of words remembered, although it does have the disadvantage of being a less objective method since the actual wording used by a subject may be very different from that used in the passage.) Both comprehensibility ratings and recall scores were highest when the subject had seen the complete context picture before listening to the passage.

Provision of the context picture after presentation of the passage, or provision of a partial context, had little effect on either ratings of comprehensibility or recall. Essentially similar results were obtained from other experiments reported in the same paper using different passages and verbal contexts.

These results suggest that knowledge of the overall theme of a passage is useful only if it is available at the time the passage is read or heard. However, Thorndyke (1977) has argued that the experiments by Bransford and Johnson (1972) and by Dooling (Dooling and Lachman, 1971; Dooling and Mullet, 1973) do not reflect the processes normally involved in understanding and remembering discourse. His objection to these studies was that the passages these investigators used made very little sense unless subjects did have some prior knowledge of their content. Of course, the passages had been constructed with precisely this intention. However, in real life such referentially obscure and ambiguous material is rare and Thorndyke therefore investigated memory for passages which were relatively coherent even when their precise theme was not specified in advance.

Thorndyke's approach to the study of discourse interpretation was rather different from that adopted in earlier studies. It has its roots in the study of the grammar of stories, or **story grammar**, as this approach is often known. There is not space here to discuss the story grammar approach in detail, and readers who are interested in this topic are advised to read the recent reviews of this and alternative approaches contained in Brown and Yule (1983: Chapter 3) and Johnson-Laird (1983: Chapter 14). For present purposes it is sufficient to note that the story grammar approach is an attempt to characterise the structure of stories by a set of rules. Some of these rules are concerned with the different components which go to make up a traditional story – the kind of story which is orally handed down from generation to generation. Thorndyke argued that such stories are easy to remember because they have a particular structure. Two aspects of this structure are relevant to the present discussion. First traditional stories have a high degree of internal organisation in which the various sub-sections of the story plot are presented in a logical order. Second, information about the overall theme of the story is given near the beginning. This information about the theme is very similar to the thematic titles used by Dooling.

Thorndyke argued that both the internal organisation of the story and knowledge of the theme are of assistance in remembering the information contained in the story. This is because both assist a reader or listener to relate individual events and pieces of information into an organised framework. For example, if we consider one of the stories which Thorndyke (1977) used we can see that it has a high degree of internal organisation. Furthermore, the theme of the story is made clear early on:

(1) There once was an old farmer (2) who owned a very stubborn donkey. (3) One evening the farmer was trying to put his donkey into its shed. (4) First the farmer pulled the donkey (5) but the donkey wouldn't move. (6) Then the farmer pushed the donkey (7) but still the donkey wouldn't move. (8) Finally the farmer asked his dog to bark loudly at the donkey (10) and thereby frighten him into the shed. (11) But the dog refused. (12) So then the farmer asked his cat (13) to scratch the dog (14) so the dog would bark loudly (15) and thereby frighten the donkey into the shed. . . .

Thorndyke presented subjects with four versions of this passage. In the *story* condition the passage was presented in the original version shown above. The *narrative after-theme* condition was identical except that sentence (3) which explains the theme of the passage was given at the end. In the *narrative no-theme* condition sentence (3) was removed altogether. In a fourth condition subjects were given a *description* in which not only was sentence (3) removed but also the internal structure of the story was disrupted by altering the temporal sequencing of events and removing the causal connection between them. Thorndyke predicted that this last condition would be the most difficult to understand and to remember and that the story condition would be the easiest. The two narrative conditions were expected to be of intermediate difficulty with the after-theme condition being easier than the no-theme.

The passages were presented either visually, one line at a time, or auditorially. In the latter case the passage was read at slightly slower than normal reading rate with care being taken to ensure that inflections or intonation did not carry across sentence boundaries. At the end of presentation subjects rated the passage for comprehensibility and then wrote down as much of it as they could remember, as close to verbatim as possible. In spite of this instruction Thorndyke actually followed the procedure of Bransford and Johnson (1972) and scored the amount of information recalled irrespective of whether the exact wording was remembered. In order to do this Thorndyke split the two passages he used into *propositions*. In order to give you some idea of the boundaries of the propositions these are numbered in the extract given above.

As you would expect, the results of Thorndyke's experiment showed that both comprehensibility and recall were highest in the story condition and lowest in the description condition with the two narrative conditions producing intermediate scores. For our present discussion, the most interesting finding concerns the difference between these two narrative conditions: both comprehensibility and recall were better in the after-theme condition than in the no-theme condition, although the recall difference did not reach significance.

This finding conflicts with those of Bransford and Johnson (1972) and Dooling and Mullett (1973) who found that providing information about the theme or context of a passage *after* it had been presented did not improve performance, and so concluded that such information only affected the organisation carried out when the passage was memorised. However, as has already been pointed out, Thorndyke's study differed from the two earlier ones in that he used passages which maintained clear temporal sequencing, and clear clausal connections in both narrative conditions. Therefore, it was possible for subjects to carry out a certain amount of integration of information even when they did not know the theme of the passage. This degree of organisation was sufficient to allow them to remember a large part of the information in the passage so that when the theme was finally presented the remembered information could be re-structured. In contrast, in both of the earlier studies structural integration was virtually impossible without knowing the overall theme, so that most of the information contained in the passage was lost by the time the important contextual/thematic information was supplied. Thus, providing such information after presentation of the passage was of little assistance.

An interesting insight into the kind of restructuring which had occurred in memory when subjects discovered what the theme of the passage was in Thorndyke's experiment comes from recall in the narrative after-theme condition. 75 per cent of subjects in this condition included a statement about the overall theme of the passage at the beginning of their recall protocols even though this information had actually been presented at the end of the passage and subjects were instructed to recall the passage verbatim.

7.4.2   General context effects

One aspect of the integration of information presented in discourse which Thorndyke's experiment ignores is that the listener or reader may also call on more general knowledge in order to integrate information into an organised whole. This more general knowledge concerns both what the speaker or listener may know about the discourse topic, and what he/she knows about conventions which are normally followed in speaking and writing. The ability to draw on such knowledge is an essential aspect of discourse interpretation and it is often employed by subjects in the kind of memory experiments which we have just described.

We noted that in Thorndyke's (1977) experiment the difference between recall scores in the two narrative conditions did not reach significance. One reason for this is probably that subjects who were not told the overall theme of the passage until the end were able to draw on their knowledge of similar stories which they had heard before. When we have attempted to replicate Thorndyke's finding with undergraduate students we have invariably found that subjects are very good at guessing the overall theme even when they are not explicitly told what it is.

The relation of information in a particular discourse to information which the subject already possesses about the discourse topic has also been investigated in memory studies. We will just mention one study, that of Pompi and Lachman (1967). This showed that after reading a prose passage with a clear and colourful theme, subjects tended to make false positive recognition errors which were elaborations of the theme of the passage. For example, after reading a passage about a battle during a war, subjects falsely recognised words such as rifle and colonel as having occurred in the passage. (A similar finding emerged in the Dooling and Lachman (1971) experiment discussed earlier where more words closely related to the theme of the passage were incorrectly recalled when subjects were told the title of the passage before being presented with it.)

The process of schematic integration which occurs in discourse interpretation thus involves not only the relation of ideas expressed within the discourse, but also the relation of specific information contained in the discourse to the pre-existing knowledge of the discourse topic which the listener or reader has.

Another way in which pre-existing knowledge is important in discourse interpretation is in the drawing of **inferences** and we will end this chapter with a brief discussion of some of the research on this very complex topic.

7.5 Drawing inferences

The fact that the interpretation of a sentence often requires a listener or speaker to go beyond literal meaning was first highlighted in psycholinguistics by Johnston, Bransford and Solomon (1973). Their argument was that when sentences are interpreted people draw **inferences** from the explicit information. The drawing of inferences is an essential part of discourse interpretation because very often essential information is implied rather than being made explicit. For example, suppose that you are presented with the following passage, used by Johnston et al.:

> The river was narrow. A beaver hit the log that a turtle was sitting on and the log flipped over from the shock. The turtle was very surprised by the event.

When you read this you may have made the inference that the turtle was knocked into the water when the beaver hit the log. Johnston et al. argued that such inferences are stored in memory along with the information explicitly contained in the passage, with the result that when subjects are given a recognition test they will falsely identify the inference as having occurred in the passage. This was what happened. The sentence *A beaver hit the log and knocked the turtle into the water* was falsely identified as a sentence from the passage. In a control condition with a passage which was identical except that the turtle was '*sitting beside*' the log (where the inference that the turtle fell into the water would have been inappropriate) there was no such false recognition.

The inferences involved in the Johnson et al. experiment are what we might think of as optional inferences. Thorndyke (1976) has argued that sometimes inferences are *necessary* in order to link successive sentences. We will call inferences of this type **bridging inferences** in order to distinguish them from all the possible inferences which could be drawn from a particular sentence.

Thorndyke attempted to compare memory for optional and bridging inferences. He devised passages containing critical sentences which could give rise to several possible inferences. Consider a sentence like *The school teacher swung her hand at little Mary who was misbehaving.* Possible inferences might be that the teacher was angry, that she actually hit Mary, that she hurt her, or that she swung her hand and missed. Thorndyke inserted another statement further on in the passage which was either neutral with respect to possible inferences or which supported particular inferences. For example, a neutral statement following on from the sentence about Mary and her teacher was *Mary heard some birds singing outside the classroom window.* This does not require any bridging inferences to link it to the earlier sentence. However, complete interpretation of the statement *Mary noticed that her lip was bleeding* requires the bridging inference that the teacher actually struck and hurt Mary. The potential inference that Mary was not actually hit would be disconfirmed by the same statement. Other possible inferences, such as that the teacher was angry, would remain appropriate but would not be essential for interpretation.

Thorndyke argued that bridging inferences should be stored as an integral part of a subject's memory of a passage. Potential inferences which were inconsistent with subsequent information should be rejected and therefore not remembered. Potential inferences which were neither confirmed nor disconfirmed by subsequent information might or might not be remembered. He tested this prediction by presenting subjects with a recognition test consisting of statements from the passages together with the three types of inference. He found that in the neutral condition, where no particular inference was confirmed or disconfirmed by subsequent information, all potential inferences were falsely identified as having occurred in a passage about 25 per cent of the time. In the other condition, where later information required the drawing of bridging inferences, such inferences were falsely recognised 58 per cent of the time. Potential inferences which were disconfirmed by a later statement were invariably rejected, and inferences which were neither confirmed nor disconfirmed were falsely identified as often as they had been in the neutral condition.

One question which arises from the conclusion that bridging inferences are falsely identified as having been present in a passage concerns *when* such inferences are drawn. One difficulty with testing recognition memory is that inferences might be made only at the time of the recognition test. For this reason, more on-line measures of processing have also been used to study inferences since this allows some measure to be taken of when inferences are made.

Haviland and Clark (1974) investigated the processing demands involved in drawing inferences by measuring reaction time in a comprehension task. They compared performance in two conditions. In one – the **direct antecedent** condition – a target sentence had a direct relation to a context sentence presented immediately before it. In the other **indirect antecedent** condition the information in the target sentence could only be related to the context sentence by the making of a bridging inference. For example, the target sentence *The beer was warm* was preceded by the context *We got some beer out of the trunk* in the direct antecedent condition and by the context *We checked the picnic supplies* in the indirect antecedent condition. In the latter case it is necessary to make the bridging inference that the picnic supplies included beer in order to relate the context and target sentences.

Haviland and Clark found that the time taken to understand the target sentence was significantly greater in the indirect antecedent condition (1016 milliseconds) than in the direct antecedent condition (835 milliseconds). However this difference might not have reflected the additional time taken to draw an inference in the indirect antecedent condition, but rather that there was repetition of a noun in the direct antecedent condition but not in the indirect antecedent condition. Haviland and Clark (1974) therefore devised pairs of context and target sentences in which the amount of repetition was the same in the direct and indirect antecedent conditions. This was achieved by repeating one noun in the indirect antecedent condition as in the following: *Ed wanted an alligator for his birthday. The alligator was his favourite present.* Linking these sentences requires the inference that Ed received an alligator for his birthday. Haviland and Clark found that the reaction time difference between the two conditions remained and therefore concluded that the additional time taken to comprehend the target sentence in the indirect antecedent condition arose because of the need to draw a bridging inference.

7.6   Overview

If you have read chapters 6 and 7, it cannot have escaped your notice that whereas research into the recognition and comprehension of single words has centred around detailed theories which attempt to provide a comprehensive description of *all* aspects of single word processing, research into the comprehension of sentences and discourse is much more fragmented. The main reason why there is currently no overall theory of language comprehension is that the relatively simple models which have been empirically tested have proved to be inadequate. An example of this kind of theoretical inadequacy is well illustrated by the research into the clausal hypothesis of language processing which we discussed in this chapter.

Early work on this topic supported a fairly strong version of the clausal hypothesis, according to which discourse is processed at the single-word level until a clause boundary is reached, at which point processing across the entire clause is instituted. Once an integrated representation of the clause as a unit is created, the specific words making up the clause can be discarded from memory to make way for the words of the next clause. As we saw in this chapter, more recently it has been found that this account of processing cannot be correct for at least three reasons: (a) there is evidence that syntactic and semantic processing is not delayed until the end of the clause; (b) there is evidence that information about the specific wording *is* retained after the end of a clause if that clause contains nonspecific words which subsequent clauses will disambiguate; (c) specific wording will also be retained if it has pragmatic significance.

Another way in which initially simple models of language comprehension have had to be modified is illustrated by another topic we discussed in this chapter, namely, the relation between syntactic and semantic processing. We argued in this chapter for an *interactive* model of these two kinds of processing rather than for a model in which syntactic and semantic analyses are carried out independently. We made a somewhat similar point in Chapter 6 when we showed that the identification of single words in both spoken and written language is influenced by contextual factors. This suggests that it is not only at the levels of syntactic and semantic analysis that language processing is interactive. Phonological analysis also interacts with syntactic and semantic analysis.

There is also evidence in favour of the view that what we might think of as *pragmatic* factors influence language comprehension. Here, we mean by 'pragmatic' those aspects of language processing which stem from general knowledge about the world and about the way in which people normally convey information in language. In this chapter, we illustrated such pragmatic influences on processing by discussing context effects. As we saw, discourse processing is influenced by context in at least two ways. There are effects of *specific* context (for example, the piece of discourse currently being processed has to be fitted into and has its processing guided by the preceding and already-processed discourse); and there are effects of *general* context (for example, the listener/reader can draw upon his background knowledge of what the world is like to guide his discourse interpretation).

We concluded this chapter by discussing another aspect of language comprehension which forms a major part of pragmatic processing, namely the way in which understanding of what is spoken or written often involves going beyond an interpretation of what is explicitly stated. We distinguished between *optional* inferences (not required for understanding discourse but naturally suggested once a discourse interpretation has been decided upon) and *bridging* inferences (necessary for establishing the links between apparently unrelated elements in the discourse).

What emerges from our discussion of these different aspects of sentence and discourse comprehension is that only a very complex model will suffice to explain the inter-relation of all the different factors which appear to form a part of language comprehension. This is a theme which will re-emerge when we consider acquired disorders of language in Chapter 9. However, we now wish to complicate the picture of language processing even further by considering what is known about the way in which speakers *produce* language.

8 Producing language

8.1 Introduction

So far in our discussion of adult language processing we have been concerned mainly with language perception and comprehension. This is not because language production is an unimportant aspect of language processing, but simply because almost all the research into normal adult language use has been on comprehension rather than production. As we saw in Part II, this has not been the case with child language, where both comprehension and production have been extensively studied, with comparisons being made between the child's spontaneous use and understanding of particular linguistic forms. As we will see in Chapter 9, language production has also been a major area of study for researchers concerned with acquired language disorders in adults. Indeed, it is possible to argue that in both the fields of child language and acquired disorders the earliest studies to be carried out were almost exclusively concerned with production.

Why, then, have the majority of studies of normal adult language processing been concerned with language comprehension? One answer is that studies of comprehension are generally very much easier to carry out in a controlled way than studies of spontaneous production. When subjects are required to press a button as soon as they are able to understand a sentence, or when subjects are asked to recall a passage, it is clear what constitutes a 'correct' response. It is therefore possible to take completely objective measures of performance such as number of errors, reaction time, or number of correctly recalled propositions. In studies of spontaneous speech, it is not possible to predict precisely what a subject may say. Therefore, the traditional methodology of cognitive psychology, which has typically been developed in order to investigate performance in tasks where correct and incorrect performance can be clearly distinguished, is often inappropriate for studying language production. However, as we will see in this chapter, it is possible to carry out systematic studies of production; and the results of such studies have an essential contribution to make to our understanding of language processing.

The production of single words is easily enough described in the context of the information-processing model developed in Chapter 6. All that is required is retrieval of an item from an output lexicon (phonological output lexicon for spoken production, or orthographic output lexicon for written production). The next step up in complexity is the production of sentences. One of the people who has been developing an information-processing model intended to describe how production of spoken sentences is achieved is Garrett (1975, 1980, 1982). We will present an outline of the ideas behind this model.

8.2 Garrett's model of sentence production

This model is set out in schematic form in Figure 13. We will discuss how the model works by considering how one might go about producing a sentence to describe a particular event, the event taking place in Figure 14.

If you wanted to tell someone what was going on here, there are many different sentences that you might use. 'A boy is hitting a girl with a flower' or 'A girl is being hit with a flower by a boy' or 'There's a girl, and a boy is hitting her with a flower' are all possible examples, and there are many others. So it is obviously quite implausible to propose that sentence production involves *selecting*, from a set of pre-existing sentences, the one you want to produce, because there are far too many different possible thoughts one might want to convey, and far too many different ways of conveying each thought. Sentence production must be a process of *constructing*, rather than *selecting*, sentences.

Any theory of sentence production, then, will be a theory which describes what the constructive processes are which, when applied to some thought which a speaker wishes to convey to someone else,

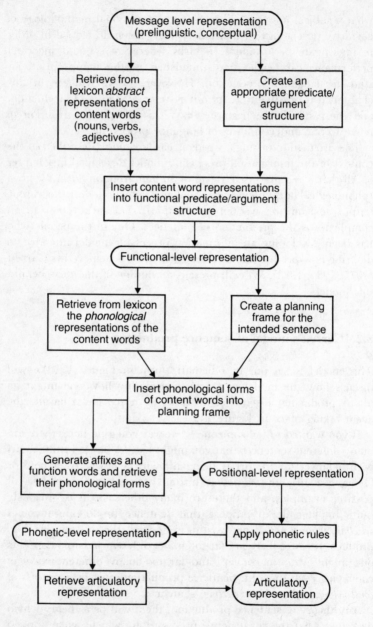

FIGURE 13 Garrett's model of sentence production

FIGURE 14   Picture of a boy hitting a girl with a flower

result in the formulation and production of an appropriate sentence. Garrett's model offers one view as to what these constructive processes might be as far as the production of *spoken* sentences is concerned. According to his model, sentence production consists of transforming an initial **message-level representation** (roughly speaking, a non-linguistic representation of the basic idea the speaker wishes to convey) into a final **articulatory representation** (a pattern of movements of the speech musculature occurring as the constructed sentence is actually spoken aloud). Intervening between these two levels of representation are three others, so the whole process of sentence construction involves a sequence of five different levels of representation. The model is meant to describe what operations the speaker performs upon each level of representation to generate the next level. We will discuss each of the five levels in turn, and describe the operations performed upon them.

The first level in Garrett's model is **the message-level representation**. As we have said, this is a non-linguistic conceptual representation of what the speaker wants to convey in a sentence – the idea, in our example, that there was a boy, a girl and a flower, that the boy hit the girl, and that he used a flower to do it. In order to create the next level of representation (the functional level, described below) two distinct procedures are needed:

(a) **Lexical retrievel**: the lexicon is searched, and retrieved from it are abstract codes representing the content words (nouns, verbs, adjectives, some adverbs) that the message level representation specifies – in our example, codes representing the words *boy*, *girl*, *flower*, and *hit*.

(b) **Creation of a functional predicate/argument structure**. In a sentence like 'The boy hit the girl with a flower', one can think of the verb as a predicate which has a number of arguments – that is, one could represent the sentence as HIT (BOY, GIRL, FLOWER). Different verbs will require different kinds of predicate/argument structure. HIT always needs at least three arguments (the hitter, the person hit, and the thing used to hit – we might call these the **AGENT**, the **ACTED-UPON** and the **INSTRUMENT**). Verbs like SLEEP have only one argument (the AGENT). So whatever verb is chosen will determine what functional predicate/argument structure is created – for HIT, it will be HIT (AGENT, GOAL, INSTRUMENT) because part of the lexical specification for the verb HIT is that it must have three arguments and they must be AGENT, ACTED-UPON, INSTRUMENT.

We should emphasise at this point that Garrett is much less specific than we are being in describing the model. For example, he does not commit himself, as we have, to a particular account of what the predicate/argument structure is like. Here and elsewhere we have been more committed than he in the interests of clarity of exposition.

Lexical retrieval yields three noun codes. Creation of the predicate/argument structure yields a structure with three arguments. When each noun code is matched up with its appropriate argument (e.g. when it is established that the boy is the agent, the girl the acted-upon, and the flower the instrument), we have reached the second level of representation of the sentence – **functional-level representation**.

The functional-level representation is linguistic, unlike the previous level. A sentence's functional-level representation specifies in linguistic terms what is being done, by whom, to whom, and with what, if all of this information is contained in the message-level representation. But specific details of sentences are not represented. No distinction is made, for example, between active versus passive sentences. Whether you are going to say 'The boy hit the girl with a flower' or 'The girl was hit by the boy with a flower' makes no difference at this level, because these two sentences have exactly the same functional-level representation. If one represents the sentence as, roughly speaking, HIT [boy = agent, girl = acted-upon, flower = instrument] then clearly this representation applies just as well to the active and to the passive sentences we have just given (and to many other sentences too, such as 'The boy hit the girl, and he used a flower to do it' or 'There was boy, and he had a flower, and he hit the girl with it'). Since eventually the speaker must produce one or other of these approximately interchangeable sentences, the next procedure must be to operate upon the functional-level representation in such a way as to decide upon the details of the specific sentence that is to be produced – to commit oneself, for example, to a passive or an active sentence. We discuss later in the chapter (see section 8.4) the kinds of factors that determine whether a speaker decides to use an active or a passive sentence and factors that determine other such decisions about sentence structure.

In Garrett's model, the specific form of a sentence is represented at **positional-level**, which is generated from functional-level representation. To produce positional-level representation from functional-level representation of a sentence, once again two distinct procedures are needed:

(a) **Lexical retrieval**. This is the 'second pass' through the lexicon. Its function is to retrieve the *phonological forms* of the content words (nouns, verbs, adjectives or adverbs) whose abstract codes were selected from the lexicon earlier on.

(b) **Creation of a planning frame for the sentence**. If you decide to use an active sentence to describe Figure 14, you might create a frame such as 'The N V-ed the N with a N ': this is the right kind of frame for an active sentence with three nouns and a verb. The selection of a particular planning frame commits the speaker to using certain function words and affixes and not others. For example, if Figure 14 is to be described by an active sentence in the present tense (e.g. 'The boy is hitting the girl with a flower') the main verb will require an *-ing* affix, whereas if the planning frame is that of a passive sentence (e.g. 'The girl is being hit by the boy with a flower') the auxiliary verb will require an *-ing* affix (but the main verb will not) and the preposition *by* will be needed. The selected affixes and function words are represented within the planning frame in phonological form, and, as we have already noted, the phonological forms of the content words have been retrieved from the lexicon: when all these phonological representations are put together under the control of the planning frame, we have the positional-level representation for the sentence, a level at which a specific sentence is represented in phonological form.

At the fourth level, phonetic rules about English are applied to this positional-level representation in order to create the corresponding **phonetic-level representation**. At this level, phonetic details about the intended sentence – e.g. the difference between the pronunciations of the plural -s in *cats, dogs,* and *churches* – are specified.

The final level in Garrett's model – **the articulatory-level representation** – is generated from the phonetic level. This level is the articulatory representation of the sentence: a set of instructions from the speech musculature which, when followed, cause the sentence to be spoken.

In Chapter 9 we discuss briefly how this model can be used to interpret various types of disturbance of sentence production seen in people with language disorders due to brain damage; a more detailed account of such interpretations is given by Schwartz (1985). The model has also been used to explain some aspects of sentence production in normals, such as slips of the tongue and hesitations: for more on this, see Garrett (1982).

Spontaneous speech consists of sequences, not just single sentences, and there are some properties of spontaneous speech which can only be appreciated when one examines language production above the sentence level; hence this is the topic we next discuss.

8.3   Encoding units in spontaneous speech

As we mentioned in the previous chapter (Section 7.1) spontaneous speech and written language have many important differences. The most striking difference is that whereas formal written language consists of clearly segmented sentences which are normally completely grammatical, spoken language is not clearly divided into sentences, and typically contains many errors. These errors range from inadvertent use of an incorrect word to grammatical errors of various kinds. (As we pointed out in Chapter 1, both kinds of error frequently arise from performance limitations of the speaker rather than from competence limitations.) Furthermore, spontaneous speech, even in the most articulate speakers, is filled with hesitations (during which speakers say such things as 'er' and 'um', or repeat a word or syllable) and silences. This is well illustrated by the following extract, taken from an undergraduate's description of the events depicted in a puppet film. Since the student is describing a series of very simple events which he has just been watching, it might be expected that he would produce a highly fluent and error-free description with no hesitations. However, as you can see, this was not the case. (In order to identify the false starts and repetitions, these have been emboldened. Short pauses are indicated by a + sign and longer pauses by a ++ sign.)

> **Well** Mrs Toad is having a sale in her shop ++ she has laid out her
> **caish** + cash register ++ an' a number of pots of tea ++ it's gonna be
> a special sale **because** ++ so she has **th'** + a sign up saying + prices
> are slashed + so she hopes lots of customers will be coming along + to
> visit her ++ while she's waiting for customers + she goes about setting
> out the rest **of** + of the shop ++ for things in the sale ++ an' she brings on
> + large cans **of tin** + of tea ++ **for** + she can only carry one at a time
> + so she walks on with one and puts it on the counter ++

Both unfilled pauses and other types of hesitation – false starts, repetitions, filled pauses (in which speakers say things like *er* and *um*) – have been analysed in studies of spontaneous speech. As we will see, hesitations are an important subject of study because of what they can reveal about the mechanisms being employed when people produce spoken language.

8.3.1 *Pauses and hesitations in spontaneous speech*

Goldman-Eisler (1968) carried out an extensive study of the pause patterns of spontaneous speech. She found that the proportion of time taken up by pauses varied considerably between subjects, although there was also considerable variation within subjects depending on the topic of conversation. In interviews of eight subjects the mean proportion of utterance time taken up by pauses varied across the subjects from 4 to 54 per cent. The variation across topics showed a spread of 13 to 63 per cent. A similar pattern emerged when subjects were asked to describe picture stories. The proportion of time spent in silence varied between 16 and 62 per cent, with most subjects pausing between 40 and 50 per cent of their total speaking time.

Pausing thus seems to be an integral part of spontaneous speech. However, this does not tell us whether pausing is a *necessary* part of language production. An ingenious experiment by Beattie and Bradbury (1979) suggests that it is. This experiment used an operant conditioning technique in order to modify subjects' spontaneous pause patterns while they were telling stories. A light came on whenever a subject paused for longer than 600 milliseconds, although subjects were merely told that the light indicated when their story-telling was poor. The presence of the light was sufficient to *reduce* the number of long pauses by 35 per cent. However, this reduction was accompanied by a very marked *increase* in the amount of repetition; subjects began repeating syllables, words and even whole phrases to a much greater extent than they had done when they were pausing naturally. By the end of the conditioning procedure the number of such repetitions had increased by 104 per cent.

This result suggests that unfilled pauses are necessary for planning spontaneous speech. When the amount of pausing drops below what it would naturally be for a given speaker in a particular situation, the number of errors which the speaker makes increases. So if pauses are necessary, it is legitimate to ask what a speaker is doing during these periods of silence. The most plausible explanation is that pauses are used by a speaker for planning what to say next. However, it is perhaps important to point out that there are presumably at least two distinct stages in planning what to say next. One concerns planning *what* to say, the other *how* to say it. It is not always possible to distinguish these two planning processes in experiments, particularly in considering pauses. However, it is a distinction which we should keep in mind.

Studies of pause patterns in speech have been carried out since the 1950s. The early studies (such as those of Lounsbury, 1954 and

Goldman-Eisler, 1958) were based on probabilistic models of language, in which the major concern was the predictability of the next word from the word or words which had gone before. These studies, therefore, looked for links between pause patterns and the predictability of successive words. However, as we showed in Chapter 7, there is good evidence that links between successive words are much less important for language processing than the relation of individual words to larger linguistic units, particularly clauses.

More recent studies of pause patterns in spontaneous speech have studied the relationship between pauses and syntactic units. A study by Beattie (1983) analysed pauses occurring in the speech of five subjects involved in academic discussion. (This was either a discussion between a teacher and an undergraduate, or between two members of a seminar group.) Two types of hesitation were considered: **unfilled pauses** of 200 milliseconds or more; and **filled pauses** consisting of sounds like *er, ah* and *um*.

Beattie found that over half of both the filled and unfilled pauses occurred *immediately before* the beginning of a clause. In addition, there was a strong tendency for the remaining pauses to occur in the first half of a clause rather than the second half. At first sight, this finding suggests very strongly that the clause is an important unit in the planning of spontaneous speech. However, the overall pattern which is presented by Beattie's data suggests a rather more complicated picture. If the clause is the main unit of encoding then we would expect to find that almost *all* clauses in the speech corpus Beattie analysed should contain pauses, particularly in initial position. This was not so. Overall, only just over 30 per cent of clauses had a filled or unfilled pause in clause-initial position.

Before we consider why this was so, it is important to realise that in the kind of discussions which Beattie analysed 'automatic' speech is rare. Discussions of academic topics typically involve a great deal of thought and the production of novel utterances, rather than a series of well-practised utterances like 'Hello' and 'How are you?'. In other words, we can assume that most of the speech analysed by Beattie was actually being planned as the discussions proceeded. This planning appeared to have a cyclical character because Beattie's data showed that for each speaker there were both **hesitant** and **fluent** phases following one after the other. The difference between these two phases was particularly noticeable in the production of long clauses (between 6 and 10 words long). During a **hesitant** phase, a speaker would pause more often and for longer periods in the long clauses, than during a **fluent** phase. This suggests that during a fluent phase a speaker has already done a major part of the planning *before* beginning to speak a clause.

Beattie concludes that it is only during the hesitant phase of a speech cycle that the clause is a major unit of speech planning. However, even in the hesitant phase, the planning of short clauses appears to have occurred during preceding utterances, since over 80 per cent of four-word clauses did not contain a pause in initial position, and nearly 75 per cent of three-word clauses did not contain any pauses at all.

During the fluent phase, planning takes place over a larger unit than the clause. Beattie suggests that this is because much of the semantic planning for this phase has been carried out during the preceding hesitant phase. In the corpus analysed by Beattie, the higher order units of planning (which spanned a complete hesitant/fluent cycle) were in the region of 8.8 clauses in length. These higher order units are probably semantic in nature as Butterworth (1975, 1976) has suggested.

However, even though the general semantic content of a series of utterances may have been worked out, detailed semantic and syntactic planning still has to proceed. Since this may take a considerable time, speakers typically begin to speak *before* they have completed all the necessary planning for a particular speech cycle. Planning of the final stages of a cycle is completed during the hesitant phase.

8.3.2   Gaze patterns in spontaneous speech

Further evidence about the amount of cognitive planning being carried out in fluent and hesitant phases of spontaneous speech comes from studies of the gaze patterns of a speaker. We would expect to find that, if more planning is occurring during hesitant phases, speakers should also look less at their listeners during these phases. This is because it has been assumed (e.g. by Argyle and Cook, 1976) that monitoring the behaviour of a listener involves a certain amount of attention and often increases the speaker's level of arousal. For both reasons, the amount of looking at the listener should go down during a phase of speech production which involves a large amount of cognitive planning.

Kendon (1967) found that speakers do tend to look at listeners more during fluent speech than during hesitant speech. Speakers looked at listeners 50 per cent of the time while speaking fluently compared with only 20 per cent of the time during hesitant speech. A similar result was obtained by Beattie (1983) in an analysis of gaze patterns during tutorials at the University of Cambridge. He found that speakers tended to look most at listeners during the most fluent phases of speech. Furthermore, if speakers did not avert their eyes during the planning (hesitant) phases in their speech, there was a marked increase in speech disturbances. There were more false starts, repetitions and parenthetic remarks during hesitant phases in which a speaker looked at a listener *and* more of these disturbances in the immediately following 'fluent' phase. This suggests that if a planning phase of speech is disrupted, then the following phase which forms part of the same semantic cycle will no longer be fluent because the prior semantic planning necessary for fluent speech has not been completed.

Evidence about the patterns of gaze which speakers normally adopt thus supports the view that the hesitant phase of speech is one in which planning of current and following utterances (within the same cycle) is carried out.

8.4   Errors in spontaneous speech

So far in this chapter we have considered what patterns of gaze and the distribution of pauses can tell us about the kind of units which might be involved in the planning of spontaneous speech. In this section, we will consider another aspect of speech which can also provide valuable insights into the nature of language production. This is the study of **errors** in spoken language.

It is important to point out here that considerable attention has been paid both to errors made by *normal* speakers and errors made by speakers who have a particular *acquired disorder* of spoken language. In this chapter we will be concerned only with errors made by normal speakers. However, a complete picture of error patterns can only emerge by comparing errors made by normal speakers with those made by speakers with a language disorder. We discuss the different kinds of error produced by adults suffering from an acquired disorder of language in Chapter 9.

8.4.1   *Errors in the production of items from 'closed' and 'open' classes*

One of the questions frequently asked by researchers studying errors in the production of words in spontaneous speech is whether there are differences in the error patterns for different *clashes* of word, the most frequently considered being **open** and **closed** classes of vocabulary items.

You may remember that we discussed the distinction between *open* and *closed* classes in Chapter 3 when we described research into early syntactic development in children's speech. Words which fall into the **open** class are those which are potentially unlimited in number because new words can be added to the language as the need arises. These words – *nouns, verbs, adjectives* and some *adverbs* – are also referred to as **content** words because they express the main meaning in an utterance. Words in the **closed** class, on the other hand, are used in order to express grammatical relations between words. Thus, words such as *articles* (a/the), *conjunctions* (and/but/because), *demonstratives* (this/that), *pronouns* (he/she/it), *auxiliary verbs*, many *adverbs* and *prepositions* (up/down/behind/between/in, etc.) fall into the closed class. New words *cannot* be added to this class – hence its name. Since words in the closed class have a syntactic rather than a semantic role in utterances they are also known as **function** words. In addition to whole words, the closed class also contains **affixes**. These are word segments which are added to the beginning or end of a word in order to form a slightly different (but related) word, or to indicate tense or number. Affixes used to mark tense or number (e.g. *he is paint**ing*** or *he paint**s***) are known as **inflectional affixes** and those used to derive related words (e.g. *paint**er*** or ***re**paint*) are known as **derivational affixes**. Since we wish to discuss both words and affixes we will use the more general term **lexical item** (rather than *word*) for the remainder of this chapter.

Like many distinctions, that between open and closed classes of lexical items is not an absolute one. In particular, *prepositions*, which are part of the closed class because of the fixed size of their numbers and their grammatical function, often express an essential aspect of the meaning of an utterance. However, for the moment we will accept the division of lexical items into open and closed classes.

Stemberger (1984) has carried out a recent study of lexical errors produced by normal adult native speakers of English in natural speech settings. He divided the errors collected into three categories: **substitution errors** (where an incorrect lexical item is produced instead of the target); **loss errors** (where a speaker fails to produce any lexical item); and **addition errors** (where a speaker produces *more* lexical items than intended). Stemberger gives the following examples of errors of each type (ϕ indicates where a lexical item has been omitted):

substitution: Oh, you did the *wash*. (dishes)

That happened *at* a couple of other people. (to)

loss: I just wanted to ϕ that. (to ask that)

You wouldn't have to worry ϕ that. (about that)

addition: I've been *keep* thinking that.

I don't want to strain*ed* it.

Stemberger compared the frequencies with which these three types of error occurred with open and closed class lexical items. He found that open class lexical items were mostly involved in substitution errors, while closed class lexical items were most frequently lost or added. The most extreme difference occurred between open class items and affixes. 96 per cent of errors in the production of open class items were substitution errors, and only 4 per cent loss or addition errors, whereas for affixes there were only 24 per cent substitution errors but 76 per cent loss and addition errors.

Since addition errors occurred least frequently for both open and closed classes of lexical items, the major type of error occurring with closed class lexical items was loss. This might suggest that the major difficulty with closed class items is that they are harder to access than open class items. However, although addition errors occurred with a generally low frequency, they were considerably more frequent for closed than for open class items. So it seems unlikely that closed class items were more difficult to retrieve than open class items. Indeed, since closed class items are among the most frequent lexical items in spoken and written English, it seems extremely unlikely that they should be difficult to retrieve.

Stemberger also investigated **phonological errors**. These are errors of *pronunciation*, as the following two examples illustrate:

I thought I heard a *thollow hud*. (hollow thud)
But shells don't go *shoft* do they? (soft)

Stemberger found that the great majority of phonological errors occurred with open class lexical items. In fact, phonological errors were nine times more frequent with open class items than with closed class items, even though there were *more* closed than open class items in Stemberger's corpus. This difference persisted even when potentially confounding factors such as stress and syllable position were taken into account.

These findings suggest that, for speech production, there are two different processing vocabularies, one for open class items and the other for closed class items. Production of lexical items from each of these two classes has its own distinct error pattern; production of words from the open class is characterised by a high frequency of substitution and phonological errors, while production of words from the closed class is characterised by a high frequency of loss and addition errors and very few phonological errors. In addition, Stemberger notes that lexical items from the closed class are less likely to be involved in **sequencing errors** (in which lexical items occur in the wrong *order* in an utterance) and in **shift errors** (in which an item appears either too early or too late in an utterance). An example of each of these kinds of error is shown below:

sequencing error: You just count *wheels* on a *light*. (intended: You just count lights on a wheel)
shift error: We tried *it making* – making it with gravy.

We have just suggested that one way of interpreting these apparently different patterns of error in the production of open and closed class lexical items is to argue for the existence of two *separate* vocabularies which are accessed during the production of spoken language. This view has been put forward by Garrett (1980; 1982). However, Stemberger (1984) has recently argued that the grounds for treating open and closed class lexical items as coming from two separate vocabularies are not convincing since many of the differences in error patterns for the two classes can be explained by differences in the *frequency* of items in the two classes, and by differences in the potential frequency with which certain kinds of error can occur for items in the two classes. This issue is also relevant to Chapter 9, in which we discuss the pattern of lexical errors in patients with acquired disorders of the production of spoken language.

8.4.2 *The Full Listing Hypothesis*

Another question which has been addressed by studies of lexical errors in speech production is whether every word-form which a speaker knows is explicitly listed in that speaker's mental lexicon. This is known as the **Full Listing Hypothesis**. An alternative to having a separate entry for every word-form is that only **base forms** are listed in the lexicon, together with a set of lexical rules for deriving all regularly inflected forms of the base item, and a listing of all irregularly inflected forms. According to this view, there would be an entry for a base form like *sing*, but not for the present participle *singing*, or the 3rd person singular present *sings*. Instead, there would be a set of lexical rules indicating which affix had to be added to produce each inflected form. However, an irregular inflection like *sung* would be listed, so that the lexical rule for the formation of the regular plural present tense would not be inappropriately applied to the base to give *singed*. We will call this the **Stem + Lexical Rules Hypothesis**. (It has also been suggested that *derivations* from a stem might not be listed explicitly, so that there would be no separate listing of a word like *singer*, only a listing of the lexical rule for the formation of an agentive.)

The plausibility of the Full Listing Hypothesis versus that of the Stem + Lexical Rules Hypothesis has been investigated by looking at errors in speech production. These often show a dissociation between the stem of a lexical item and its affix. This is particularly striking in the case of **inflections**. Consider the following example of a sequencing error taken from Stemberger (1984) which we considered earlier:

You just count *wheels* on a *light*.

Note that the inflection occurring with the transposed lexical item has remained in its grammatically correct position, rather than moving with the base item to which it would normally have been attached. (If the *s* inflection *had* moved with its base, the speaker would have said: You just count *wheel* on a *light***s**.)

There are many other examples of dissociation between base and inflection, and several other examples from Stemberger's corpus which we quoted earlier illustrate this. However, in order to accept that such examples are evidence in favour of a Stem + Lexical Rules Hypothesis of entries in a mental lexicon, it is necessary to show that similar patterns of dissociation do *not* occur for other word-final fragments. As Butterworth (1983) points out, there are cases where similar exchanges do occur for other word-final fragments. For example, Garrett (1980) gives the following examples which involve transposition of **derivational** affixes:

square it face*ly* (face it squarely)
I've got a load of cook*en* chick*ed* (. . . chicken cooked)

Fromkin (1973) gives the example of a speaker erroneously producing *fran sanisko* for San Francisco, in which the final segment of Francisco is produced in its correct position but the preceding segment is not. Here what is transposed is not an affix at all, but just a syllable.

In order to accept that the data from speech errors are contrary to the Full Listing Hypothesis, it is necessary to show that the fate of inflections is different from that of other word-final fragments. As we have just seen, this is not the case. So, as Butterworth (1983) concludes, the data derived from the speech errors of normal speakers is not decisive in rejecting the Full Listing Hypothesis. However, as with our discussion of open and closed lexical classes, the evidence from patients with acquired disorders of spoken and written language is also highly relevant. Such patients are discussed in Chapter 9.

8.5   Formulating sentences

As we mentioned in Chapter 7, it is probably inappropriate to think of normal spontaneous speech as consisting of *sentences*.

However, since much of the research which we want to discuss in the following section is concerned with the formulation of sentences, we will use this term in order to avoid confusion. Since the arguments we wish to make are not dependent on whether speakers actually produce sentences, this simplification will not affect our discussion.

Our principle concern in this section of the chapter will be factors which affect the kind of syntactic form which speakers use on a particular occasion. We will discuss two issues, the existence of various alternative ways of expressing essentially similar information, and the relation between the accessibility of particular lexical items and the production of particular syntactic forms.

8.5.1 *Syntactic paraphrases*

One question which has concerned psycholinguists for many years is why there exist in English (and in other languages) several alternative syntactic options (or paraphrases) for expressing essentially the same information. For example, the following three sentences all express the same basic meaning:

(a) The dog chased the tabby cat
(b) The tabby cat was chased by the dog
(c) The cat the dog chased was a tabby

It was an implicit assumption of much of the early research carried out in psycholinguistics in the 1960s (see Greene, 1972 for a review) that certain syntactic forms were exactly equivalent in meaning. This assumption was necessary for the commonly held view that complex syntactic forms (like negatives, passives and interrogatives) might be constructed by applying **transformational rules** to simpler syntactic forms. According to this view (e.g. Miller and McKean, 1964), passive sentences were constructed by the application of a *passive transformation* rule to an active, and negative sentences by application of a *negative transformation* rule to an affirmative. It was further assumed that passive negative sentences were constructed by the application of *two* transformational rules (passive and negative).

However subsequent research has shown that both negatives and passives are used in response to the presence of particular pragmatic factors. In the case of negatives, these factors are different from those associated with use of affirmatives, and in the case of passives these factors are different from those associated with the use of actives.

The use of negative forms was investigated by Wason (1965) and Greene (1970a; b) who showed that the natural function of a negative is to signal denial or contradiction of a prior assertion. Comprehension of negative sentences is facilitated when negation is being used to fulfil one of these functions. For example, in Greene's (1970a) experiment subjects were asked to sort pairs of statements according to whether the statements in a pair had the *same* or a *different* meaning. She argued that if the second statement in a pair contained a *negative* then it would be more natural for the meaning of the two statements to be *different*, whereas if the two statements were both *affirmative* it would be more natural for the two statements to have the same meaning.

Greene found subjects' performance in her sorting task supported this claim. For statement pairs containing a negative, sorting was faster when the two statements meant something different than it was when the two statements meant the same. Thus, it took subjects less time to decide that the following sentences had a *different* meaning:

x exceeds y
x does not exceed y

than to decide that the following two sentences had the *same* meaning:

y exceeds x
x does not exceed y.

Pairs of active and passive sentences were included as controls and performance with these showed the opposite pattern. A *different meaning* pair like:

x exceeds y
x is exceeded by y

took longer to sort than a *same meaning* pair like:

y exceeds x
x is exceeded by y.

Unfortunately for our present discussion, Greene did not investigate the *production* of negatives, only comprehension. However, it seems reasonable to assume that pragmatic factors in comprehension will also be present in production. Direct evidence about pragmatic factors in production comes from studies of the passive.

Turner and Rommetveit (1967) and Tannenbaum and Williams (1968) manipulated subjects' focus of attention while they were describing events depicted in simple line drawings. They predicted that when a subject's attention was on the *actor* a situation would be described using an *active*, whereas when attention was on the *acted-upon* (the recipient of action), greater use would be made of the passive.

In the experiment carried out by Tannenbaum and Williams, focus of attention was manipulated by prior presentation of a preamble concerning either the acted or acted-upon depicted in the line drawing. Subjects were told whether to produce an active or a passive sentence to describe the picture, and production latency was measured. The prediction was that when a subject's attention had been focused on the acted-upon it would be easier (and so take less time) to produce a passive, whereas an active would be easier when the preamble concerned the actor. This was confirmed by the pattern of response latencies; there was a significant interaction between prior focus and sentence voice.

In the Turner and Rommetveit experiment (which was carried out with children) attentional focus was manipulated either by asking subjects a question about actor or acted-upon, or by presenting one part of the line drawing before revealing the whole drawing. In the latter case either the actor or the acted-upon was revealed first. Both techniques were successful in manipulating the way in which the line drawing was described. When the acted-upon was presented first, or emphasised through questioning, significantly more passives were produced than when the actor received prior attentional focus.

Subsequent experiments have revealed that the concept of

attentional focus can be broken down into two separate factors: one concerns the *intrinsic* importance of actor and acted-upon; the other concerns *informational* aspects of actor and acted-upon. In the case of intrinsic importance, the factor that has been most extensively studied is **animacy**. Experiments by Prentice, Barrett and Semmel (1966), Harris (1977; 1978) and Dewart (1979) have shown that the passive is likely to be used when the acted-upon is more animate than the actor. For example, a collision between a pedestrian and a car is very likely to be described by a speaker as a *boy being run over by a car*, rather than as a *car knocking a boy down*.

This pattern emerged clearly in the experiment by Harris (1978) in which both adults and children were asked to describe pictures in which the animacy of actor and acted-upon was systematically varied. Actor and acted-upon were either human (e.g., a girl, a milkman), animal (e.g. a cow, a horse) or inanimate (e.g. a bicycle, a ball) and the depicted action involved either an actor and acted-upon of the same class (e.g. two humans) or a different class (e.g. a human and an animal).

The number of passives produced in response to the different pictures varied considerably. As predicted, most passives were produced when the acted-upon was more animate than the actor and least when the actor was more animate than the acted-upon. The difference between these conditions was striking: 154 passives were produced when the acted-upon was more animate and only 3 when the actor was more animate. 17 passives were produced when actor and acted-upon came from the same class.

Animacy is, however, only one of the factors which influences selection of a passive form to describe a particular situation. In most situations, a particular sentence will form part of a larger discourse and, when this is so, another important factor affecting use of the passive is whether actor or acted-upon is the **theme** of a discourse (i.e. what the discourse is about). When an acted-upon, rather than an actor, is thematic, use of the passive increases.

This was demonstrated by an experiment reported in Harris (1977) in which both animacy and discourse theme were manipulated. Subjects (children aged between 4:6 and 9:9) were presented with sequences of pictures. At the beginning of each sequence, a picture of a human, an animal or object was presented, and the sequence was introduced as being a 'story' about whoever or whatever was depicted in this initial picture. Each picture in the sequence showed the thematic person, animal or object in interaction with other people, animals and objects. For example, in one sequence the following events (all involving a girl) were depicted:

> *a girl following a boy*
> *a girl stroking a rabbit*
> *a girl cleaning a car*
> *a soldier carrying a girl*
> *a dog licking a girl*
> *a bus knocking over a girl*

The results of this experiment showed that both the animacy of the actor and acted-upon, and whether actor or acted-upon was thematic, affected subjects' use of passives. When the acted-upon was more animate than the actor 133 passives were used, compared with only 16 when this pattern was reversed. When the acted-upon was thematic, 155 passives were produced, but when the actor was thematic, only 44 were produced. The effects of animacy and thematisation were additive: the greatest number of passives (96) occurred when the acted-upon was both thematic *and* more animate than the actor, and the least (only 1) when the actor was thematic *and* more animate than the acted-upon.

One way of viewing these results is to suggest that what determines use of the passive rather than the active is selection of the acted-upon as the first noun to be mentioned. This is because there is considerable evidence that it is normal in English to put more animate nouns and thematic information in sentence-initial position. (See Halliday, 1967 and Harris, 1977 for a discussion of this view.) We will therefore broaden our discussion of factors involved in the formulation of sentences to consider evidence concerning the accessibility of lexical items.

8.5.2 *Lexical accessibility and syntactic structure*

The possible role of lexical accessibility in determining the syntax of a speaker's utterances has been considered at length by Bock (1982). She argues that there are good reasons for supposing that variables such as frequency, concreteness and prior priming – all of which influence the speed with which individual words can be accessed (see Chapter 6) – will affect sentence production. More specifically, Bock argues, syntactic alternatives are employed in order to place lexical information, that has already been retrieved, earlier in an utterance than lexical information which has not been retrieved.

The reasons for adopting this view that syntactic production and the accessibility of individual lexical items are closely related are twofold. First, there are *a priori* grounds for supposing that it would be inefficient to have a production system in which words are accessed *before* the constituent in which they are to appear. We can assume that the processing resources available for language production are limited, and attempts to hold items for future as well as current constituents would result in an unnecessary drain on processing resources. However, since access to lexical items appears to be at least partly an *automatic* process in which words are accessed as a result of unplanned factors (such as prior mention by the present speaker or an earlier speaker), it seems plausible to suggest that the production system should be able to adapt in order to incorporate automatically accessed lexical items into current constituents. Hence the existence of syntactic alternatives which allow word order to be varied.

The second reason for Bock's claim about relations between syntactic form and lexical accessibility in production is an empirical one. This is the finding that the same kinds of factors responsible for increasing lexical accessibility of *single words* (mainly in studies of word recognition, but also in some studies of production) are also responsible for affecting word order in *sentences*. So, for example, in the case of the passive both animacy and prior access of a particular word (occurring when a noun is thematic) are factors which have been shown to influence single word identification. This was illustrated by Glanzer and Koppenaal (1977), who showed that animate words are more likely to be recalled from a list than inanimate words; and many experiments have established the existence of priming effects in word recognition (see Chapter 6).

It would, however, be incorrect to assume that syntactic aspects of language production could only be influenced by *automatic* accessing of particular lexical items. It is also likely that in some cases syntax is influenced by the *controlled* access of particular lexical items – the desire to convey certain items of information earlier, rather than later, in an utterance. On yet other occasions the access of lexical items will be *constrained* by the selection of particular syntactic options which are required in order to convey particular communicative intentions.

Thus, it would seem that, like other aspects of language processing we have discussed in this book, sentence production appears to have both top-down and bottom-up components. We need to bear this in mind in the next chapter when we consider some of the problems of lexical retrieval experienced by patients exhibiting an acquired language disorder.

8.6 Overview

The production of written or spoken language at the single-word level (as, for example, when you answer a question like 'What is the large grey animal with tusks and a trunk?' or write down the name of a picture shown to you) is not difficult to explain. It involves retrieval of single items from a lexical output system of the kind described in Chapter 6.

Language production, however, is normally the production of syntactically structured *sequences* of words. We described Garrett's ideas about the various processes required for the production of spoken sentences, and the various factors (discourse theme, animacy, lexical accessibility) which determine the choice a speaker makes between different sentences expressing the same meaning – passives versus actives, for example.

In practice, spontaneous speech does not consist of fluent sequences of grammatically correct sentences, but is hesitant, sometime repetitive and grammatically incorrect. There is good evidence that these imperfections are imposed by performance limitations. The speaker's ability to plan utterances is not sufficiently good to allow planning and production to co-occur smoothly and without interference; and so there are periods when production must suffer if planning is to proceed. Hence errors at a variety of levels (from the interchanging of elements of adjacent words up to the abandoning of whole sentences) are inevitable.

9 Acquired disorders of language

9.1 Introduction

In Chapter 4, we discussed developmental disorders of language: developmental dysphasia, developmental dyslexia, and developmental dysgraphia. The term 'developmental' here indicates that there has been a failure to acquire the relevant linguistic skill (the use of spoken language, reading or writing) at the normal rate, during the course of development.

There is another way in which language disorder can occur, however. In people who had achieved entirely normal linguistic skills, brain damage can reduce or even abolish such skills. Here the term 'acquired disorder of language' is used; and this is the topic of this chapter. The chapter has two aims. The first is to describe the various forms that acquired language disorders can take – that is, the various different ways in which language processing can be impaired by various forms of brain damage. The second aim is to discuss these patterns of language impairment in relation to the models of normal language processing we have described in previous chapters. If one can demonstrate clear relationships between specific patterns of impairment and specific models of normal processing, then, one can use the patterns of impairment as evidence for or against the models, and one can use the models to explain how the patterns of impairment come about – why patients with language disorders behave in certain ways and not in other ways.

Neurologists of the nineteenth century, such as Broca and Dax, were able to show that damage to the brain often leads to very obvious disturbances in various aspects of cognition. This is particularly the case for damage to the left hemisphere of the brain; and this led to the concept of cerebral dominance: the idea that the left hemisphere dominated the right as far as their contributions to cognitive processing were concerned. It was soon realised, however, that for certain mental processes – visuospatial processing and visual object recognition, for example – it was the *right* hemisphere of the brain which was the important one. For all aspects of specifically linguistic processing, however, it remained the case that, in almost all people, the left hemisphere was the important one; and so in people with acquired disorders of language it was almost always the case that the left hemisphere had been damaged.

The concept of an acquired disorder of cognition is, of course, much broader than the concept of an acquired disorder of language, but the latter concept is still extremely general; and neurologists in the second half of the nineteenth century made it more specific in a variety of ways. It was recognised, for example, that in some people with an acquired disorder of language, it was only the *production* of language that was impaired, with language *perception* and *comprehension* still normal, whilst the opposite pattern (impaired perception or comprehension with intact production) could be seen in other patients. It was also recognised that there were patients whose language disorder affected only the processing of written language (reading and writing) and others where it was only the processing of spoken language that was impaired. Further refinements developed: for example, Dejerine (1982) described a patient whose disorder in the processing of written language was confined to its perception – that is, this patient could still write normally, even though his reading had been severely impaired by brain damage.

It had thus become clear by the turn of the century that acquired language disorder was by no means a single entity: instead, a variety of different patterns of disorder could be observed. Hence a set of terms emerged for describing these different patterns, and this set of terms is still in use today.

Aphasia or **acquired dysphasia** is used to refer to any acquired disorder in the ability to process *spoken* language. If one wishes to distinguish between an input defect (impairment in the perception or comprehension of spoken language) and an output defect (impairment in the production of spoken language), then the terms

receptive aphasia versus **expressive aphasia** can be used. **Alexia** or **acquired dyslexia** is used to refer to any acquired disorder of reading, and **agraphia** or **acquired dysgraphia** to refer to any acquired disorder of writing or spelling. **Anomia** (or, occasionally, **dysnomia**) is used to refer to an impairment in the ability to produce the right single word when, for example, trying to name an object or to produce a specific word in spontaneous speech. This is also often referred to simply as 'word-finding difficulty'.

We have already illustrated ways in which the research on the effects of brain damage on mental processes had taken the form of defining increasingly more specific patterns of disorder. The general idea that cognitive processing can be impaired was made more specific by showing that particular domains of cognition, such as language, can be selectively impaired with other domains such as memory or attention intact. This concept of a general language impairment was, in turn, made more specific with the idea that particular sub-abilities (e.g. the production of spoken language) can be impaired whilst other sub-abilities involved in language (e.g. speech perception) are spared. It should be clear how such findings are of relevance to theories about normal language processing. If a theory of normal language processing were proposed in which there were a single processing system responsible for dealing with spoken language – a system used both for *perceiving* and for *producing* speech – then one ought never to see patients with intact speech perception and impaired speech production, nor patients with the opposite disorder. The fact that both these forms of aphasia *are* frequently observed suggests that there are separate systems for perceiving and producing speech; and we have already seen in Chapter 6 that research on normal subjects suggests the same conclusion. More examples of arguments along these lines are given later in this chapter.

A patient with a language disorder caused by brain damage will normally exhibit various different symptoms of the disorder, not just a single symptom. A collection of symptoms is called a **syndrome**. Hence the neurologists of the late nineteenth and early twentieth centuries, having recognised that various different patterns of language disorder existed, went on to attempt to define these as syndromes – for example, to define several different categories of aphasia, each category being defined as a list of the symptoms that are seen in patients belonging to that category.

There are two very different uses to which the concept of syndrome can be put, and it is important to appreciate the distinction between these uses which we will refer to as the **theoretical** and the **clinical**. The theoretical use is as follows: if there exists a syndrome such that *every* patient who exhibits symptom x also exhibits symptoms y and z, it would seem reasonable to try to explain this by developing a theory in which there exists a single processing system whose properties are such that, if the system were malfunctioning, all three symptoms x, y and z would automatically occur. One starts off with a syndrome and uses it to develop a theory of normal processing.

The clinical use is different: here one uses syndromes to help one be aware that, for example, if you notice symptom x in a patient, you ought to test for the presence of symptoms y and z, since they are very likely to be present.

The difference between these two uses of syndromes becomes clear if one considers the following situation: suppose, after years of finding that, every time a patient exhibits symptom x, symptoms y and z are also exhibited, a patient comes along who has symptom x but not symptom y. This makes no difference as far as the clinical use of the concept of syndrome is concerned: it remains true that if you see x it is a good idea to look for y and z (since they are so likely to be present). But the single patient with x and not y does make a great deal of difference as far as the theoretical use of the concept is concerned. The pattern of symptoms in this patient refutes the theory that the reason why x, y and z co-occur is that they all reflect damage to a single system (since if that theory were true you could *never* get x without y); indeed, this patient shows that there actually is no syndrome (in the *theoretical* sense) defined by the joint occurrence of all three symptoms.

We have discussed this point because we are about to describe various syndromes of aphasia, and it is important to realise that one can think of each syndrome in the theoretical sense or in the clinical sense. We will return to this point later.

9.2 Syndromes of aphasia

It is perhaps not surprising that two of the major varieties of aphasia are named after two nineteenth-century neurologists, Broca and Wernicke. We will begin by describing Broca's aphasia and Wernicke's aphasia, and then go on to describe other frequently seen forms of aphasia.

9.2.1 *Broca's aphasia*

Figure 15 depicts a fairly everyday household scene. Before you read on, write down a description, about half a page in length, of what is going on in the scene.

FIGURE 15   The assessment of aphasia and related disorders

Here is a spoken description of what is going on in Figure 15 given by a patient with Broca's aphasia (from Funnell, 1983):

(Points to the water on the floor and laughs) 'Ah . . . ah . . . girl and boy, ah oh er er dear . . . girl (points to the woman) cof (points to the cloth) and, er oh er dear me . . . er (points to the water) um steps (points to the stool) er steps um window, curtains . . . a pot and an er (points to the water) oh dear me . . . OK.'

The nature of this description is even clearer if one deletes the pauses, interjections, and the ums and ahs; the patient describes the picture thus: 'Girl and boy, girl, cloth and steps, steps, window, curtains, a pot and an . . .'

This kind of spoken language production is characteristic of Broca's aphasia. Its basic features are:

(a) speech is effortful, extremely hesitant, contains long pauses and is very non-fluent;
(b) virtually no grammatical structure is evident – certainly no proper sentences, and a few or no function words, prefixes or suffixes;
(c) what is produced consists largely of specific nouns, and verbs are notably under-represented;
(d) even those words which can be produced are often poorly articulated;
(e) the comprehension of speech, at least for single words and simple sentences, is often very good despite the very severe deficit in the production of speech.

9.2.2 Wernicke's aphasia

The pattern of symptoms exhibited in Wernicke's aphasia is in many respects exactly the opposite of that shown in Broca's aphasia. Here is how a patient with Wernicke's aphasia gave an account of what is going on in Figure 15 (Funnell, 1983):

'Well it's a it's a it's a place and it's a g-girl and a boy . . . and the-they've got obviously something which is is made some made made made well it's just beginning to go and be rather unpleasant (ha! ha!) um and this is in the this is the the woman and she's put putting some stuff and the it's it's that's being really too big t-to do and nobody seems to have got anything there at all at all and er it's . . . I'm rather surprised that but there you are this this er this stuff this is coming they were both being one and another er put here and er um um I suppose the idea is that the er two people should be fairly good but I think it's going somewhere and as I say it's down again . . . let's see what else has gone er the the this is just I don't know how she di' how they did this but it must have been fairly hard when they did it and er I think there isn't v-very much there I think.'

The basic features of Wernicke's aphasia are:

(a) speech is effortless, fluent and rapid;
(b) what is said is generally grammatically complex and well-structured, with an abundance of function words, prefixes and suffixes;
(c) those content words which are produced are very rarely words with specific meanings such as *knife, hair, dig* or *spill*. Instead, the content words are mostly very general nouns such as *place, something, stuff* and very general verbs such as *got, put* or *did*;
(d) the comprehension of speech is severely impaired; sometimes even single spoken words cannot be understood even though they are correctly perceived.

9.2.3   Conduction aphasia

In this syndrome, the central deficit is in the ability to repeat back what has been heard. This ability is impaired far more than other aspects of the patient's language. In severe cases, even the ability to repeat single words is not intact; for example, a patient, KC, was not perfect even when single common concrete nouns were spoken to him, with his task being to repeat back each one immediately. The kinds of errors he made are illustrated by these responses:

'face'   – 'pace, no, p, p . . .'
'woman' – 'woolden, wooden, no . . .'
'girl'   – 'curn, cur . . . no'

The failures in repetition are not caused by difficulties in hearing the words themselves. We know this, firstly, because KC was perfect at understanding the *meanings* of words spoken to him (as tested by word-to-picture matching) and, secondly, because KC always knew whether his attempt at a repetition was right or wrong. If KC repeated 'girl' as 'curn' because that is how he *heard* it, he would not know his response was wrong.

In cases of conduction aphasia, comprehension of spoken words and simple spoken sentences can be intact. Speech is usually fluent and grammatical, sometimes with occasional mispronunciations of individual speech sounds and sometimes with word-finding difficulties. Here is a sample from conversation with two psychologists, the topic of conversation being the linguistic difficulties – particularly, the intrusions of completely unwanted and irrelevant words – KC experienced in the first few weeks after his stroke.

KC   'What worried me most er at the beginning and now the treat . . . and now fading to a great degree, was the extraordinary presence of another absence er of another kind of speaking. Absolutely real. I mean a real belief that I have the word "tiger" or "leopard" or whatever. An absolute knowledge for it, and I see the picture of it, and it's *quite* wrong. It has no connection with this.'

MC   'Where do the words come from, do you think?'

KC   'God knows! But I actually know that I, I, I . . . li, line, thinking er er myself. I would *think* of "tiger" or what not, that it might mean, and this thing has no trans . . . has no relation to, to, to, to, to, the, the, the sounds that I was looking. . . .'

MC   'To the word you are looking at?'

KC   'Yes, yes. I was imagining a totally different one. And this was, for a time, for about er three, three, three or four . . . weeks was still quite strong.'

KC's conversational speech may not be entirely normal – but it is remarkable in comparison to his extremely impaired ability to repeat back single words.

You might be curious as to why this disorder of repetition is called conduction aphasia. The answer is that the earliest attempt to explain the disorder was that the brain regions for understanding and for producing speech were intact, and what was damaged was the neural pathway which *conducted* information between these two pathways. The consequence of this damage was, on this theory, that when the patient heard speech he could understand it but could not transmit what he had heard to the brain region for speech production, and so could not repeat it. There are all kinds of reasons why this explanation will not work; we mention it only to explain the origin of the term 'conduction aphasia'.

9.2.4   *Transcortical aphasia*

Just as Wernicke's aphasia is in some sense the opposite of Broca's aphasia, so transcortical aphasia is in some sense the opposite of conduction aphasia, because in transcortical aphasia it is repetition which is the *best*-preserved of the patient's linguistic abilities, with the patient being extremely poor at understanding speech. In some such patients, speech production is not eliminated, but what is said is usually entirely meaningless and incomprehensible (this syndrome is known as transcortical sensory aphasia). In others, there is no spontaneous or elicited speech output (this is known as transcortical motor aphasia). In both syndromes, however, repetition is remarkably preserved.

A severe case of transcortical aphasia is described in detail by Whitaker (1976). This patient, HCEM, had no spontaneous speech, could not write and could not name objects. She had some ability to read, but almost no comprehension of spoken or written words. Her ability to repeat what she heard was the only language task which she could perform at all well. She could repeat sentences such as 'The window was broken by John'. Remarkably, when she was given ungrammatical sentences to repeat, she often produced a grammatically correct version: she repeated 'She write she mother a letter' as 'She wrote her mother a letter', and 'Do you want to go movies?' as 'Do you want to go to the movies?'. In contrast, she never corrected *semantic* anomalies when repeating (for example, she faithfully repeated such anomalous sentences as 'I put on your clothes in the morning' or 'Eat your milk').

Why is this called transcortical aphasia? Again, the term comes from the earliest attempts at explaining the disorder. The idea was that since repetition is so good the pathways across the cortex (hence *trans*cortical) from the brain regions for perceiving speech to the brain regions for producing speech are intact. However, these regions are cut off from the rest of the brain (hence, roughly speaking, disconnecting speech from thought). Again, we mention this explanation not to advocate it, but to explain the origin of the term.

9.2.5 Anomic aphasia

As we have seen, word-finding difficulty is common in various kinds of aphasia. Sometimes it is this which is the patient's most obvious symptom: comprehension of speech is very good and spontaneous speech can be well-articulated, grammatical and fluent, except that every so often the patient stops speaking because he simply cannot find the word he wants to say. Approximate synonyms, or else circumlocutions, are chosen to fill the gap. This is anomic aphasia.

9.2.6 Global aphasia

Global aphasia could be thought of as the most extreme form of aphasia. In patients who suffer this form of aphasia no language ability is spared: speech comprehension, spontaneous speech, repetition (and reading and writing) are all absent or minimal.

9.3 The theoretical interpretation of aphasic syndromes

What do these syndromes tell us about the language-processing system as it exists in intact brains? Can we use theories of the normal language-processing system to explain the various patterns of abnormality of language behaviour seen in different kinds of aphasic syndromes?

The answer to such questions depends in the first place upon what we mean by 'syndrome'. Let us use Broca's aphasia to illustrate this point. Earlier in this chapter, we distinguished between the syndrome as a theoretical entity and the syndrome as a clinical observation. In the first case, a syndrome is a set of symptoms which inevitably co-occur, the reason being that a single underlying malfunction of the language-processing system is responsible for all the symptoms. In the second case, a syndrome is a set of symptoms which frequently (but not necessarily invariably) co-occur; if there are occasional instances (no matter how rare) where some of the symptoms are present and others absent, then one cannot explain the syndrome as due to a single underlying defect generating all the symptoms.

Various attempts have been made to regard Broca's aphasia as a syndrome in the first of these senses – that is, to argue that there is a single underlying deficit in the language processing system which is responsible for all the symptoms of Broca's aphasia. Different people have had different views on what this single deficit might be: we will mention three such views.

On one interpretation, the form of brain damage suffered in Broca's aphasia has simply made the production of spoken words very effortful. So the patient says very little and is very non-fluent. Why is it that content words tend to be preserved and function words omitted? Because the patient is trying to communicate in the fewest possible words, and a sentence missing its function words is easier to understand than a sentence missing its content words. One of the many major problems for this idea is that Broca's aphasics usually show better performance with content than with function words even when the task is reading aloud single words: the patient given *tie, and, the* and *ant* to read aloud might well succeed with *tie* and *ant* but not with *and* or *the*. There is no reason (as there might be with spontaneous speech) why the patient should choose to utter the isolated content words here and not the isolated function words.

Another single-deficit interpretation of Broca's aphasia is that it is a *phonological* deficit (Kean, 1977): an impairment of the aspects of the language-processing system that relate to phonology (the sounds of words, as distinct from their meanings or spellings). Kean has proposed that what is omitted in spontaneous speech are the elements of sentences which are *unstressed* – commonly, prefixes, suffixes and function words. However, this analysis also fails to explain why even the reading aloud of single function words (where there is no question of stress patterns in a sentence) is so often impaired in Broca's aphasia.

Perhaps the most widely held single-deficit theory of Broca's aphasia is that it is a *syntactic* deficit. The patient's ability to employ syntactic knowledge is impaired – so spontaneous speech is grammatically very simple, or even ungrammatical, and words which are primarily important in establishing grammatical structure (function words) are especially affected.

The trouble with all of these theories of Broca's aphasia, and others like them, is that they assume that a single deficit is involved, i.e. that the syndrome is a 'theoretical syndrome'; and it is becoming increasingly clear that this is not so. It is perfectly correct that, if you compare a group of Broca's aphasics with a control group and measure (a) rate of spontaneous speech; (b) number of function words used; (c) number of prefixes and suffixes used; (d) number of verbs used; (e) complexity of grammatical structure; and (f) accuracy of pronunciation, you will find that the Broca's aphasics have a lower mean than the control group on all six measures. What you will *not* find, however, is that every individual Broca's patient is lower on all six measures (see, e.g. Berndt, 1985). Some patients classified as Broca's aphasics have dysfluent speech but normal complexity of grammatical structure; others have reduced occurrence of function words, prefixes and suffixes but fluent speech; and so on. In general, an individual Broca's aphasic is likely to show only some *subset* of the six symptoms listed above.

Thus, it seems that it is misguided even to try to find a single-deficit theory of Broca's aphasia, because Broca's aphasia is a clinical syndrome, not a theoretical syndrome. Most patients with effortful, poorly articulated speech will have ungrammatical speech output with good speech comprehension, but not all – any two of these symptoms can exist without the third, so one cannot offer a single theory accounting for all three symptom at once.

Although we have illustrated this point with reference to Broca's aphasia, it is generally true for all the aphasic syndromes. All are clinical syndromes, not theoretical syndromes. They are of value in guiding the clinician's testing of aphasic patients, but are not of direct value in relation to theorising about the language-processing system and how it can go wrong after brain damage, because one cannot answer such question as 'In Broca's aphasia, how is the language-processing system malfunctioning?

This does not at all mean that the study of aphasia and theories about the language processing system have nothing to say to each other. On the contrary, investigation into relationships between these two approaches to language is currently flourishing. This kind of research does not depend upon the concept of a syndrome, however. Instead of generalising findings from one patient to others by treating them all as representing instances of a single syndrome, the approach is to treat them all as people in whom a language-processing system which, before their neurological damage, was the same for all of them, has been impaired in some specific way. The nature of the impairment of the system might be different for every patient, so each patient is unique; yet all the impairments shown by all the patients are interpreted with reference to a single theory of the language processing system.

How this approach works will become clearer when we come to discuss acquired disorders of reading and spelling later in the chapter; but we will give one example relating to disorders of spoken language – specifically, to contrasting patterns of disordered sentence production.

Schwartz (1985) has discussed ways in which the model of normal sentence production proposed by Garrett (1980, 1981, 1982), which we described in Chapter 8, might be used to interpret defects of sentence production seen in patients with any form of expressive aphasia. Consider the example from Funnell (1983) which we gave earlier in this chapter, of a patient with Broca's aphasia attempting to describe the scene shown in Figure 15. This patient's verbal output consisted almost entirely of content words – there were almost no function words and no grammatical structure. This pattern can be described economically in terms of Garrett's model if we propose that, of the two processes applied to the message-level representation in order to create the functional-level representation, one has been completely disabled, with the other remaining almost intact. The nearly intact process is that which selects major lexical items (content words) from the lexicon: hence the patient produces appropriate content words (though we cannot explain why verbs are poorly produced relative to nouns). The abolished process is that which generates the functional predicate/argument structure for a sentence. If this structure is not generated the patient will be left with a collection of content words but no argument structure in which to insert them. Hence the eventual output can only be an unstructured sequence of content words. Other symptoms frequently seen in the sentence production of Broca's aphasics would need to be explained as due to additional deficits in the sentence-production system (e.g. if there is a specific problem with prefixes and suffixes, that would be seen as arising during attempts to construct the positional-level representation).

The contrasting pattern characteristic of Wernicke's aphasia and illustrated by the second of the patients of Funnell (1983) – whose attempt at a description of Figure 15 we also quoted earlier in this chapter – could be interpreted, in terms of Garrett's model, as arising when there is a defect of the process which selects the required major lexical items from the lexicon. However, the process which creates the functional predicate/argument structure remains relatively intact. Hence when the Wernicke's aphasic is seeking to create a functional-level representation by applying these two processes to the message-level representation, the patient will be left with an appropriate argument structure but no content words to insert into it. If this structure gives any clues as to what *kinds* of words the missing ones are – if one can deduce from the structure that one missing word is a verb of action, another is an animate noun, and so on – the patient can insert very general content words by using such deductions (words like *did, person, thing*). Thus one would expect to see grammatically structured and grammatically correct sentence production with the specific content words needed replaced by extremely general ones: as is evident in the productions of Funnell's patient.

We refer the interested reader to Schwartz (1985) for more illustrations of ways of applying Garrett's model to aphasic sentence production, since we do not have space here to consider this work further: we must now turn from considering disorders of spoken language to a discussion of disorders of written language – reading disorders (acquired dyslexias) and writing disorders (acquired dysgraphias).

9.4 Acquired dyslexias and their relationships to a model of normal reading

In Chapter 6 we set out a *dual-route* model of reading aloud, distinguishing between a *lexical* procedure and a *non-lexical* procedure for converting print to speech. The lexical procedure works by retrieving previously learned information about the specific letter string being read (and so cannot be used for reading non-words aloud, since the reader has never seen these before). The non-lexical procedure works by applying *rules* specifying how a particular letter or letter group is to be pronounced (and so cannot be used for reading exception words aloud correctly, since such words disobey the rules: if you apply the rules to read an exception word aloud, you will produce an *incorrect* pronunciation, such as reading *pint* as if it rhymed with *mint, hint, lint*, etc.).

If the reading system does include these two separate processing components, it might be possible that neurological damage could impair one component whilst leaving the other intact, to produce a specific pattern of acquired dyslexia. Let us explore this possibility further. Suppose the lexical procedure had been damaged whilst the non-lexical procedure remained intact. What effect would this have on the reading system as a whole? 'Non-words and regular words could still be read aloud accurately (because the non-lexical procedure can handle both these types of stimuli correctly); but exception words would suffer. If the patient cannot use the lexical procedure to read, say, *pint*, and so has to fall back upon the non-lexical procedure, a reading error will result: *pint* will be read with a short *i* (as in *mint*). Thus the pattern we would expect to see if the lexical procedure is damaged but the non-lexical procedure remains intact – if these procedures really are separate – is good reading of regular words and non-words with bad reading of exception words. Furthermore, the wrong reading responses with exception words should demonstrate the application of rules to these words, as in the *pint* example. Such errors are known as regularisation errors.

This pattern of acquired dyslexia is in fact seen. It is known as **surface dyslexia** (Marshall and Newcombe, 1973; Coltheart, Masterson, Byng, Prior and Riddoch, 1983; Patterson, Marshall and Coltheart, 1985). Thus surface dyslexia is one of a set of syndromes of acquired dyslexia, just as Broca's aphasia is one of a set of syndromes of acquired aphasia.

9.4.1 *Surface dyslexia*

The clearest case of surface dyslexia so far described is that of Bub, Cancelliere and Kertesz (1985). This patient was actually normal at reading regular words and non-words (in terms of accuracy and reading time), but made many errors in reading exception words. Almost all her errors here were regularisations: for example, she read *have* as if it rhymed with '*cave*', *lose* as if it rhymed with '*hose*', *own* as if it rhymed with '*down*', and *steak* as if it rhymed with '*beak*'.

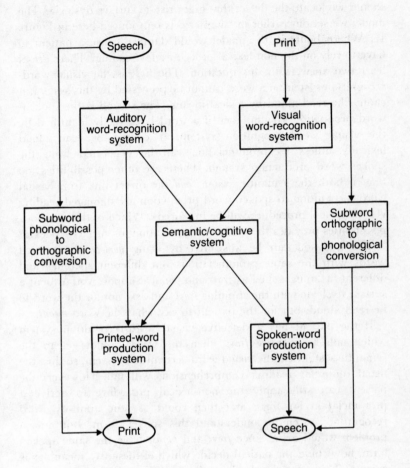

FIGURE 16 An information processing model of language

Precisely where, within the lexical procedure for reading aloud, should we locate the defect that gives rise to surface dyslexia? The model we set out earlier in Chapter 6 is reproduced here in Figure 16. Whereabouts in the model would damage cause a patient to have to rely on the non-lexical procedure for reading? There are at least two answers to this question. The first is the visual word-recognition system: if a word cannot be processed by this system, it cannot be read aloud by lexical means. The second is the spoken-word production system: even if a word is correctly identified by the visual word-recognition system, it cannot be read aloud lexically unless its pronunciation can be generated from the spoken-word production system. There are other possibilities too (e.g. if both the semantic system *and* the direct link from visual word recognition to spoken word production are damaged reading via the lexical procedure will be impaired). Which of these various possibilities provides the correct interpretation for surface dyslexia?

The question can be answered by using *homophones*: printed words with the same pronunciations but different spellings and different meanings, such as *frays* and *phrase*. Suppose you present a surface dyslexic with the stimulus *frays* and ask, not for the word to be read aloud, but for the patient to say what the word *means*.

If the patient has a defective visual word-recognition system which fails to identify *frays*, then the word cannot get to the semantic system via the visual word-recognition system, so this, the usual route for reading comprehension, will fail. However, the patient can still apply the non-lexical procedure to derive a pronunciation for *frays*, and then could use the auditory word recognition system to understand this spoken form. But now a problem would arise: since *frays* and *phrase* have the same spoken form, how could the patient decide which of these two meanings is correct? This reasoning leads to the prediction that, if the locus of impairment in surface dyslexia is within the visual word recognition system, the patient will sometimes confuse one homophone with another when asked to define single printed words – will say, for example, that the printed word *frays* means 'a part of a sentence'. By exactly the same reasoning, it would be predicted that a patient who reads *pint* with a short *i* (a regularisation error) would fail to understand this word, because the only route to understanding print is via pronunciation, and the patient's pronunciation represents a non-word (*pint* with a short *i*).

On the other hand, if the deficit is located within the spoken word production system, the patient will be able to get from print to semantics correctly. So *frays* will not be confused with *phrase*, and *pint* will be understood correctly as referring to beer or milk, even if it is read aloud incorrectly.

So which of these two patterns does one actually see in surface dyslexia? The answer is both. In some patients (e.g. Coltheart et al., 1983), only the first pattern is seen, so that the way a printed word is comprehended is via pronunciation; in others (e.g. Kay and Patterson, 1983) one does see examples where a word is read aloud wrongly but comprehended correctly.

This shows that even a single symptom (regularisation errors in reading aloud) can arise in different ways in different patients. We have already argued that the concept of a syndrome is not of use as far as theoretical analysis of language disorders is concerned, because it is not the case that a small number of syndromes (defined as sets of symptoms which *always* co-occur) actually exist. It is much more nearly true to say that no two patients ever show exactly the same constellation of symptoms. We have now shown that, even for a single symptom shared by a set of patients the explanation of that symptom might be different for different patients. So not only is it unwise to try to group patients, in terms of syndromes, it is not even possible to group them in terms of symptoms – that is, even a set of patients all showing the same symptom may not be homogeneous even with respect to that symptom.

How, then, can researchers generalise from one patient to others? By referring the patients to a specific model of language processing. In our surface dyslexia example, it does not matter that there are different kinds of surface dyslexics, so long as each of the patterns of surface dyslexia can be interpreted with reference to the same model of reading. If this cannot be done, then that counts as evidence against whatever model one is using.

Although we have illustrated these points with reference to surface dyslexia, they are generally applicable: they apply to the investigation of any form of language disorder – expressive or receptive, spoken language or written language. That is why we have digressed. To return to the main point: we introduced surface dyslexia as the pattern of acquired dyslexia which would be expected if neurological damage had affected the lexical procedure for reading aloud and spared the non-lexical procedure. What of the opposite pattern? If the lexical procedure were spared and the non-lexical procedure damaged, what symptoms should follow? It should be obvious, from the discussion of dual-route reading models in Chapter 6, that the answer is that all words (exception or regular) would be read well, but non-words would not. This pattern of acquired dyslexia is also seen: it is known as **phonological dyslexia**.

9.4.2   *Phonological dyslexia*

The clearest case of phonological dyslexia so far described is that of Funnell (1983a). Her patient, WB, was almost normal at reading words, his accuracy being 85–90 per cent (even with complex words like *satirical* or *preliminary*). In contrast, he could not read non-words aloud at all, scoring 0 per cent correct even with simple non-words like *cobe* or *nust*. The same pattern in less extreme form is shown by patients described by Beauvois and Derouesne (1979), Shallice and Warrington (1980) and Patterson (1982).

These two disorders, surface dyslexia and phonological dyslexia, have extremely straightforward interpretations in terms of the model of reading we set out in Chapter 6. The two other forms of acquired dyslexia which have been clearly defined are, for different reasons, less straightforward to interpret, these disorders being **letter-by-letter reading** and **deep dyslexia**.

9.4.3   *Letter-by-letter reading*

This form of acquired dyslexia is sometimes called **pure alexia** or **alexia without agraphia**, the reason being that, as a rule, these patients have no impairment of writing or spelling, and so they contrast with patients having other kinds of acquired dyslexia, all of whom have had impaired writing and spelling as well as impaired reading. The letter-by-letter reader will usually be able to write a passage well, and then be unable to read what he has written. The reading difficulty is not due to some very peripheral visual defect, since the patient may be perfect at identifying letters (e.g. Warrington and Shallice, 1980).

The disorder gets its name from the way the patient behaves when trying to read a word: the letters of the word will usually be named aloud, from left to right, very slowly. This process might take minutes if a word is long. If the patient gets to the end of the word having named all the letters correctly, the word is likely then to be read aloud correctly. An illustrative case of this form of acquired dyslexia is described by Patterson and Kay (1982).

How should this disorder be interpreted in relation to a model of normal reading? Clearly, the problem is somewhere at a very early stage of the reading system. The problem is that there is no stage in the model in Figure 16 where damage should cause the specific behaviour of identifying words by slow serial identification of their individual letters. Perhaps the best one can do is to say that communication from the letter detector to the word detector level, which is normally both fast and parallel, has become slow and serial, but this is a rather *ad hoc* explanation, and certainly much less satisfying than the interpretations offered by the model for surface dyslexia and phonological dyslexia.

9.4.4   Deep dyslexia

In this kind of acquired dyslexia, described for example by Marshall and Newcombe (1966, 1973) and by Coltheart, Patterson and Marshall (1980), the most striking symptom is the semantic error in reading aloud. The patient, asked to read aloud the single printed word *artist*, produces the response 'picture', or reads *sepulchre* as 'tomb'. Deep dyslexics exhibit several other reading symptoms too. Non-words cannot be read aloud at all; abstract words like *truth* or *equality* are much less likely to be read aloud correctly than concrete words like *blood* or *cathedral*; visual errors such as reading *bush* as 'brush' or *forge* as 'ford' occur; function words, and the prefixes and suffixes on affixed words, cause particular difficulties.

Two approaches have been taken to the interpretation of deep dyslexia in relation to models of normal reading. It is clear that the complex pattern of symptoms could not be a consequence of just one or two loci of damage within the normal reading system, and Morton and Patterson (1980) have offered an interpretation in which the disorder is explained as occurring when a number of different loci in the normal reading system are all damaged. In contrast, Coltheart (1980) and Saffran, Bogyo, Schwartz and Marin (1980) suggested that in deep dyslexia the normal reading system cannot operate at all, and that the reading that the patient can manage is mediated by an alternative processing system located in the right hemisphere, a system which might play no role at all in normal reading. This issue is still unresolved: for further discussion, see Coltheart (1984), Patterson and Besner (1984a,b), Rabinowicz and Moscovitch (1984), and Zaidel and Schweiger (1984).

Having described the four best-documented forms that acquired dyslexia can take, we will conclude this chapter with a brief discussion of acquired dysgraphia. The discussion will be brief because much less work has so far been done on acquired dysgraphia than on acquired dyslexia.

9.5 Acquired dysgraphia

The basic considerations which in Chapter 6 led to the view that the reading system involves two different processing procedures, one lexical and the other non-lexical, apply also to the spelling system. We must be able to spell without relying on access to stored lexical information because we can spell non-words, and could not have learned their spellings beforehand. But spelling cannot solely rely on this route: to be able to spell words like *yacht* or *choir* we must have access to specific lexical information about how each word is spelled. So current models of spelling (e.g. Ellis, 1982) frequently include two procedures for going from speech to print, a lexical spelling procedure (retrieving the correct spelling from a lexicon of spellings) and a non-lexical spelling procedure (applying a system of rules specifying correspondences between sounds and letters). It is not surprising, then, that very recently varieties of dysgraphia have been recognised in which there are various patterns of impairment to one or other of these two routes.

In **phonological dysgraphia**, the spelling of real words is preserved whilst the spelling of non-words is impaired. For example, the patient described by Shallice (1981b) could spell more than 90 per cent of the words dictated to him, but could produce plausible spellings for almost no non-words. In the converse disorder, which unfortunately has been given several different names (**surface dysgraphia**, **phonological spelling**, and **lexical agraphia**), the spelling to dictation of non-words is good, but words are commonly misspelled, and the misspellings are usually phonologically correct – e.g. 'search' – *surch*, 'spade' – *spaid* and 'come' – *cumme*. Hatfield and Patterson (1983) describe a representative case of this kind of acquired dysgraphia. It is clear that, within the framework of a dual-route model of spelling, phonological dysgraphia is the pattern you would expect if the non-lexical procedure for spelling is selectively damaged, and surface dysgraphia is the pattern expected if it is the lexical procedure for spelling that is the damaged one.

Other patterns of acquired dysgraphia are beginning to be identified too. We will mention one, called **deep dysgraphia** because of its analogy to deep dyslexia. A patient described by Bub and Kertesz (1982) made semantic errors in writing to dictation; for example 'desk' – *chair*, 'give' – *take* and 'yacht' – *boat*. The patient could not write non-words to dictation, spelled concrete nouns better than abstract nouns, and was poor at spelling function words. None of these impairments appeared when the patient was asked to read words and non-words rather than to spell them.

9.6 Overview

According to the ideas outlined in Chapter 6, the language processing system is made up of a number of information-processing *modules*, each responsible for a specific information-processing task (such as recognising letters, for example, or producing spoken words). In Chapter 6, we used this approach to the understanding of language processing to interpret the results of various different sorts of experiments involving the comprehension and production of single words in skilled users of language.

This general approach can also be used to interpret the patterns of impairment to language processing seen in patients with acquired disorders of language produced by neurological damage. If the sentence production system includes one component whose task is to retrieve specific content words from the mental lexicon, and another component whose task is to create a linguistic structure into which these content words are to be inserted, then one would not be surprised to find some patients whose speech consists of unstructured sequences of specific content words, and others whose speech has correct linguistic structure but lacks specific content words. We saw in Chapter 8 that Garrett's model of sentence production does contain these two components; and the examples of spontaneous speech by aphasic patients we gave in sections 9.2.1 and 9.2.2 illustrate the two patterns which occur if one of the components is damaged and the other spared.

Similarly, models of normal reading aloud which distinguish a lexical from a non-lexical procedure for reading aloud provide straightforward interpretations of two contrasting patterns of acquired dyslexia (surface dyslexia and phonological dyslexia), and models of normal *spelling* which distinguish lexical from non-lexical procedures for spelling allow us to interpret two contrasting patterns of acquired *dysgraphia* (surface dysgraphia and phonological dysgraphia).

If you think back to Chapter 5 where we discussed developmental disorders of language, you will recall that the situation there was rather similar. It was possible to establish plausible relationships between what is known about normal language acquisition, especially learning to read, and what is known about developmental disorders of language, especially developmental dyslexia.

Thinking about language acquisition and skilled language use in terms of the particular forms of information-processing that go on when any linguistic task is being performed, and thinking about language disorders explicitly as patterns of impairments and preservations of different forms of information-processing, thus provides a particularly powerful way of illuminating both normal and disordered linguistic capacities. It is to be hoped that future research into the nature of language processing will continue to relate findings about the performance of both skilled and impaired language users on the wide range of tasks which go together to make up out ability to acquire and use language – for it is only by attempting to do so that it will ultimately be possible for psychologists to develop a comprehensive model of language processing.

References

Aaronson, D., and Scarborough, H.S. (1976). Performance theories for sentence coding: some quantitative evidence. *Journal of Experimental Psychology: Human Perception and Performance, 2,* 56–70.

Abrams, K., and Bever, T.G. (1969). Syntactic structure modifies attention during speech perception and recognition. *Quarterly Journal of Experimental Psychology, 21,* 280–90.

Adams, M.J. (1979). Models of word recognition. *Cognitive Psychology, 11,* 133–76.

Argyle, M., and Cook, M. (1976). *Gaze and Mutual Gaze.* Cambridge University Press: Cambridge.

Barr, R. (1974/5). The effect of instruction on pupil reading strategies. *Reading Research Quarterly, 10,* 555–82.

Barrett, M.D. (1979). Semantic development during the single-word stage of language acquisition. Unpublished doctoral thesis, University of Sussex.

Bartlett, F. (1932). *Remembering.* Cambridge Press: Cambridge, Massachusetts.

Bates, E., Kintsch, W., Fletcher, C.R., and Giuliani, V. (1980). Recognition memory for surface forms in dialogue: explicit vs. anaphoric reference. In *Papers from the Parasession on Pronouns and Anaphora.* Chicago Linguistics Society: Chicago.

Beattie, G. (1983). *Talk: An Analysis of Speech and Non-Verbal Behaviour in Conversation.* Open University Press: Milton Keynes.

Beattie, G., and Bradbury, R.J. (1979). An experimental investigation of the modifiability of the temporal structure of spontaneous speech. *Journal of Psycholinguistic Research, 8,* 225–48.

Beauvois, M.-F., and Derouesne, J. (1979). Phonological alexia: three dissociations. *Journal of Neurology, Neurosurgery and Psychiatry, 42,* 1115–24.

Berndt, R.S. (1985). Symptom co-occurrence and dissociation in the interpretation of agrammatism. In Coltheart, M., Job, R., and Sartori, G. (eds.). *The Cognitive Neuropsychology of Language.* Lawrence Erlbaum Associates: London.

253

Bever, T.G. (1970). The cognitive basis for linguistic structures. In Hayes, J.R. (ed.), *Cognition and the Development of Language*, Wiley: New York.

Bishop, D. (1982). Comprehension of spoken, written and signed sentences in childhood language disorders. *Journal of Child Psychology and Psychiatry*, *23*, 1–20.

Bloom, L. (1970). *Language Development: Form and Function in Emerging Grammars*. MIT Press: Cambridge, Massachusetts.

Bock, J.K. (1982). Towards a cognitive psychology of syntax: information processing contributions to sentence formulation. *Psychological Review*, *89*, 1–47.

Bonavia, D. (1977). China's war of words. *Visible Language*, *11*, 75–8.

Bower, T.G.R. (1977). *A Primer of Infant Development*. Freeman: San Francisco.

Bowerman, M. (1973). *Learning to Talk: A Cross Linguistic Study of Early Syntactic Development, with Special Reference to Finnish*. Cambridge University Press: Cambridge.

Bradley, L., and Bryant, P.B. (1983). Categorising sounds and learning to read: a causal connection. *Nature*, *301*, 419–21.

Braine, M.D.S. (1963). The ontogeny of English phrase structure: the first phase. *Language*, *39*, 1–13.

Bransford, J.D., and Franks, J.J. (1971). The abstraction of linguistic ideas. *Cognitive Psychology*, *2*, 331–50.

Bransford, J.D., and Johnson, M.K. (1972). Contextual prerequisites for understanding: some investigations of comprehension and recall. *Journal of Verbal Learning and Verbal Behavior*, *11*, 717–26.

Brown, G., and Yule, G. (1983). *Discourse Analysis*. Cambridge University Press: Cambridge.

Brown, R.W. (1973). *A First Language: The Early Stages*. Allen & Unwin: London.

Brown, R.W., and Bellugi, V. (1964). Three processes in the child's acquisition of syntax. *Harvard Educational Review*, *34*, 133–51.

Brown, R.W., and Fraser, C. (1964). The acquisition of syntax. In Bellugi, V., and Brown, R. (eds.), The Acquisition of Language. *Monographs of the Society for Research in Child Development*, *29*, 43–70.

Bruner, J.S. (1975a) The ontogenesis of speech acts. *Journal of Child Language*, *2*, 1–19.

Bruner, J.S. (1975b). From communication to language – a psychological perspective. *Cognition*, *3*, 255–87.

Bub, D. and Kertesz, A. (1982). Deep agraphia. *Brain and Language*, *17*, 146–65.

Bub, D., Cancelliere, A., and Kertesz, A. (1985). Whole-word and analytic translation of spelling to sound in a non-semantic reader. In Patterson, K.E., Marshall, J.C., and Coltheart, M. (eds.), *Surface Dyslexia: Cognitive and Neuropsychological Studies of Phonological Reading*. Lawrence Erlbaum Associates: London.

Burroughs, E.R. (1912). *Tarzan of the Apes*. Republished by Ballantine Books, New York, 1963.

Butterworth, B.L. (1975). Hesitation and semantic planning in speech.

Journal of Psycholinguistic Research, 4, 75–87.

Butterworth, B.L. (1976). Semantic planning, lexical choice and syntactic organisation in spontaneous speech. Unpublished paper, University of Cambridge.

Butterworth, B.L. (1983). Lexical representation. In Butterworth, B.L. (ed.), *Language Production, Volume 2*. Academic Press: London.

Byng, S., Coltheart M., Masterson, J., Prior, M., and Riddoch, M.J. (1984). Bilingual biscriptal deep dyslexia. *Quarterly Journal of Experimental Psychology, 36A*, 417–33.

Campbell, R. (1983). Writing non-words to dictation. *Brain and Language, 19*, 153–78.

Campbell, R. and Butterworth, B. (1985). Phonological dyslexia and dysgraphia in a highly literate subject. *Quarterly Journal of Experimental Psychology, 37A*, 435–75.

Caplan, D. (1972). Clause boundaries and recognition latencies for words in sentences. *Perception and Psychophysics, 12*, 73–6.

Carroll, J.M., and Bever, T.G. (1976). Sentence comprehension: a case study in the relation of knowledge and perception. In Carterette, E., and Friedman, J. (eds.), *The Handbook of Perception, Volume 7: Language and Speech*. Academic Press: New York.

Chomsky, N. (1957). *Syntactic Structures*. Mouton: The Hague.

Chomsky, N. (1959). Review of *Verbal Behavior* by B.F. Skinner, *Language, 35*, 26–58.

Chomsky, N. (1965). *Aspects of the Theory of Syntax*. MIT Press: Cambridge, Massachusetts.

Chomsky N. (1976). *Reflections on Language*. Temple Smith: London.

Clarke, R., and Morton, J. (1983). Cross modality facilitation in tachistoscopic word recognition. *Quarterly Journal of Experimental Psychology, 35A*, 79–96.

Cohen, A.S. (1974/5). Oral reading errors of first-grade children taught by code emphasis approach. *Reading Research Quarterly, 10*, 616–50.

Coltheart, M. (1978). Lexical access in simple reading tasks. In Underwood G. (ed.), *Strategies of Information Processing*. Academic Press: London.

Coltheart, M. (1980a). Deep dyslexia: a right hemisphere hypothesis. In Coltheart, M., Patterson, K., and Marshall, J.C. (eds.), *Deep Dyslexia*. Routledge & Kegan Paul: London.

Coltheart, M. (1980b). Reading, phonological recoding, and deep dyslexia. In Coltheart, M., Patterson, K., and Marshall, J.C. (eds.), *Deep Dyslexia*. Routledge & Kegan Paul: London.

Coltheart, M. (1983). Writing systems and reading disorders. In Henderson, L. (ed.), *Orthographies and Reading*. Lawrence Erlbaum Associates: London.

Coltheart, M., (1984). The right hemisphere and disorders of reading. In Young, A. (ed.), *Functions of the Right Cerebral Hemisphere*. Academic Press: London.

Coltheart, M. (1985). Cognitive neuropsychology and the study of reading. In Posner, M.I., and Marin, O.S.M. (eds.), *Attention and Performance XI*.

Lawrence Erlbaum Associates: Hillsdale, New Jersey.

Coltheart, M., Davelaar, E., Jonasson, J.T., and Besner, D. (1977). Access to the internal lexicon. In Dornic, S. (ed.), *Attention and Performance VI*. Lawrence Erlbaum Associates: Hillsdale, New Jersey.

Coltheart, M., and Freeman, R. (1974). Case alternation impairs word identification. *Bulletin of the Psychonomic Society, 3*, 102–4.

Coltheart, M., Masterson, J., Byng, S., Prior, M., and Riddoch, M.J. (1983). Surface dyslexia. *Quarterly Journal of Experimental Psychology, 35A*, 469–95.

Coltheart, M., Patterson, K., and Marshall, J.C. (eds.). (1980). *Deep Dyslexia*. Routledge & Kegan Paul: London.

Cromer, R.F. (1974). The development of language and cognition: the cognition hypothesis. In Foss, B. (ed.), *New Perspectives in Child Development*. Penguin Books: Harmondsworth.

Cromer, R.F. (1978). The basis of childhood dysphasia: a linguistic approach. In Wyke, M. (ed.), *Developmental Dysphasia*. Academic Press: London.

Cromer, R.F. (1979). The strengths of the weak form of the cognition hypothesis for language acquisition. In Lee, V. (ed.), *Language Development*. Croom Helm: London.

Cromer, R.F. (1983). Hierarchical planning disability in the drawings and constructions of a special group of severely aphasic children. *Brain and Cognition, 2*, 144–64.

Cross, T.G. (1977). Mothers' speech adjustments: the contributions of selected child listener variables. In Snow, C.E., and Ferguson, C.A. (eds.), *Talking to Children: Language Input and Acquisition*. Cambridge University Press: Cambridge.

Cross, T.G. (1978). Mother's speech and its association with rate of linguistic development in young children. In Waterson, N., and Snow, C.E. (eds.), *The Development of Communication*. Wiley: Chichester.

Cross, T.G., Johnson-Morris J.E. and Nienhuys, T.G. (1980). Linguistic feedback and maternal speech: comparisons of mothers addressing hearing and hearing-impaired children. *First Language, 1*, 163–89.

Curtiss, S. (1977). *Genie: A Psycholinguistic Study of a Modern-Day 'Wild Child'*. Academic Press: New York.

Dejerine, J. (1892). Contribution à l'etude anatomo-pathologique et clinique des differentes variétés de cécité verbale. *Memoires de la Societe de Biologie, 4*, 61–90.

De Villiers, J.G., and De Villiers, P.A. (1978). *Language Acquisition*. Harvard University Press: Harvard.

Dewart, M.H. (1975). A psychological investigation of sentence comprehension by children. Unpublished Ph.D. thesis, University of London.

Dewart, M.H. (1979). Children's hypotheses about the animacy of actor and object nouns. *British Journal of Psychology, 70*, 525–30.

Diringer, D. (1968). *The Alphabet*. Hutchinson: London.

Doctor, E., and Coltheart, M. (1980). Phonological recoding in children's reading for meaning. *Memory and Cognition, 80*, 195–209.

Dooling, D.J. (1971). Some context effects in the speeded comprehension of sentences. Unpublished Ph.D. thesis, SUNY at Buffalo.

Dooling, D.J. (1972). Some context effects in the speeded comprehension of sentences. *Journal of Experimental Psychology, 93*, 56–62.

Dooling, D.J., and Lachman, R. (1971). Effects of comprehension on retention of prose. *Journal of Experimental Psychology, 88*, 216–22.

Dooling, D.J., and Mullett, R.L. (1973). Locus of thematic effects in retention of prose. *Journal of Experimental Psychology, 97*, 404–6.

Ellis, A.W. (1982). Spelling and writing (and reading and speaking). In Ellis, A.W. (ed), *Normality and Pathology in Cognitive Functions*. Academic Press: London.

Ellis, R., and Wells, G. (1980). Enabling factors in adult-child discourse. *First Language 1*, 46–62.

Evans, J. (1980). Some comparisons of speech modifications made by four-year-olds when explaining a task to either a two-year-old sibling or an adult. Unpublished M.Sc. thesis. University of London.

Firth, I. (1972). Components of reading disability. Unpublished Ph.D. thesis, University of New South Wales.

Fischler, I., and Bloom, P.A. (1979). Automatic and attentional processes in the effects of sentence contexts on word recognition. *Journal of Verbal Learning and Verbal Behavior, 18*, 1–20.

Fischler, I., and Bloom, P.A. (1980). Rapid processing of the meaning of sentences. *Memory and Cognition, 8*, 216–25.

Flores d'Arcais, G.B. (1978). The perception of complex sentences. In Levelt, W.J.M., and Flores d'Arcais, G.B. (eds.), *Studies in the Perception of Language*. Wiley: Chichester.

Flores d'Arcais, G.B. (1982). Automatic syntactic computation in sentence comprehension. *Psychological Research, 44*, 231–42.

Flores d'Arcais, G.B., and Schreuder, R. (1983). The process of language understanding: a few issues in contemporary psycholinguistics. In Flores d'Arcais, G.B., and Jarvella, R.J. (eds.), *The Process of Language Understanding*. Wiley: Chichester.

Fodor, J.A. (1983). *Modularity of Mind*. MIT Press: Cambridge, Massachusetts.

Fodor, J.A., Bever, T.G., and Garrett, M.F. (1974). *The Psychology of Language: An Introduction to Psycholinguistics and Generative Grammar*. McGraw Hill: New York.

Forster, K.I. (1979). Levels of processing and the structure of the language processor. In Cooper, W.E., and Walker, E.C.T. (eds.), *Sentence Processing: Psycholinguistic Studies Presented to Merrill Garrett*. Lawrence Erlbaum Associates: Hillsdale, New Jersey.

Forster, K.I., and Olbrei, I. (1974). Semantic heuristics and syntactic analysis. *Cognition, 2*, 319–47.

Forster, K.K., and Ryder, L.A. (1971). Perceiving the structure and meaning of sentences. *Journal of Verbal Learning and Verbal Behavior, 10*, 285–96.

Fowler, W. (1962). Teaching a two-year-old to read: an experiment in early childhood learning. *Genetic Psychology Monographs, 66*, 181–283.

Freedman, P., and Carpenter, R. (1976). Semantic relations used by normal and language-impaired children at Stage 1. *Journal of Speech and Hearing Research, 19*, 784–95.

Friedman, R.B. (1980). Identity without form: abstract representations of letters. *Perception and Psychophysics, 28*, 53–60.

Frith, U. (1980). Unexpected spelling problems. In Frith, U. (ed.), *Cognitive Processes in Spelling*. Academic Press: London.

Frith U. (1984). Specific spelling problems. In Malatesha, R.N., and Whitaker, H.A. (eds.), *Dyslexia: A Global Issue*. Martinus Nijhoff: The Hague.

Frith, U. (1985). Beneath the surface of developmental dyslexia. In Patterson, K.E., Marshall, J.C., and Coltheart, M. (eds.), *Surface Dyslexia: Cognitive and Neuropsychological Studies of Phonological Reading*. Lawrence Erlbaum Associates: London.

Fromkin, V. (1973). *Speech Errors as Linguistic Evidence*. Mouton: The Hague.

Funnell, E. (1983a). Phonological processes in reading: new evidence from acquired dyslexia. *British Journal of Psychology, 74*, 159–80.

Funnell, E. (1983b). Ideographic communication and word-class differences in aphasia. Unpublished Ph.D. thesis. University of Reading.

Gallagher, T., and Darnton, B. (1977). Revision behaviors in the speech of language disordered children. Paper presented to the American Speech and Hearing Association, Chicago.

Garnica, O. (1977). Some prosodic and paralinguistic features of speech to young children. In Snow, C.E., and Ferguson, C.A. (eds.), *Talking to Children: Language Input and Acquisition*. Cambridge University Press: Cambridge.

Garrett, M.F. (1975). The analysis of sentence production. In Bower, G. (ed.), *Pychology of Learning and Motivation, Volume 9*. Academic Press: New York.

Garrett, M.F. (1980). Levels of processing in sentence production. In Butterworth, B.L. (ed.), *Language Production, Volume 1*. Academic Press: London.

Garrett, M.F. (1982). Production of speech: observations from normal and pathological language use. In Ellis, A.W. (ed.), *Normality and Pathology in Cognitive Functions*. Academic Press: London.

Garrett, M.F., Bever, T.G., and Fodor, J.A. (1966). The active use of grammar in speech perception. *Perception and Psychophysics, 1*, 30–2.

Garrod, S., and Trabasso, T. (1973). A dual-memory information processing interpretation of sentence comprehension. *Journal of Verbal Learning and Verbal Behavior, 12*, 155–67.

Gelb, I.J. (1952). *A Study of Writing*. University of Chicago Press: Chicago.

Gibson, E.J., and Levin, H. (1975). *The Psychology of Reading*. MIT Press: Cambridge, Massachusetts.

Glanzer, M., and Koppenaal, L. (1977). The effect of encoding tasks on free recall: stages and levels. *Journal of Verbal Learning and Verbal Behavior, 16*, 21–8.

Goldman-Eisler, F. (1958). The predictability of words in context and the length of pauses in speech. *Language and Speech, 1,* 226–31.

Goldman-Eisler, F. (1968). *Psycholinguistics: Experiments in Spontaneous Speech.* Academic Press: London.

Gough, P. (1972). One second of reading. In Kavanagh, J.P., and Mattingly, I.G. (eds.), *Language by Eye and by Ear.* MIT Press: Cambridge, Massachusetts.

Greene, J.M. (1970a). The semantic function of negatives and passives. *British Journal of Psychology, 61,* 17–22.

Greene, J.M. (1970b). Syntactic form and semantic function. *Quarterly Journal of Experimental Psychology, 22,* 14–27.

Greene, J.M. (1972). *Psycholinguistics: Chomsky and Psychology.* Penguin: Harmondsworth.

Halle, M. (1972). On a parallel between conventions of versification and orthography and on literacy among the Cherokee. In Kavanagh, J.F. and Mattingly, I.G. (eds.), *Language by Ear and by Eye.* MIT Press: Cambridge, Massachusetts.

Halliday, M.A.K. (1967). Notes on transitivity and theme in English, Part 2. *Journal of Linguistics, 3,* 199–244.

Harris, M. (1976). The influence of reversibility and truncation on the interpretation of the passive voice by young children. *British Journal of Psychology, 67,* 419–28.

Harris, M. (1977). Syntactic and semantic factors in the acquisition of the passive by young children. Unpublished Ph.D. thesis, University of London.

Harris, M. (1978). Noun animacy and the passive voice: a developmental approach. *Quarterly Journal of Experimental Psychology, 30,* 495–504.

Harris, M., Jones, D., and Grant, J. (1983). The non-verbal context of mothers' speech to children. *First Language, 4,* 21–30.

Hatfield, F.M., and Patterson, K.E. (1983). Phonological spelling. *Quarterly Journal of Experimental Psychology, 35A,* 451–68.

Haviland, S.E., and Clark, H.H. (1974). What's new? Acquiring new information as a process in comprehension. *Journal of Verbal Learning and Verbal Behavior, 13,* 512–21.

Haynes, C. (1982). Vocabulary acquisition problems in language disordered children. Unpublished M.Sc. thesis, Guys Hospital Medical School, University of London.

Herriot, P. (1969). The comprehension of active and passive sentences as a function of pragmatic expectations. *Journal of Verbal Learning and Verbal Behavior, 8,* 166–9.

Hoar, N. (1977). Paraphrase capabilities of language impaired children. Paper presented to the Boston University Conference on Language Development, Boston, Massachusetts.

Holmes, J.M. (1973). Dyslexia: a neurolinguistic study of traumatic and developmental disorders of reading. Unpublished Ph.D. thesis, University of Edinburgh.

Holmes, V.M., and Forster, K.I. (1970). Detection of extraneous signals during sentence recognition. *Perception and Psychophysics, 7,* 297–301.

Howe, C.J. (1980). Mother-child conversation and semantic development.

In Giles, H., Robinson, W.P., and Smith, P.M. (eds.), *Language: Social Psychological Perspectives*. Pergamon: Oxford.

Humphreys, G.W., Quinlan, P.T., and Evett, L.J. (1983). Automatic orthographic priming: implications for processing orthography. *Working Papers of the London Linguistics Group*, Volume 5.

Hupet, M., and Le Boudec, B. (1977). The given-new contract and the constructive aspect of memory for ideas. *Journal of Verbal Learning and Verbal Behavior, 16*, 69–75.

Hymes, D. (1971). *On Communicative Competence*. University of Pennsylvania Press: Pennsylvania.

Inhelder, B. (1963). Observations sur les aspects opératifs et figuratifs de la pensée chez des enfants dysphasiques. *Problemes de Psycholinguistique, 6*, 143–53.

Jarvella, R.J. (1971). Syntactic processing of connected speech. *Journal of Verbal Learning and Verbal Behavior, 10*, 409–16.

Jensen, H. (1970). *Sign, Symbol and Script*. George Allen & Unwin: London.

Job, R., Sartori, G., Masterson, J., and Coltheart, M. (1984). Developmental surface dyslexia in Italian. In Malatesha, R.N., and Whitaker, H.A. (eds.), *Dyslexia: A Global Issue*. Martinus Nijhoff: The Hague.

Johnson, M.K., Bransford, J.D., and Solomon, S.K. (1973). Memory for tacit implications of sentences. *Journal of Experimental Psychology, 98*, 203–5.

Johnson-Laird, P.N. (1968). The intepretation of the passive voice. *Quarterly Journal of Experimental Psychology, 20*, 69–73.

Johnson-Laird, P.N. (1983). *Mental Models*. Cambridge University Press: Cambridge.

Johnston, J.C. (1978). A test of the sophisticated-guessing theory of word perception. *Cognitive Psychology, 10*, 123–54.

Johnston, J.C. (1981). Understanding word perception: clues from studying the word-superiority effect. In Tzeng, O., and Singer, H. (eds.), *Perception of Print: Reading Research in Experimental Psychology*. Lawrence Erlbaum Associates: Hillsdale, New Jersey.

Johnston, J.C., and McClelland, J.L. (1973). Visual factors in word perception. *Perception and Psychophysics, 14*, 365–70.

Johnston, J.C., and McClelland, J.L. (1980). Experimental tests of a hierarchical model of word identification. *Journal of Verbal Learning and Verbal Behavior, 19*, 503–24.

Johnston, J., and Schery, T. (1976). The use of grammatical morphemes by children with communication disorders. In Morehead, D., and Morehead, A. (eds.), *Normal and Deficient Child Language*. University Park Press: Baltimore, Maryland.

Karanth, P. (1985). Dyslexia in a Dravidian language. In Patterson, K.E., Marshall, J.C., and Coltheart, M. (eds.), *Surface Dyslexia: Cognitive and Neuropsychological Studies of Phonological Reading*. Lawrence Erlbaum Associates: London.

Karmiloff-Smith, A. (1979a). *A Functional Approach to Child Language: A Study of Determiners and Reference*. Cambridge University Press:

Cambridge.

Karmiloff-Smith, A. (1979b). Language development after five. In Fletcher, P. and Garman, M. (eds.), *Language Acquisition*. Cambridge University Press: Cambridge.

Kay, J., and Lesser, R. (1985). The nature of phonological processing in oral reading: evidence from surface dyslexia. *Quarterly Journal of Experimental Psychology, 37A*, 39–82.

Kay, J., and Patterson, K.E. (1983). Routes to meaning in surface dyslexia. In Patterson, K.E., Marshall, J.C., and Coltheart, M. (eds), *Surface Dyslexia: Cognitive and Neuropsychological Studies of Phonological Reading*. Lawrence Erlbaum Associates: London.

Kean, M.L. (1977). The linguistic interpretation of aphasic syndromes. *Cognition, 5*, 9–46.

Keenan, E.O., and Klein, E. (1975). Coherency in children's discourse. *Journal of Psycholinguistic Research, 4*, 365–80.

Keenan, J., MacWhinney, B., and Mayhew, D. (1977). Pragmatics in memory: a study of natural conversation. *Journal of Verbal Learning and Verbal Behavior, 16*, 549–60.

Kendon, A. (1967). Some functions of gaze direction in social interaction. *Acta Psychologica, 26*, 22–63.

Kintsch, W., and Bates, E. (1977). Recognition memory for statements from a classroom lecture. *Journal of Experimental Psychology: Human Learning and Memory, 3*, 150–9.

Kress G. (1982). *Learning to Write*. Routledge & Kegan Paul: London.

Ladefoged, P., and Broadbent, D.E. (1960). Perception of sequence in auditory events. *Quarterly Journal of Experimental Psychology, 12*, 162–70.

Lehmann, W.P. (ed.), (1975). *Language and Linguistics in the People's Republic of China*. University of Texas Press: Austin, Texas.

Leonard, L.B. (1979). Language impairment in children. *Merrill-Palmer Quarterly, 25*, 205–32.

Leonard, L.B., Camarata, S., Rowan, L.E., and Chapman, K. (1982). The communicative functions of lexical usage by language impaired children. *Applied Linguistics, 3*, 109–25.

Leonard, L.B., Steckol, K., and Schwartz, R. (1978). Semantic relations and utterance length in child language. In Peng, F., and von Raffler, W. (eds.), *Language Acquisition and Developmental Kinesics*. Bunka Hyoren: Tokyo.

Leong, C.K. (1973). Hong Kong. In Downing, J. (ed.)., *Comparative Reading*. Macmillan: New York.

Lounsbury, F.G. (1954). Transitional probability, linguistic structure, and systems of habit-family hierarchies. In Osgood, C.E., and Sebeok, T.A. (eds.), *Psycholinguistics: A Survey of Theory and Research Problems*. University Press: Indiana.

Lynn, R. (1963). Reading readiness and the perceptual abilities of young children. *Educational Research, 6*, 10–15.

McClelland, J. (1976). Preliminary letter identification in the perception of words and non-words. *Journal of Experimental Psychology: Human Perception and Performance, 2*, 80–91.

McClelland, J.L., and Johnston, J.C. (1977). The role of familiar units in perception of words and non-words. *Perception and Psychophysics, 22,* 249–61.

McClelland, J.L., and Rumelhart, D.E. (1981). An interactive activation model of context effects in letter perception: Part 1. An account of basic findings. *Psychological Review, 88,* 375–407.

McNeill, D. (1966). The creation of language by children. In Lyons, J., and Wales, R.J. (eds.), *Psycholinguistic Papers.* University of Edinburgh Press: Edinburgh.

McShane, J. (1980). *Learning to Talk.* Cambridge University Press: Cambridge.

Manelis, L. (1974). The effect of meaningfulness in tachistoscopic word perception. *Perception and Psychophysics, 16,* 182–92.

Maratsos, M.P. (1973). Nonegocentric communication abilities in preschool children. *Child Development, 44,* 697–700.

Marcel, A.J. (1980). Surface dyslexia and beginning reading: a revised hypothesis of the pronunciation of print and its impairments. In Coltheart, M., Patterson, K., and Marshall, J.C. (eds.), *Deep Dyslexia.* Routledge & Kegan Paul: London.

Margolin, D.I. (1984). The neuropsychology of writing and spelling: semantic, phonological, motor, and perceptual processes. *Quarterly Journal of Experimental Psychology, 36A,* 459–90.

Marsh, G., Friedman, M., Welch, V., and Desberg, P. (1981). A cognitive-developmental theory of reading acquisition. In MacKinnon, G.E., and Waller, T.G. (eds.), *Reading Research: Advances in Theory and Practice.* Academic Press: New York.

Marshall, J.C., and Newcombe, F. (1966). Syntactic and semantic errors in paralexia. *Neuropsychologia, 4,* 169–76.

Marshall, J.C., and Newcombe, F. (1973). Patterns of paralexia: a psycholinguistic approach. *Journal of Psycholinguistic Research 2,* 175–99.

Marslen-Wilson, W.D. (1975). Sentence perception as an interactive parallel process. *Science, 189,* 226–8.

Marslen-Wilson, W.D. (1978). Sequential decision processes during spoken word-recognition. Paper presented at Psychonomic Society meeting, San Antonio, Texas.

Marslen-Wilson, W.D., and Tyler, L.K. (1980). The temporal structure of spoken language understanding. *Cognition. 8,* 1–71.

Marslen-Wilson, W.D., Tyler, L.K., and Seidenberg, M. (1978). Sentence processing and the clause boundary. In Levelt, W.J.M., and Flores d'Arcais, G.B. (eds.), *Studies in the Perception of Language.* Wiley: Chichester.

Marslen-Wilson, W.D., and Welsh, A. (1978). Processing interactions and lexical access during word-recognition in continuous speech. *Cognitive Psychology, 10,* 29–63.

Martlew, M., Connolly, K., and McCleod, C. (1978). Language use, role and context in a five-year-old. *Journal of Child Language, 5,* 81–99.

Martin, S.E. (1972). Non-alphabetic writing systems: some observations. In Kavanagh, J.F., and Mattingly, I.G. (eds.), *Language by Eye and by*

Ear. MIT Press: Cambridge, Massachusetts.

Menyuk, P. (1978). Linguistic problems in children with developmental dysphasia. In Wyke, M. (ed.), *Developmental Dysphasia*. Academic Press: London.

Messer, D.J. (1978). The integration of mothers' referential speech with joint play. *Child Development*, *49*, 781–7.

Messer, D. (1980). The episodic structure of maternal speech to young children. *Journal of Child Language*, *7*, 29–40.

Miller, G.A. (1968). The psycholinguists. In *The Psychology of Communication: Seven Essays*. Penguin Books: Harmondsworth.

Miller, G.A., and McKean, K.O. (1964). A chronometric study of some relations between sentences. *Quarterly Journal of Experimental Psychology*, *16*, 297–308.

Mitchell, D.C., and Green, D.W. (1978). The effects of context and content on immediate processing in reading. *Quarterly Journal of Experimental Psychology*, *30*, 609–36.

Morton, J. (1968). Considerations of grammar and computation in language behavior. In Catford, J.C. (ed.), *Studies in Language and Language Behavior*. University of Michigan Press: Ann Arbor, Michigan.

Morton, J. (1969). Interaction of information in word recognition. *Psychological Review*, *76*, 165–78.

Morton, J. (1970). A functional model for memory. In Norman, D.A. (ed.), *Models of Human Memory*. Academic Press: New York.

Morton, J. (1978). Facilitation in word recognition: experiments causing change in the logogen model. In Kolers, P.A., Wrolstad, M.E., and Bouma, H. (eds.), *Proceedings of the Conference on the Processing of Visible Language*. Plenum: New York.

Morton, J., and Patterson, K.E. (1980). A new attempt at an interpretation, or an attempt at a new interpretation. In Coltheart, M., Patterson, K., and Marshall, J.C. (eds.), *Deep Dyslexia*. Routledge & Kegan Paul: London.

Nelson, K. (1973). Structure and strategy in learning to talk. *Monographs of the Society for Research in Child Development*, *38*, 1–2.

Nicolaci-da-Costa, A. (1983). Number markers in non-redundant and redundant sentences: interpretation and use by young children. Unpublished doctoral thesis, University of London.

Nicolaci-da-Costa, A., and Harris, M. (1983). Redundancy of syntactic information: an aid to young children's comprehension of sentential number. *British Journal of Psychology*, *74*, 343–52.

Patterson, K.E. (1982). The relation between reading and phonological coding: further neuropsychological observations. In Ellis, A.W. (ed.), *Normality and Pathology in Cognitive Function*. Academic Press: London.

Patterson, K.E., and Besner, D. (1984a). Is the right hemisphere literate? *Cognitive Neuropsychology*, *1*, 315–42.

Patterson, K.E., and Besner, D. (1984b). Reading from the left: a reply to Rabinowicz and Moscovitch and to Zaidel and Schweiger. *Cognitive Neuropsychology*, *1*, 365–80.

Patterson, K.E., and Kay, J. (1982). Letter-by-letter reading:

psychological descriptions of a neurological syndrome. *Quarterly Journal of Experimental Psychology, 34A*, 411–42.

Patterson, K.E., and Marshall, J.C., and Coltheart, M. (eds.). (1985). *Surface Dyslexia: Cognitive and Neuropsychological Studies of Phonological Reading.* Lawrence Erlbaum Associates: London.

Peterson, C.L., Danner, F.W., and Flavell, J.H. (1972). Developmental changes in children's response to three modifications of communicative failure. *Child Development, 43*, 1463–8.

Phillips, J. (1973). Syntax and vocabulary of mothers' speech to young children: age and sex comparisons. *Child Development, 44*, 182–5.

Piaget, J. (1926). *The Language and Thought of the Child.* Routledge & Kegan Paul: London.

Piaget J. (1970). *Genetic Epistemology.* Columbia University Press: Columbia, Ohio.

Piaget, J., and Inhelder, B. (1966). *The Psychology of the Child.* Routledge & Kegan Paul: London.

Pompi, R.F., and Lachman, R. (1967). Surrogate processes in short-term retention of connected discourse. *Journal of Experimental Psychology, 75*, 143–50.

Prentice, J.L., Barrett, L.S., and Semmel, M.I. (1966). Repetition and animacy in active and passive sentence construction. *Studies in Language and Language Behavior. Progress Report No. 2*, University of Michigan.

Rabinowicz, B., and Moscovitch, M. (1984). Right hemisphere literacy: a critique of some recent approaches. *Cognitive Neuropsychology, 1*, 343–50.

Reicher, G.M. (1969). Perceptual recognition as a function of meaningfulness of stimulus material. *Journal of Experimental Psychology, 81*, 274–80.

Rumelhart, D.E., and McClelland, J.L. (1982). An interactive activation model of context effects in letter perception: II. The contextual enhancement effect and some tests and extensions of the model. *Psychological Review, 9*, 60–94.

Sachs, J., and Devin, J. (1976). Young children's use of age-appropriate speech styles in social interaction and role-playing. *Journal of Child Language, 3*, 81–98.

Sachs, J.S. (1967). Recognition memory for syntactic and semantic aspects of connected discourse. *Perception and Psychophysics, 2*, 437–42.

Saffran, E.M., Bogyo, L.C., Schwartz, M.F., and Marin, O.S.M. (1980). Does deep dyslexia reflect right-hemisphere reading? In Coltheart, M., Patterson, K., and Marshall, J.C. (eds.), *Deep Dyslexia.* Routledge & Kegan Paul: London.

Sakamoto, T., and Makita, K. (1973). Japan. In Downing, J. (ed.), *Comparative Reading.* Macmillan: New York.

Sasanuma, S. (1980). Acquired dyslexia in Japanese: clinical features and underlying mechanisms. In Coltheart, M., Patterson, K., and Marshall, J.C. (eds.), *Deep Dyslexia.* Routledge & Kegan Paul: London.

Sasanuma, S. (1985). Surface dyslexia and dysgraphia: how are they manifested in Japanese? In Patterson, K.E., Marshall, J.C., and

Coltheart M. (eds.), *Surface Dyslexia: Cognitive and Neuropsychological Studies of Phonological Reading*. Lawrence Erlbaum Associates: London.

Scarborough, D.L., Cortese, C., and Scarborough, H.S. (1977). Frequency and repetition effects in lexical memory. *Journal of Experimental Psychology: Human Perception and Performance, 3*, 1–17.

Schaffer, H.R. (1975). Social development in infancy. In Lewin, R. (ed.), *Child Alive*. Temple Smith: London.

Schaffer, H.R., Hepburn, A., and Collis, G.M. (1983). Verbal and non-verbal aspects of mothers' directives. *Journal of Child Language, 10*, 337–55.

Schultz, E.E. and Kamil, M.L. (1979). The role of some definite references in linguistic integration. *Memory and Cognition, 7*, 42–9.

Schwartz, M. (1985). Classification of language disorders from the psycholinguistic viewpoint. In Oxbury, J., Wyke, M., Whurr, R., and Coltheart, M. (eds.), *Aphasia*. Butterworths: London.

Seymour, P.H.K. (1973). A model for reading, naming and comparison. *British Journal of Psychology, 64*, 35–49.

Seymour, P.H.K., and Elder, L. (1985). Beginning reading without phonology. *Cognitive Neuropsychology* (in press).

Seymour, P.H.K., and McGregor, C.J. (1984). Developmental dyslexia: a cognitive experimental analysis of phonological, morphemic and visual impairments. *Cognitive Neuropsychology, 1*, 43–82.

Shallice, T. (1981a). Neurological impairment of cognitive processes. *British Medical Bulletin, 37*, 187–92.

Shallice, T. (1981b). Phonological agraphia and the lexical route in writing. *Brain, 104*, 413–29.

Shallice, T., and Warrington, E.K. (1980). Single and multiple component central dyslexic syndromes. In Coltheart, M., Patterson, K., and Marshall, J.C. (eds.), *Deep Dyslexia*. Routledge & Kegan Paul: London.

Shatz, M. (1983). On mechanisms of language acquisition: can features of the communicative environment account for development? In Wanner, E., and Gleitman, L.R. (eds.), *Language Acquisition: The State of the Art*. Cambridge University Press: Cambridge.

Shatz, M., and Gelman, R. (1973). The development of communication skills: modifications in the speech of young children as a function of the listener. *Monographs of Social Research and Child Development, 38*, 5.

Sinclair, A., Sinclair, H., and De Marcellus, O. (1971). Young children's comprehension and production of passive sentences. *Archives de Psychology, 41*, 1–22.

Skinner, B.F. (1957). *Verbal Behavior*. Appleton Century Crofts: New York.

Slobin, D.I. (1966). Grammatical transformations and sentence comprehension in childhood and adulthood. *Journal of Verbal Learning and Verbal Behavior, 5*, 219–27.

Slobin, D.I. (1971). *Psycholinguistics*. Scott Foresman: London.

Smith, N., and Wilson, D. (1979). *Modern Linguistics: The Results of Chomsky's Revolution*. Penguin Books: Harmondsworth.

Snow, C.E. (1972). Mother' speech to children learning language. *Child Development, 43*, 549–65.

Snow, C.E. (1977). The development of conversation between mothers and babies. *Journal of Child Language, 4*, 1–22.

Steckol, K.F., and Leonard, L.B. (1979). The use of grammatical morphemes by normal and language-impaired children. *Journal of Communication Disorders, 12*, 291–301.

Steedman, M.J., and Johnson-Laird, P.N. (1977). A pragmatic theory of linguistic performance. In Smith, P.T., and Campbell, R.N. (eds.), *Advances in the Psychology of Language: Formal and Experimental Approaches*. Plenum: New York.

Stemberger, J.P. (1984). Structural errors in normal and agrammatic speech. *Cognitive Neuropsychology, 1*, 281–313.

Strohner, H., and Nelson, K.E. (1974). The young child's development of sentence comprehension: influence of event probability, non-verbal context, syntactic form and strategies. *Child Development, 45*, 567–76.

Stubbs, M. (1983). *Discourse Analysis*. Basil Blackwell: Oxford.

Tallal, P., and Piercy, M. (1978). Defects in auditory perception in children with developmental dysphasia. In Wyke, M. (ed.), *Developmental Dyslexia*. Academic Press: London.

Tannenbaum, P.H., and Williams, F. (1968). Generation of active and passive sentences as a function of subject and object focus. *Journal of Verbal Learning and Verbal Behavior, 7*, 246–50.

Taylor, T.J. (1984). Editing rules and understanding: the case against sentence-based syntax. *Language and Communication, 4*, 105–27.

Temple, C.M. (1984). Developmental analogues to acquired phonological dyslexia. In Malatesha, R.N., and Whitaker, H.A. (eds.), *Dyslexia: A Global Issue*. Martinus Nijhoff: The Hague.

Temple, C.M., and Marshall, J.C. (1983). A case study of developmental phonological dyslexia. *British Journal of Psychology, 74*, 517–34.

Thorndyke, P.W. (1976). The role of inferences in discourse comprehension. *Journal of Verbal Learning and Verbal Behavior, 15*, 437–46.

Thorndyke, P.W. (1977). Cognitive structures in comprehension and memory of narrative discourse. *Cognitive Psychology, 9*, 77–100.

Trevarthen, C. (1975). Early attempts at speech. In Lewin, R. (ed.), *Child Alive*. Temple Smith: London.

Turner, E.A., and Rommetveit, R. (1967). Experimental manipulation of the production of active and passive voice in children. *Language and Speech, 10*, 169–80.

Turvey, M.T. (1973). On peripheral and central processes in vision. *Psychological Review, 80*, 1–52.

Walker, S.F. (1984). *Learning Theory and Behaviour Modification*. Methuen: London.

Wang, W.S.-Y. (1973). The Chinese language. *Scientific American, 228*, 50–63.

Warrington, E.K., and Shallice, T. (1980). Word-form dyslexia. *Brain, 103*, 99–112.

Wason, P.C. (1965). The contexts of plausible denial. *Journal of Verbal Learning and Verbal Behavior, 4*, 7–11.

Wheeler, D. (1970). Processes in word recognition. *Cognitive Psychology, 1*,

59–85.

Whitaker, H. (1976). A case of isolation of the language function. In Whitaker, H., and Whitaker H.A. (eds.), *Studies in Neurolinguistics, Volume 2*. Academic Press: new York.

Winnick, W.A. and Daniel, S.A. (1970). Two kinds of response priming in tachistoscopic recognition. *Journal of Experimental Psychology, 84*, 74–81.

Zaidel, E., and Schweiger, A. (1984). On wrong hypotheses about the right hemisphere: commentary on K. Patterson and D. Besner, 'Is the right hemisphere literate?'. *Cognitive Neuropsychology, 1*, 351–64.

Author index

Subject index